Thinking Through Utilitarianism

A Guide to Contemporary Arguments

Thinking Through Utilitarianism

A Guide to Contemporary Arguments

Andrew T. Forcehimes and Luke Semrau

Hackett Publishing Company, Inc.
Indianapolis/Cambridge

Copyright © 2019 by Hackett Publishing Company, Inc.

All rights reserved
Printed in the United States of America

22 21 20 19   1 2 3 4 5 6 7

For further information, please address
  Hackett Publishing Company, Inc.
  P.O. Box 44937
  Indianapolis, Indiana 46244-0937

  www.hackettpublishing.com

Cover design by Brian Rak and E.L. Wilson
Interior design by Laura Clark
Composition by Aptara, Inc.

Library of Congress Control Number: 2019948112

ISBN-13: 978-1-62466-831-9 (cloth)
ISBN-13: 978-1-62466-830-2 (pbk.)

The paper used in this publication meets the minimum requirements of American National Standard for Information Sciences—Permanence of Paper for Printed Library Materials, ANSI Z39.48–1984.

∞

Preface

What does morality demand of you? Once this question is posed, the importance of finding the answer is immediately apparent. It is also apparent that answering this question actually involves answering many questions. Some concern right action. Some concern value. This book is about the answers given by Utilitarianism. If its answers are correct, then morality demands that you do the best you can, and this requires that you bring about the happiest world available to you.

Why take Utilitarianism seriously? We could point out that those accepting the theory have historically found themselves on the right side of history. In the 1800s, for example, Jeremy Bentham advocated animal welfare, prison reform, the decriminalization of homosexuality, universal suffrage, and anticolonialist policies. It is tempting to conclude that such foresight is explained by having landed on the ethical truth. Or instead we could note even the most ardent critics of Utilitarianism recognize the theory's appeal. Consider a few representative remarks from leading contemporary ethicists:

> T. M. Scanlon: Utilitarianism occupies a central place in the moral philosophy of our time. It is not the view which most people hold; certainly there are very few who would claim to be act utilitarians. But for a much wider range of people it is the view towards which they find themselves pressed when they try to give a theoretical account of their moral beliefs.

> Philippa Foot: Utilitarianism tends to haunt even those of us who will not believe in it. It is as if we for ever feel that it must be right, although we insist that it is wrong.

> Judith Jarvis Thomson: Many of us who work in moral philosophy spend a lot of time worrying about utilitarianism. Our problem isn't merely that it continues to have its friends, though it does; our problem is deeper, lying in the fact that we haven't found—and its friends are delighted to draw our attention to the fact that we haven't found—a way of positively killing it off. No amount of mowing and tugging seems to work: it keeps on reappearing, every spring, like a weed with a long root.

> Christine Korsgaard: To later generations, much of the moral philosophy of the twentieth century will look like a struggle to escape from utilitarianism. We seem to succeed in disproving one utilitarian doctrine, only to find ourselves caught in the grip of another.

The strongest reason to take Utilitarianism seriously, however, is that you likely already accept some of its central commitments. That is, you may already be something of a Utilitarian. Consider three attractive claims endorsed by some of the greatest moral philosophers in history.

The first claim holds that you make a mistake—you've acted wrongly—whenever you make the world less valuable than it would have been had you done something else instead. Some philosophers think you can recognize that this claim is true simply by understanding it. Consider how you would react if a friend said to you: "Yesterday I faced a choice between two actions. If I chose to do the first it would be good. But if I chose to do the second it would be even better. I chose to do the first." Without needing any more information, you would probably conclude that your friend made the wrong choice. What could speak in favor of taking the worse option? This line of thought led G. E. Moore to assert, "It seems to me quite self-evident that it must always be our duty to do what will produce the best effects upon the whole."

The second claim posits a tight connection between welfare and value. Specifically, the value of the world is determined solely by the levels of welfare found there. One way to see the appeal of this idea is to note what you'd have to accept if you denied it, namely, that something could be good or bad without being good-for or bad-for someone. Suppose, for example, a villain threatened to unleash a machine on the world unless you agreed to his demands. Suppose further that it was revealed that the machine cannot make causal contact, even indirectly, with any sentient creature. Without needing any more information, you would probably conclude that, precisely because this machine will not change the lives of anyone, this villain's demands can safely go unmet. Since it will not influence welfare levels, this innocuous machine cannot make the world worse or better. Examples like these prompted Henry Sidgwick to write:

> I think that if we consider carefully such permanent results as are commonly judged to be good, other than qualities of human beings, we can find nothing that, on reflection, appears to possess this quality of goodness out of relation to human existence, or at least to some consciousness or feeling.

The third claim asserts that welfare is determined solely by pleasure and pain. That pleasure is good-for and pain is bad-for the subject experiencing them is obvious to anyone who has ever felt them. But should we also accept that one's welfare only depends on pleasure and pain? Reflect on how your welfare has changed over the course of your life. What events mattered? You may have accomplished something important, failed horribly, had friends, been betrayed, experienced beauty, fell ill, and many other things. In each case notice that, when an event influenced your welfare, pleasure or pain were close at hand. Accomplishments, friendships, and beauty are pleasant. Failure, betrayal, and sickness are painful. This striking correlation led Jeremy Bentham to maintain, "A thing is said to promote the interest, or to be for the interest, of an individual, when it tends to add to the sum total of his pleasures: or, what comes to the same thing, to diminish the sum total of his pains."

Combining these three ideas brings us very close to Utilitarianism's answer to what morality demands of you. Together they suggest that an action is permissible if and only if the performance of any other available action would not have brought about a greater sum total of pleasure minus pain.

Whatever its initial appeal, and despite its impressive philosophical pedigree, Utilitarianism is, and has been, rejected by the majority of moral philosophers. Here is a typical example of how this rejection goes from Douglas Portmore:

> Utilitarianism's counterintuitive implications [are] too much for even me to stomach.... First, utilitarianism implies that agents are morally required to commit murder whenever doing so will produce the most aggregate utility, and, thus, even when the net gain would be quite small, as small as, say, one *utile*. And let me just stipulate that a utile is the smallest possible unit of utility: equivalent to someone's experiencing the mildest of pleasures for the briefest of moments. Second, utilitarianism implies that agents should sacrifice, not only their disposable income, but even their own lives and the lives of those whom they love most whenever doing so will produce the most aggregate utility, and, thus, even when the net gain would be as small as one utile. I find these implications utterly absurd.

In the cases Portmore describes, making the world the happiest place you can is indeed counterintuitive. This suggests that Utilitarianism has gone wrong somewhere. Yet it doesn't reveal where. Utilitarianism is a combination of commitments. Which is responsible for these troubling implications? It is unclear. We could avoid the implications by rejecting any one of the three claims we've considered. We could deny that it's always permissible to bring about the best. Or we could deny that the value of a world is determined solely by welfare. Or we could deny that welfare is determined solely by pleasure and pain. We've reached a standoff without a clear path forward. We have a few claims, each of which is independently attractive. But together they deliver a result we're loath to accept.

Our goal is to offer a guide to such impasses. It would not be inaccurate to describe this book as a detailed stress test: Does Utilitarianism fail? If so, where precisely does the failure occur? Seeing how the theory performs under pressure, we believe, is one of the best ways to understand it. More importantly, however, we also believe that thinking through Utilitarianism is one of the best ways to refine your own moral view.

The book is organized accordingly. After the introductory material (Part I), we devote a chapter to each of five normative principles (Part II) and a chapter to each of four evaluative principles (Part III). These nine chapters, which are largely self-contained, all follow the same pattern. Each introduces a principle, presents a forceful challenge to that principle, and then develops a response on behalf of Utilitarianism. Each chapter concludes by drawing attention to the weakest part of this response. Taking this dialectical approach puts Utilitarianism on full display. You'll know what the view amounts to because you'll know what it takes to accept or reject it. If you find a counterexample targeting a specific principle to be genuine, then you'll know exactly which principle should be jettisoned. If you find a principle compelling, you'll know what you think needs to be retained when you go looking for an alternative ethical theory. If, however, you find that, in the end, the specific principles stand up to scrutiny, then you should accept Utilitarianism. It passes the stress test.

Reflecting our general strategy, we've written the book in a style that invites you to engage with the material. Books that provide an overview of a philosophical topic are helpful. They have their place. But this is not that kind of book. Being told about what philosophers have been debating is like hearing about a boxing match that happened decades ago. Even the best commentary leaves you feeling far from the action. This problem is somewhat mitigated when recent academic work is addressed. Yet contemporary philosophical debates are rarely carried out in a clear and orderly fashion. There is a lot of abstruse language, digressions, and people talking past one another. In this book, we've tried to bring you close to the action without the background noise. So rather than surveying existing work on the topic or providing an overview of the main themes, this book runs like a prolonged, highly controlled debate.

We've attempted to present the material in a neutral tone, but we've erred on the side of pushing the debate forward in an engaging way. We've presented Utilitarianism as forcefully as we can, so that you're well positioned to evaluate the theory. We hope to have made vivid the most serious challenges Utilitarianism faces, as well as the maneuvers that can be made to rebuff these challenges. To aid in this process, nearly each section of each chapter ends with a premise-to-conclusion argument. These allow you to identify the claims on which the arguments turn. By considering these arguments, you'll be able to locate, if you reject Utilitarianism, specifically what it is that you find objectionable. And this, in turn, will enable you to track what commitments you incur in rejecting it. That way, even if you conclude the view is a failure, you can learn much from engaging with it.

A final remark. We carefully examine a set of principles that, if accepted, commit one to Utilitarianism. (To view all these principles in one place, see Appendix A.) However, as the remark from Korsgaard above suggests, you need not accept each of these principles to qualify as a Utilitarian. In contemporary ethics, a large number of distinct views fly under Utilitarianism's banner. (To view many of these alternatives, see Appendix B.) We regard the flatfooted version around which this book is organized to be the most defensible. We focus on a specific version of the view because we want to convey the complexities involved in fully working out an ethical theory and because, as Hume once wrote, "'Tis impossible to refute a system, which has never yet been explain'd. In such a manner of fighting in the dark, a man loses his blows in the air, and often places them where the enemy is not present."

* * *

To ease readability, we've adopted a number of conventions. Sections, subsections, figures, and tables are numbered according to their chapter. Hence, §6.7.2 is the second subsection of the seventh section of Chapter 6, Figure 11.1 is the first figure in Chapter 11, and so on. When important matters—principles, cases, key terms, and distinctions—first appear we will set them apart from the main text with additional indentation on the left and additional line spacing above and below. This is a visual indication of their significance, and it makes it easier to refer back to them later. We'll also adjust the typography. When we introduce a core principle—one of the members of the set of principles that together imply Utilitarianism—we will use small capitals, for example, WELFARISM. When we introduce a case, we will give it a name and underline it, for example, Mineshafts. For everything else that's important, we will use italics, for example, *Agent-Favoring Option*. When such matters appear again later in the chapter, we drop all typographical emphasis and simply capitalize the first letter of each word. This indicates that you can find it set off from the text earlier in the chapter. In later chapters, we will cease capitalizing. If, at any point, you run across a term you are unfamiliar with, there's a good chance you can find it defined in the Glossary.

A few comments on writing. First, with generic personal pronouns, we default with "she." When two generic personal pronouns are used together, to avoid ambiguity, we will assign the first "she" and the second "he." Second, though some people understand the terms to have different meanings, we use "ethics" and "morality" interchangeably. Third, to avoid cumbersome locutions, we'll often personify nonagents. For example, we'll say, "Utilitarianism tells us that this act is impermissible." Finally, on occasion, qualifications pile up around a specific term. When context makes the intended meaning obvious, we'll drop the qualifications. For instance, if it's clear we are talking about "intrinsic good-simpliciter," we will just say "good." When confusion might arise or when we are giving a definition, we'll retain the qualifications.

To avoid distraction, we have tried to keep references to a minimum and to include direct quotations only when seeing the original wording is crucial. When we have drawn on the ideas of others, we mention this in a note. This is to acknowledge our intellectual debts, which are extensive, but also to indicate where the ideas are explored in more detail. Each chapter ends with a list of references. These also serve as our recommended reading list for each topic. We've marked with an asterisk readings that are well suited for pedagogical purposes.

Acknowledgments

ATF

This book began with Steve Cahn. He had the idea to do an anthology on contemporary Utilitarianism. Organizing the readings with him shaped much of the structure of this work. Eventually the idea of an anthology was abandoned. But without Steve, the writing of this book would have never started. I am grateful for his constant support and guidance.

I wish to thank Luke Semrau for taking on this project with me. I am lucky to have been able to spend so much time enjoying the company of such a powerful interlocutor.

Most of this manuscript was written while I was a visiting research fellow at Leeds University (IDEA CETL). I wish to express my gratitude to Leeds for their hospitality and to Chris Megone for working tirelessly to arrange the visit. I presented Chapter 8 as part of the IDEA Research Seminar series and received many helpful comments. Nanyang Technological University offered generous financial support through a Start Up Grant (No. M4081673.100). I wish to thank my colleagues for covering my duties while I was away. And I especially wish to express my gratitude to Chenyang Li for making my leave of absence possible.

Matthew Hammerton offered many helpful suggestions on Chapters 1–4. Douglas Portmore provided invaluable feedback on Chapter 6 and Chapter 7. Travis Timmerman greatly improved Chapter 6. I benefited from a number of discussions with Paul Snowdon concerning Chapter 4 and Chapter 8. More importantly, Paul and Katzi Snowdon offered much warmth and care during our time in London. I also wish to express appreciation to Brian Rak and Maura Gaughan at Hackett for their diligent assistance in bringing this project to press. A number of anonymous reviewers made many important suggestions and prevented some bad mistakes. I am very indebted to all of these people for the time and energy they sacrificed.

I owe the most to my wife, Hiu Chuk Winnie Sung, and our Baba and Mama. You embody *Analects* 6.30 (夫仁者己欲立而立人己欲達而達人). Thank you for showing me the way.

LBS

Andrew Forcehimes generously invited me to write this book with him. I cannot easily overstate how much I've learned from him in the process.

Magdi, who is an inspiring human, has never hesitated to help me.

Travis Timmerman, Douglas Portmore, and anonymous reviewers offered helpful feedback. Naturally, the remaining faults are our own.

Contents

Part I. Introductory Material ... 1
1. A Brief Introduction to Utilitarianism ... 2
   1.1 Introduction ... 2
   1.2 The Ethical Domain ... 2
       1.2.1 Deontic Properties ... 6
       1.2.2 Reason Properties ... 9
       1.2.3 Evaluative Properties ... 13
   1.3 Utilitarianism ... 17
       1.3.1 Utilitarianism's Answer to the Relevance Question ... 19
       1.3.2 Utilitarianism's Answer to the Significance Question ... 21
       1.3.3 Utilitarianism's Answer to the Combinatorial Question ... 22
       1.3.4 Utilitarianism's Deontic Verdicts ... 23
   1.4 Being a Utilitarian ... 25
       1.4.1 Utilitarianism and Self-Effacement ... 26
       1.4.2 The Approximation Strategy of a Utilitarian ... 29
   1.5 Conclusion ... 34
2. An Argument from the Classical Utilitarians ... 36
   2.1 Introduction ... 36
   2.2 Bentham's Argument from the Burden of Proof ... 37
   2.3 Mill's Argument from Desire as Sole Evidence ... 44
   2.4 Sidgwick's Argument from Temporal Insensitivity ... 50
   2.5 Conclusion ... 56

Part II. Normative Principles ... 59
3. Maximizing Is Sufficient and Constraints ... 60
   3.1 Introduction ... 60
   3.2 One for Two ... 61
   3.3 The Argument from One for Two ... 63

	3.4	Why Are Constraints Puzzling	65
	3.5	The Standard Story of Action Argument against Non-Consequentialism	66
	3.6	The Collective Self-Defeat Argument against Agent-Relative Consequentialism	69
	3.7	The No Approach Succeeds Argument against Constraints	73
	3.8	Decision-Deontic Confusion	74
	3.9	Conclusion	77
4.	**Maximizing Is Necessary and Demandingness**		79
	4.1	Introduction	79
	4.2	Endless Self-Sacrifice	80
	4.3	The Argument from Endless Self-Sacrifice	81
	4.4	The Minimal Beneficence Argument against Existence Internalism	84
	4.5	The Moral Reasons Ubiquity Argument against Rational Options Abound	86
	4.6	Impermissibility-Blame Confusion	89
	4.7	Conclusion	93
5.	**Objectivism and Action Guidance**		95
	5.1	Introduction	95
	5.2	Mineshafts	97
	5.3	The Action Problem Argument against Objective Consequentialism	98
	5.4	The Argument from Ambiguous Ability	101
	5.5	The Centrality Problem Argument against Objective Consequentialism	105
	5.6	The Deontic Force Argument against Impermissibility Aversion	108
	5.7	Conclusion	111
6.	**Actualism and Control Sensitivity**		113
	6.1	Introduction	113
	6.2	Sequential Doses	115
	6.3	The Argument from Diachronic Identical Control	117
	6.4	The Ensuring Control Argument against Diachronic Identical Control	119
	6.5	The Argument for Only Irreversible Actions Are Available	124

	6.6	The Argument from Synchronic Identical Control	126
	6.7	Actualistic Consequentialism's Response to Synchronic Cases	129
		6.7.1 The Problem of Act Versions Argument against Every Act Directly	129
		6.7.2 The Best Solution Argument for Only Non-Entailed Acts Directly	133
		6.7.3 The Only Non-Entailed Acts Directly Argument against Synchronic Control Insensitivity	137
	6.8	Conclusion	138
7.	**Individualism and Overdetermination**		141
	7.1	Introduction	141
	7.2	Asteroid	142
	7.3	Individualistic Consequentialism and the Principle of Moral Harmony	144
		7.3.1 The Argument That Volitional-Focused Individualistic Consequentialism Is Unharmonious	145
		7.3.2 The Argument That Volitional-Rational-Focused Individualistic Consequentialism Is Unharmonious	147
		7.3.3 The Principle of Moral Harmony Argument against Individualistic Consequentialism	152
	7.4	A Harmonious Form of Individualistic Consequentialism	153
		7.4.1 The Pragmatic Encroachment Argument against No State Given	154
		7.4.2 The Preference Permissibility Argument against the Object-Given Preference Profile	157
		7.4.3 The Argument That Volitional-Rational-Focused Individualistic Consequentialism Is Harmonious	162
	7.5	Conclusion	163
Part III. Evaluative Principles			167
8.	**Hedonism and the Experience Machine**		168
	8.1	Introduction	168
	8.2	The Experience Machine	169
	8.3	The Argument from the Experience Machine	170
	8.4	The Argument from Self-Supervenience to Mental State Supervenience	172
	8.5	The Argument from Invariabilism and Monism to Hedonism	176
	8.6	Conclusion	181

9. Welfarism and Sadistic Pleasure — 184
- 9.1 Introduction — 184
- 9.2 Sadistic Pleasure — 185
- 9.3 The Argument from Sadistic Pleasure — 186
- 9.4 The Well-Being in Ill-Being Argument against Welfarism — 188
- 9.5 The Intrinsic Goodness Argument against Not Good — 190
- 9.6 The Argument from Innocuous Sadism — 193
- 9.7 Conclusion — 197

10. Proportionalism and Worthiness — 199
- 10.1 Introduction — 199
- 10.2 Saint or Sinner — 200
- 10.3 The Basic Value Depends on Worthiness Argument against Proportionalism — 201
- 10.4 Graphing Proportionalism — 202
- 10.5 The Fit Idea Argument against the Merit View — 204
- 10.6 The Polarity Preservation Argument against the Desert View — 208
- 10.7 The Circularity Argument against Worthiness — 212
- 10.8 Conclusion — 215

11. Additive Aggregation and The Repugnant Conclusion — 217
- 11.1 Introduction — 217
- 11.2 The Repugnant Conclusion — 218
- 11.3 The Argument from the Repugnant Conclusion — 221
- 11.4 The Argument against Additive Aggregation — 223
- 11.5 The Argument to Accept Repugnance — 224
- 11.6 The Argument for the Unreliability of Repugnance — 230
- 11.7 Conclusion — 232

Appendix A: Principles to Utilitarianism — 235
Appendix B: Alternative Principles — 237
Appendix C: Theory Assessment — 242
Glossary — 248

PART I
Introductory Material

1

A Brief Introduction to Utilitarianism

1.1 *Introduction*

The purpose of this chapter is to get you acquainted with Utilitarianism. With a firm grasp of the theory's central claims, you'll be better able to evaluate the arguments coming in later chapters. Our approach will be, at least initially, indirect. Rather than diving into Utilitarianism straightaway, we'll begin with a more general inquiry: What's an ethical theory? Answering this will occupy us for the first section of the chapter. This topic is interesting in its own right. Anyone thinking seriously about ethics should have a clear idea of what an ethical theory is and what it seeks to accomplish. But it also provides background information that will prove helpful once we turn directly to our central question: What's Utilitarianism?[1]

There is another motivation for beginning with ethical theory. One of the features of Utilitarianism that's especially attractive is that it tells a grand, unified story about ethics, with few loose ends. This story, of course, could be entirely mistaken. The remaining chapters in this book will take up that issue. But the point to emphasize is that, regardless of the details of the view, Utilitarianism offers a complete—perhaps even elegant—account of the ethical domain. This virtue is apparent only when you view the theory from a distance. Here we try to afford that perspective. We show how the structure of Utilitarianism enables it to address a wide range of issues with minimal theoretical commitments.

1.2 *The Ethical Domain*

You are already familiar with ethics. You wonder what you should do and try to do it. You also have been the unfortunate target of others acting unethically. As an agent and a patient, ethical phenomena are all too common. As a first approximation, we might say that an ethical theory is an attempt to organize these data. That is, an ethical theory attempts to provide a systematic account of all ethical

---

1. Since we want to make this chapter a manageable length, we'll answer neither of these questions in sufficient detail. For an in-depth overview of ethical theory in general, see Kagan (1998). For an in-depth overview of Utilitarianism in particular, see Bykvist (2010).

phenomena.[2] This involves completing two tasks. First, an ethical theory needs to supply a list categorizing all actions as either right or wrong. We'll call this a theory's enumerative task. Second, an ethical theory needs to explain why the acts get categorized as they do. It needs to say what it is that makes right acts right and wrong acts wrong. We'll call this a theory's explanatory task. If we have an account that can accomplish both the enumerative and explanatory tasks, then we have the makings of an ethical theory.

However, if you are not already used to ethical theorizing, this quick characterization is not terribly informative. It requires unpacking. To get a better sense of what ethical theory is about, it will be helpful to look at what separates the ethical domain from everything else.

Moral philosophy textbooks often proclaim that we can discern if a claim is ethical by attending to the use of the words "is" and "ought." On this suggestion, the claim "It ought to be that no one suffers needlessly" and the claim "You ought to keep your promises," because both use "ought," are ethical. "The cat is on the mat" and "An atom is small," because both use "is," are nonethical. Yet, despite being commonly invoked, this is-ought test is seriously deficient. Some is-statements have ethical content and some ought-statements do not. For example, consider the claims "Murder is wrong" and "Friendship is good." These claims obviously have ethical content. Whatever the is-ought test is tracking, these claims clearly fall on the ought side of that divide. Yet they both use "is." Similarly, consider the claims "The train ought to arrive in an hour" and "This seltzer water ought to remove that stain." These statements are clearly nonethical, the use of "ought" notwithstanding. There is an important distinction between ethical and nonethical claims. But we can't simply rely on "is" and "ought" to make it. Instead we need to attend to the substance of the claim. We need to focus on the kinds of properties picked out.

Imagine that you've woken in the middle of the night to the sound of a fire alarm and the smell of smoke. Your mind is racing. As you come to your senses, you utter the following:

> The apartment is engulfed in flames. That siren is incredibly loud. The firetrucks ought to arrive soon.

Each of these three claims predicates a trait to something. There is an apartment and it is claimed to be in flames. There's a siren, and it is claimed to be loud. And there is a place, and it is claimed that the firetrucks are expected to arrive there soon. In philosophical contexts, to say that something has a certain trait is to ascribe to it a

> *Property*: A property is a feature, characteristic, or quality a thing might have.

---

2. For an overview of what factors matter in judging one theory as superior to another, see Appendix C.

In the sentence "The apartment is engulfed in flames," "the apartment" is the subject and "is engulfed in flames" is the predicate. The predicate tells us that a certain property is possessed by the subject. The sentence expresses the idea that the apartment has the property of being engulfed in flames.

Notice how properties enable us to move beyond surface features of our language to focus on the content of what's being claimed. If we relied on terms such as "is" and "ought" to demarcate the ethical domain, then we would conclude that the last claim—"The firetrucks ought to arrive here soon"—is within the domain of ethics. That would be a mistake. In this instance, the "ought" indicates something about expectations. To say that "The firetrucks ought to arrive here soon" is to say of this place that firetrucks are expected to arrive. This is a descriptive claim. In fact, all three of these claims, despite superficial differences, aim to describe. Each claim predicates what are called

> *Descriptive Properties*: A property that can be ascribed with a descriptive predicate (e.g., is red, is flat, is round, is heavy).[3]

The first claim describes the apartment: it is engulfed in flames. The second describes the siren: it's loud. And the last describes the location: it is one where firetrucks are expected to soon arrive. Notice that these claims involve no assessment or evaluation. Accordingly, such claims—claims that predicate Descriptive Properties—are nonethical.

So far, we've offered only a negative characterization of ethics. We've said that it does not seek to explain descriptive facts. But we can give a positive characterization. To begin, we want to draw attention to another class of claims, ones that do have distinctively ethical content. Imagine again that your apartment is on fire. You're standing outside with your neighbors, and you utter the following:

> It is impermissible for me to stand by idly. Helping the injured is morally required. That her wounds are the most serious is a reason to help her first.

The first and second of these claims give an all things considered assessment of a particular action. They say you have certain duties. The third claim says that a fact—that her wounds are the most serious—is a reason for you to act in a certain way. Despite their differences, however, each claim concerns the regulation of behavior. All three claims predicate what are called

> *Normative Properties*: A property that can be ascribed with a normative predicate (e.g., is permissible, is impermissible, is optional, is required, is a reason for, is a reason against).

---

3. This formulation, as well as the formulation of Normative Properties, is modified from Jackson (1998: 120–22) and Streumer (2011: 326).

It is worth attending to the difference between the two different kinds of Normative Properties just mentioned. Those in the first class, which provide all things considered normative assessments, are called

> *Deontic Properties*: A property that can be ascribed with a deontic predicate (e.g., is permissible, is impermissible, is optional, is required).

Deontic Properties are of obvious importance. But sometimes we want to look more carefully at the various factors that bear on performing or not performing an action. For this we appeal to reasons. Reasons are the specific considerations that justify acting in certain ways. The fact that her wounds are the most serious counts in favor of your helping her first. This fact contributes to the justification of your starting with her. Those in the second class, which identify distinct normative contributions, we call

> *Reason Properties*: A property that can be ascribed with a reason predicate (e.g., is a reason for, is a reason against, is a strong reason, is a weak reason, is a decisive reason).

So there are two kinds of Normative Property. First, there is the property of having a certain deontic status: being permissible, impermissible, optional, and required. Second, there is the property of being a reason.

We can add to this positive characterization of ethical theory. There is another class of properties that are treated as falling within the ethical domain. To get a sense of these properties, imagine, as before, that your apartment is on fire. As emergency workers get things under control, you utter the following:

> It's good that I woke up in time to escape. Inhaling smoke is bad for that child. It is bad that our beautiful building is damaged.

These claims, like those that predicate Normative Properties, should also strike you as importantly different from descriptive claims. Rather than merely describing things, they evaluate them. Each says not only that something exists in some way but that it is valuable. These claims predicate what are called

> *Evaluative Properties*: A property that can be ascribed with an evaluative predicate (e.g., is good-for, is bad-for, is good, is bad, is valuable, is desirable).

The first claim says that a state of affairs—that you woke up in time to escape—is good. But this claim is ambiguous. We can highlight the ambiguity by looking at the second and third claims, which are also evaluative. The second says that a state of affairs—that a child inhales smoke—is bad-for someone, namely, the child. The smoke causes the child's life to go worse-for her. The third claim says that a state of affairs—that a beautiful building is damaged—is just bad. The damage makes the world a worse place.

To this point, we've suggested that we can get a clearer idea of what ethical theorizing is about by first getting clear about the difference between the ethical and nonethical domain. We're now in a position to say more specifically what this amounts to. The nonethical domain trades in Descriptive Properties, whereas the ethical domain trades in Normative and Evaluative Properties. An ethical theory gives an account of how Normative and Evaluative Properties relate to one another and how they link up to Descriptive Properties. Put in more familiar (but less precise) terminology, we might say that an ethical theory gives an account of the right and the good, their connection, and explains how each maps on to the natural world.

We've narrowed in on the domain of ethics. This goes some distance toward answering the question: What's an ethical theory? Still, there's much more to say. In the following subsections, we elaborate on both the normative and the evaluative.

1.2.1 *Deontic Properties*

An ethical theory, to complete its enumerative task, must provide a special kind of assessment for every action. It should say, for each, if it has the property of being permissible, impermissible, optional, or required. In this section, we describe each of these four Deontic Properties and how they relate to each other.

But before turning to this description, we need to explain a simplifying assumption we're going to make for the bulk of this book. Right now, you could perform a number of actions. You could continue reading, take a sip of coffee, cross your legs, and so on. All of these acts are, for you

> *Presently Available*: An action is presently available to an agent just when its performance is now under her control.

Notice that these acts are not mutually exclusive. You could continue reading while also crossing your legs and sipping coffee. Accordingly, although each of these acts is distinct, they are not

> *Alternatives*: One act is an alternative to another just when their joint performance is impossible.[4]

Only continuing reading (i.e., reading while refraining from crossing your legs and refraining from sipping coffee) is an Alternative to continuing reading while also crossing your legs and sipping coffee. You cannot do both. Likewise, only

---

4. This understanding of Alternatives follows Bergström (1966).

continuing reading is an Alternative to only sipping coffee. They are mutually exclusive.

We can now state our assumption. We will proceed as if it were sufficient for an ethical theory to assign Deontic Properties to all Alternatives. More precisely, we'll assume that if an ethical theory assigns Deontic Properties to every member of every set of Presently Available Alternatives for every agent, it has completed its enumerative task. This will greatly simplify our discussion, and for the most part is innocent. It aligns with our ordinary ways of thinking about acts. In everyday conversations, when people say that you could do this or that, they often intend for you to understand the "or" as exclusive. If, while hanging out, a friend asks, "What do you want to do next? Eat lunch or go swimming?" She's probably not proposing the combination. Normally people talk in terms of Alternatives, not distinct actions. They make the assumption we'll be making. Strictly speaking, however, the assumption is false. To complete its enumerative task, an ethical theory needs to assign Deontic Properties to all actions, not just Alternatives.[5]

With this understanding of Presently Available Alternatives in hand, we can now turn to Deontic Properties. Imagine each of your Presently Available Alternatives as a door in front of you. You can only go through one door. And on the other side of each door is the complete state of affairs you would bring about—the way the world would be—if you performed the act. Performing an act is like going through the door corresponding to that act. Above each door is a light that glows either red or green. Red-light doors correspond to actions that you ought not to perform. These actions have the property of being

> *Impermissible*: An action is impermissible if and only if refraining from the action is required.

You are physically able to open a red-light door, but you ought not to. It's ethical trespassing. Green-light doors, by contrast, correspond to actions that you are permitted to perform. These actions have the property of being

> *Permissible*: An action is permissible if and only if it is an action that is not impermissible.

You are physically able to open green-light doors, and ethically you are allowed to do so.

But among permissible actions another distinction remains. The green-light doors—the permissible actions—are either optional or required. To know which of these categories a permissible act belongs to requires looking to the Deontic Properties of the other acts that could have been performed instead. For example,

---

5. We will drop the focus on Alternatives only in §6. In §6.8, we offer a formulation of Utilitarianism that covers all distinct actions.

suppose you face a mix of permissible and impermissible actions. This, continuing with our analogy, would be like facing multiple red-light doors and multiple green-light doors. You are permitted to open any of the green-light doors. And you must refrain from opening any of the red-light doors. Since any of the many green-light doors will do, each one has the property of being

> *Optional*: An action is optional if and only if it is permissible to either perform or refrain from the action.

Because there are multiple permissible actions, and you are allowed to perform or refrain from the performance of any of them, each also has the property of being optional.

Suppose next that you face a different set of Presently Available Alternatives. All but a single act is impermissible. This is like choosing from a sea of red-light doors with a solitary green-light door. You are allowed, of course, to perform the permissible act and to open the only green-light door. But here you lack options. So we say this act also has the property of being

> *Required*: An action is required if and only if it is the uniquely permissible action available—a permissible action that is not optional.

You ought to perform any act that is required. You ought to open this door; it's what morality demands of you.

With a clear view of what each deontic predicate picks out, we can now see how each property relates to the others. These relationships are depicted in Figure 1.1.

All actions are either permissible or impermissible. Permissible actions are further categorized as optional or required. A permissible action is optional when there are other permissible actions available. A permissible action is required when there are no other permissible actions available.

Figure 1.1: *Deontic Properties*

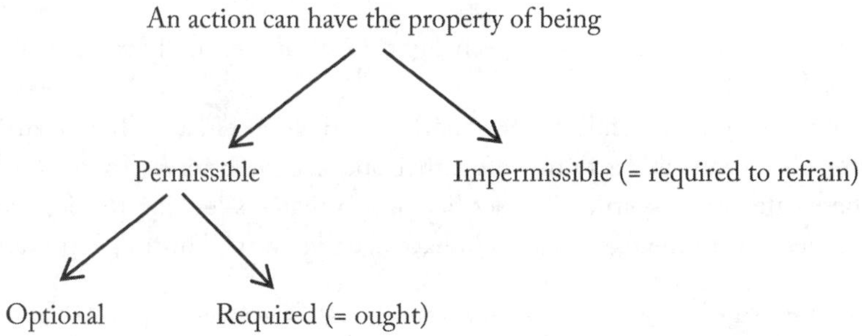

An action can have the property of being

Permissible   Impermissible (= required to refrain)

Optional   Required (= ought)

Once you see how these four Deontic Properties are related, you can see why ethical theories are usually formulated in the same way. Since all the other Deontic Properties can be understood in terms of permissibility, an ethical theory can complete its enumerative task by offering a biconditional—a set of necessary and sufficient conditions—of the form "An action has the property of being permissible if and only if this act has [Descriptive Properties]." There are, of course, many ways to fill in the blank. A Divine Command Theorist might say, "the property of being an action that God has not commanded you to refrain from" and a Utilitarian might say, "the property of being an action that maximizes the sum total of pleasure minus pain." Equipped with this biconditional, the Deontic Properties of every act can be identified. If we know the necessary and sufficient conditions for an action to be permissible, then we can infer the remaining three Deontic Properties. If an act fails the necessary conditions for permissibility, it is impermissible. If an action is among many that satisfy the sufficient condition for permissibility, then it is optional. And if an action uniquely satisfies the sufficient condition for permissibility, then it is required. If a theory can give us such a principle, it has completed its enumerative task.

Still, more work remains. Assigning Deontic Properties to all acts is not enough. To see why, notice that two different theories may assign all actions the very same Deontic Properties, but they do so for very different reasons. For example, consider a version of Divine Command Theory according to which God commands you to follow the precepts of Utilitarianism. These two theories would agree that actions with the property of maximizing the sum total of pleasure minus pain are permissible. And they would agree that actions that failed to so maximize are impermissible. They disagree, however, about the explanation. They offer very different accounts of what, ultimately, makes acts have the Deontic Properties they do. Utilitarianism says that the fact that an action maximizes the sum total of pleasure minus pain ultimately explains why it is permissible. By contrast, this Divine Command Theory says that the fact that refraining from the act was not commanded by God ultimately explains why it is permissible. To discern this difference, we need to examine the explanation each theory offers. We need to look to what each says about what ultimately accounts for the Deontic Properties of actions. In other words, we look to what the theory says is intrinsically reason providing.

1.2.2 *Reason Properties*

We've seen that an ethical theory must assign Deontic Properties to all actions. But, beyond this enumerative task, a theory must also explain why these properties are assigned as they are. It must be able to point to the various considerations that together make it the case that an action has the Deontic Properties it does. Here is where an ethical theory must turn to reasons. Reasons are the specific considerations that justify—that count in favor or against—an action. Reasons are the basic currency of the normative domain. They tell us both what matters and how much it matters. The reasons to perform or refrain from performing an action are what constitutively explain why it is permissible or impermissible.

To clarify the nature of Reason Properties, we can start with an example. Suppose you are walking to class. You were up late working on a paper, so you're tired; and the sun is beating down, so you're hot. On your way, you come across two drink sellers. One is selling cold juice. The other is selling hot coffee. Let's assume you ought to buy a drink but that you only have enough cash for one. Which ought you to buy? To answer this question, we need to consider the facts that bear on the choice. There is the fact that a cool beverage would provide some relief from the heat. And there is the fact that a jolt of caffeine would make you less tired for class. These facts are normatively relevant. When we talk about them in the context of determining what you ought to do, we say that these facts have the property of being a reason. So the fact that the juice would provide relief from the heat is a reason to buy the juice. The fact that the coffee would help wake you up is a reason to buy the coffee. These facts pick out certain Descriptive Properties that are reason providing. The descriptive facts that are reason providing are the facts that explain why an action has the Deontic Properties it does. These are the descriptive facts that matter.

Reasons thus determine which Descriptive Properties are of deontic relevance. But here we should distinguish between the two forms reasons can take. For only some reasons are part of the ultimate explanation as to why an action has the Deontic Properties it has. Consider some examples. Suppose that you like the taste of coffee. It affords you a pleasant experience. The fact that you would experience pleasure is a reason for you to buy the coffee. We can add that this fact about your pleasure has the normative force that it does independent of anything else. You don't want the pleasant experience as a means to some other end. Your pleasure itself is a reason for you to buy the coffee. Given this, we say that this fact is an

> *Intrinsic Reason*: A fact has the property of being an intrinsic reason if and only if this fact itself counts in favor of acting in a certain way; its normative force does not depend on any other fact.

By contrast, some facts are reason providing, but their normative force is derived from other facts. These facts do not feature in the ultimate explanation as to why actions have the Deontic Properties they do. For example, consider the fact that the coffee's caffeine would make you less tired for class. That fact is a reason for you to buy the coffee. Yet it's clearly not the end of the story. You don't want to be less tired for the sake of being less tired. Rather you want to be less tired because that will enable you to do other things that do matter. You might want, for example, to learn important truths in class, and if you are awake you will be better able to do so. So the fact that the coffee would make you less tired for class is a reason to buy it, but its normative force is parasitic on the fact that you will learn important truths in class if you are awake. Given this, we say that this fact is an

> *Instrumental Reason*: A fact has the property of being an instrumental reason if and only if it is not the case that this fact itself counts in favor of acting in a certain way; its normative force depends on some other fact.

The fact that the coffee would make you less tired for class is only a reason to buy it because it is suitably related to the fact that being awake gives you access to important knowledge. Now we might keep pressing, asking whether this fact is the end of the story. Does knowledge of important truths matter in its own right? Or is there something else that they are a means to? Perhaps the fact that you'd learn certain important truths is itself an Instrumental Reason. But eventually we would arrive at some fact that kicks off this chain. It is this fact that is intrinsically reason providing.

In addition to determining which descriptive facts are normatively relevant, reasons also indicate how significant these facts are. Reasons can be stronger or weaker. Suppose that it is blistering hot outside. You are in utter misery. In this case, the fact that the juice would relieve your misery is a strong reason to buy it. But let us assume that the pleasure you get from coffee is rather mild. You like it, but not that much. So the fact that you would experience pleasure is a weak reason for you to buy the coffee. While the fact that the juice would relieve your misery is a stronger reason than the fact that you would experience pleasure from the coffee. Reasons, then, not only pick out what's normatively relevant but also determine how significant each deontically relevant Descriptive Property is in its own right. Reasons tell us both what matters and how much it matters.

We are now in a position to see how reasons can explain why actions have the Deontic Properties that they do. For every act you could perform, there are some facts that count in favor of performing it, some facts that count against it, and some that are irrelevant. Take, for example, the act of buying the juice. The fact that the juice would relieve your misery from the heat is a reason to buy it, the fact that you'd miss out on the pleasant experience of the coffee is a reason against buying it, and the fact that the seller's brother has brown hair is irrelevant. The strength of the reasons to buy and not to buy determine the action's Deontic Properties. We can call this connection the

> *Reasons-Deontic Link*: An agent's Presently Available Alternative has the property of being permissible if and only if (and because) the set of intrinsic reasons for performing it have a combined strength that is at least as strong as the combined strength of the set of intrinsic reasons for performing any of her other Presently Available Alternatives.[6]

---

6. This formulation is modified from Schroeder (2015).

According to the Reasons-Deontic Link, whether an action has the property of being permissible or impermissible depends on the reasons there are for and against performing that action. If the strength of the reasons for performing it is equal to or greater than the strength of the reasons for performing any other Presently Available Alternative, then the act has the property of being permissible. If the strength of the reasons for performing it is less than the strength of the reasons for performing any other Presently Available Alternative, then the act has the property of being impermissible.

Here the analogy of tug-of-war is helpful. We can think of all of the reasons for performing an act as members of one team—let's call them the Green Team—and all of the reasons for refraining from performing the action as members of a second team, the Red Team. The facts that are irrelevant are like people outside of the game. The different members of each team are of different strengths. Some exert a lot of force, others less so. The people who exert more force are more significant members of the team, just as some descriptive facts provide stronger reasons than others.

We can link this tug-of-war analogy to our door analogy from our discussion of Deontic Properties. Suppose that the middle of the rope is tied around a switch that controls the color of the lights above the door. If the switch is not flipped, then the light will stay green. The act is permissible. Team Green—the reasons in favor of the performance of this act—tries to accomplish this goal. Team Red—the reasons against the performance of this act—tries to flip the switch. If Team Red can overpower Team Green, the act is impermissible. That is, if the reasons against performing are stronger than the reasons for performing, then the Red Team wins and the act is impermissible. If the reasons for performing are at least as strong as the reasons against, then the light stays green.

A final observation. We've suggested that the tug-of-war analogy helpfully models the interaction among reasons that explains why actions have the Deontic Properties they do. It is important that this model does not assume that reasons combine additively. We should allow for the possibility that the combined strength of the reasons in favor of performing an action is different from the sum of the strengths of each individual reason for performing the action. The tug-of-war analogy preserves this possibility. In mechanics, force is a vector quantity. It has both magnitude and direction. We could imagine testing the strength of each team member pulling alone. This is how we might think of the strength of each reason in isolation. But when team members pull together, the force they exert may not be the sum of the force of the individuals. Team members may interact, leading some to pull at different angles. This would lead to a total force that is unequal to the sum of each of their individual forces. Similarly, the strength of the reasons for or against might combine nonadditively.

Let's take stock. We suggested that an ethical theory must turn to reasons in order to explain why acts have the Deontic Properties that they do. Reasons tell us what descriptive facts are relevant and how significant they are. In this way, a theory is able to complete its explanatory task.

1.2.3 *Evaluative Properties*

We next turn to the part of the ethical domain concerned with Evaluative Properties. Yet, as noted above, value talk is fraught with ambiguity. Whatever else a theory has to say about what is valuable, there are three standard distinctions among value concepts we can expect it to accommodate.

Let us begin with the distinction, now familiar from our discussion of reasons, between intrinsic and instrumental goodness. Some things are good because they provide something else that's good, and some things are good in themselves, independent of any relation to other goods. You win the lottery. When handed the check, you might say, "This money is good!" Later, while at the beach on your dream vacation, you might say, "This pleasant experience is good!" As is apparent, there is an important distinction between these utterances. The goodness of the money depends crucially on the goodness of what it makes available to you. If the money couldn't be spent, it would cease to be good. By contrast, the goodness of the pleasant experience requires nothing else. It retains its goodness even if nothing else comes from it. As this example illustrates, we need the following distinction:

> *Intrinsic Value*: A fact has the property of being intrinsically valuable if and only if this fact is itself good or bad; its goodness or badness does not depend on how it relates to anything else.

> *Instrumental Value*: A fact has the property of being instrumentally valuable if and only if it is not the case that this fact is itself good or bad; its goodness or badness depends on how it relates to something else.[7]

It's important to note that these are not mutually exclusive categories. The same thing can be both instrumentally good or bad and intrinsically good or bad. For example, the pleasure of being complimented for a job well done is, as a pleasant experience, intrinsically good. And, insofar as this experience motivates you to do more jobs well, as an incentive it is also instrumentally good. Or, to take another example, imprisoning someone causes her suffering and so is intrinsically bad. But,

---

7. We assume that nothing we say hinges on what bears value. We thus treat the following as interchangeable: facts, true propositions, and obtaining states of affairs. For discussion, see Zimmerman (2001: 49–50).

insofar as this punishment deters other would-be criminals, it is instrumentally good.

The second key distinction is between things that are good-simpliciter or bad-simpliciter and things that are good-for someone or bad-for someone. We claimed that your pleasant experience on the beach was good. But this statement is ambiguous. Did we mean to express the idea that this pleasant experience is good-simpliciter or that it was good-for you that you had the experience? These two senses of good are importantly different. We thus need the following distinction:

> *Value-for You*: Some fact is good-for you or bad-for you if and only if it is personally good or bad.
>
> *Value-Simpliciter*: Some fact is good-simpliciter or bad-simpliciter if and only if it is impersonally good or bad.

The distinction is fairly easy to track, but we will note one helpful heuristic. The difference between these senses is often marked by the "point of view" modifier. Return to your pleasant beach experience. There are two different things we might say. First, of two lives identical in every respect except that one includes the pleasant beach experience while the other does not, we might say that the life with the additional beach experience is better-for you. And that's because the beach experience is good from your point of view. Second, of two worlds identical in every respect except that one includes the pleasant beach experience while the other does not, we might say that the one with this additional pleasure is better-simpliciter. And that's because pleasure is good from the point of view of the universe or that of an impartial spectator.

As with the distinction between Instrumental and Intrinsic Goodness, the categories picked out by this distinction are not mutually exclusive. The same thing can be good-for you or bad-for you and good-simpliciter or bad-simpliciter. For example, suppose that yesterday, at great suffering to yourself, you saved the lives of many of your fellow soldiers. What you did is good-simpliciter in that you saved many lives in a heroic act of self-sacrifice, but it is also bad-for you in that you experienced great suffering.

Your heroic act is both good-simpliciter and bad-for you. But isn't it also bad-simpliciter? After all, it is not just bad-for you that you experienced great suffering; it is bad from the point of view of the universe. This is puzzling. How can the same state of affairs be both good-simpliciter and bad-simpliciter? It can't. This puzzle arises only because we are missing an important distinction. There is, on one hand, the value of a particular part of a complete state of affairs and, on the other hand, the value of the whole thing. If we're not careful in distinguishing between the complete state of affairs and a state of affairs that's a part, then we're liable to error.

Up to this point, we've relied on your linguistic intuitions when talking about states of affairs. But in philosophy it is a technical term with a specific meaning, which we'll now make explicit. Sometimes we use "state of affairs" to refer to part of the way things might be. For example, "that you are left-handed" is a state of affairs. If you have the property of being left-handed, then we say that this state of affairs obtains or is actual. But if you don't have the property of being left-handed, then we say that this state of affairs is possible but not actual. It does not obtain. Yet, more often than not in ethics, what we want to talk about is a

> *Complete State of Affairs*: A state of affairs such that every other state of affairs is either included or precluded.

A state of affairs includes another if it is not possible for it to obtain and for the other not to obtain. For example, being the only person in your family that's left-handed includes your having hands, includes somebody having hands, includes your having a family, and so on. A state of affairs precludes another if it is not possible that it obtains and that the other also obtains. For example, being the only person in your family that's left-handed precludes your lacking arms, precludes your being right-handed, precludes your having a brother that's left-handed, and so on. Everything that's actual—our world—is a Complete State of Affairs. But there are other ways that things could be. There are different combinations of what's included or precluded. Each of these combinations is also a Complete State of Affairs. Sometimes we call these different combinations "possible worlds." This is the sense of "world"—a Complete State of Affairs—being used when people say things like "You ought to make the world as good as you can."[8]

With the notion of a Complete State of Affairs defined, we're able to make sense of what was initially puzzling. Return to your heroic act of self-sacrifice. If we focus on what happened to you—you experienced great suffering—it's clear what we should say. This state of affairs is bad-for you and bad-simpliciter. But if we expand the scope of our evaluation to the Complete State of Affairs, which includes your saving many fellow soldiers, then we'll arrive at a different judgment. The key idea is that we distinguish between something's having value in the most basic way and the overall value of the Complete State of Affairs. Putting the distinction precisely,

---

8. This paragraph, and the formulation of Complete State of Affairs, draws heavily on Plantinga (2003: 106–8).

Overall Value: The intrinsic value-simpliciter of a Complete State of Affairs.[9]

Basic Value: The Intrinsic Value-simpliciter of a state of affairs consisting purely of a single Intrinsic Value.[10]

Whereas we use Overall Value to talk about the value of the whole, we use Basic Value to talk about the value atoms, so to speak. The Overall Value of the Complete State of Affairs is thus a function of the interaction of the Basic Values it contains. So we can say that it is basically bad that you experience great suffering. However, due to the basic goods that you bring about in saving your comrades, the Complete State of Affairs is good overall.

As this example suggests, a Complete State of Affairs contains many parts, some of which are good, others bad, and still others evaluatively neutral. Given that combining the Basic Values is how we arrive at Overall Value, we need to be able to pick out just those states of affairs consisting only of what evaluatively matters and do so in a way that avoids double counting. That is, the states of affairs in question need to contain something of Intrinsic Value and nothing else. For example, "Your suffering greatly yesterday at noon" is, presumably, a state of affairs that, in the most basic way, is intrinsically bad-simpliciter. Assuming this is so, we must avoid allowing this same suffering to qualify other states of affairs as basically bad. For example, we do not want to qualify as basically valuable "your suffering greatly yesterday at noon while wearing a helmet." This state of affairs does not consist purely of an Intrinsic Value; rather it is the impure mix of the evaluative and the descriptive. Nor do we want to count the state of affairs "your suffering greatly yesterday at noon while also feeling pleased that you can help your friends." This state of affairs does not consist in a single Intrinsic Value; rather it consists of both good and bad.

Finally, we should stress, as we did with reasons, that basic goods and bads may nonadditively interact with one another. The basic goods and bads may combine in such a way that the value of the Complete State of Affairs is not the sum of its parts.

To this point we've been focusing on Normative Properties and Evaluative Properties independently of one another. You might now ask: What's the relationship between the normative and the evaluative? To answer this question, we can no longer talk about ethical theories in general. This question is substantive.

---

9. As we did in this formulation, we occasionally write as though nonobtaining states of affairs have value. What we mean is that this state of affairs would be valuable if it were to obtain. This is only to ease exposition.

10. Our formulation is inspired by Feldman's claim that, "Every basic [value] is a pure attribution of a core intrinsically valuable property" (2000: 328). For accessibility, we've followed Feldman in using this imprecise language. For a precise formulation, see Zimmerman (2001: 155–59).

Different ethical theories will answer this question differently. It's now time to turn to Utilitarianism.

1.3 *Utilitarianism*

Put roughly, Utilitarianism holds that an action is permissible if and only if, and because, it brings about the Complete State of Affairs that is best overall, and the best Complete State of Affairs is the one with the greatest sum total of pleasure minus pain. Accordingly, one way to understand Utilitarianism is to think of it as the view that lines up, in the most flatfooted way, the normative and the evaluative. Acts that have certain Deontic Properties (e.g., being impermissible) will also bring about outcomes that have certain Evaluative Properties (e.g., being less than impersonally best overall or having lower levels of total personal value). Before getting into the details of the theory, however, we should highlight why this connection forged by Utilitarianism concerning the normative and the evaluative is not farfetched. Consider three striking structural similarities made apparent from our discussion above.

First, both values and reasons come in intrinsic and instrumental forms. Of both we can ask, What ultimately matters? Remember that specific descriptive facts are reason providing. Yet not all of these facts matter for deontic assessment, only those facts that provide Intrinsic Reasons. These are the descriptive facts that make distinct normative contributions. They are what explain why an act has the deontic verdict that it does. Evaluative Properties work similarly. Some specific descriptive facts are basically good. These are the descriptive facts that make distinct evaluative contributions. They are what explain why an outcome has the Overall Value that it does. For example, your pleasant beach experience is intrinsically good. If you need a beach pass to get in, then having a beach pass is instrumentally good. Similarly, we might say that you have an Intrinsic Reason to bring about your pleasant beach experience. But you have only an Instrumental Reason to buy the beach pass.

Second, both goodness and reasons can matter more or less. Of both we can ask: How much does the relevant descriptive fact matter? Remember that specific descriptive facts provide reasons with greater strengths. This tells us how much these facts matter in deontic assessment. Evaluative Properties work similarly. Specific descriptive facts are basically good to a certain extent. Suppose you have a headache that, without intervention, will last all day. You're permitted to choose between two pills. One provides complete relief. The other provides partial relief. Here we can say that you have stronger reason to choose complete relief over partial relief. We can also say that it is better that you choose complete relief than partial relief. Relatedly, both goodness and reasons can be overpowered without being destroyed. For example, it would be best if you chose complete relief, but it would still be good if you chose partial relief. Some relief from the pain is better than none. Similarly, there is most reason for you to choose complete relief, but there is still some reason for you to choose partial relief. The goodness of partial relief, and the reasons that favor it, are overpowered by the greater goodness of complete relief and the stronger reasons for choosing it. But, in both cases, this does not eliminate what's overpowered.

Finally, both goodness and reasons can be combined. Of both we can ask: How are the component parts—basic goods and reasons—combined to produce the overall value of the Complete State of Affairs or the assignment of Deontic Properties, respectively? We need a normative combinatorial principle. That is, a principle that takes all of the Intrinsic Reasons and their strengths as inputs and delivers the assignment of Deontic Properties—an overall assessment for a given act, all things considered—as the output. Similarly, we need some evaluative combinatorial principle. That is, we need a principle that takes all the basic goods and bads as inputs and churns out Overall Value—the evaluation of a Complete State of Affairs, all things considered—as the output.

Given these three structural similarities between goodness and reasons, we can pose, for both the normative and evaluative, three central questions:

Relevance Question: What descriptive facts are relevant?

- Normative Version: What descriptive facts are intrinsically reason providing?

- Evaluative Version: What descriptive facts are basically valuable?

Significance Question: How significant is each relevant descriptive fact?

- Normative Version: What is the strength of the reason provided by a given relevant fact?

- Evaluative Version: How much Basic Value does a given relevant fact possess?

Combinatorial Question: How do the relevant descriptive facts and their significance get combined?

- Normative Version: How do we arrive at the combined strength of the set of reasons for an action?

- Evaluative Version: How do we arrive at the Overall Value of a Complete State of Affairs?

We are now in a position to see one way of constructing a very orderly ethical theory. Both versions of the Relevance Question receive a similar answer. The very same descriptive facts are relevant for both reasons and value. Both versions of the Significance Question receive a similar answer. The extent to which these facts are significant is the same for reasons and value. And both versions of the Combinatorial Question receive a similar answer. We hold that reasons and basic goodness are combined using an additive combinatorial principle.

This, however, would leave one issue discussed previously unaddressed, namely, what is good-for you and bad-for you. To remedy this omission, we could claim that these, too, pick out the same descriptive facts. That is, the facts that provide reasons and the facts that are basically good are the same descriptive facts as the facts that make your life good-for you. Moreover, we could claim that the extent to which a given descriptive fact is good-for you is identical to the extent that it is basically good and that, when the relevant actions are available, these same facts provide reasons of a strength proportional to the amount of goodness.

Return to our door analogy. Suppose you could look at the world behind one of the doors and perceive everything that ethically matters. If this orderly theory were correct, what you would see is something like the picture in Figure 1.2. Notice that we are looking at only one world, so it is instructive to note that we cannot depict all the reasons for or against opening this door. Why? Because some of the reasons for and against opening a given door will be provided by your other Presently Available Alternatives—what's behind other doors. Even if a world contains only goods, there may still be reasons against selecting it. The alternative worlds may all be better. Similarly, a world that contains only bads may still be the best of those available. The alternatives may all be worse.

Utilitarianism adopts the structure of this orderly theory. To explain exactly how, we turn now to a more detailed account of Utilitarianism's answers to the Relevance Question, the Significance Question, and the Combinatorial Question.

1.3.1 *Utilitarianism's Answer to the Relevance Question*

We'll start with Utilitarianism's answer to the Evaluative Version of the Relevance Question: What descriptive facts are basically valuable? According to Utilitarianism the answer will ultimately come to what is good-for you and what is bad-for you. There is, on this view, a necessary connection between impersonal and personal value. That which is impersonally good is that which is personally good-for someone. We can answer what things are impersonally good by answering what makes your life better-for you—what Descriptive Properties are well-being makers. We can answer what things are impersonally bad by answering what makes your life worse-for you—what Descriptive Properties are ill-being makers. This brings us to the question: What things are good-for you and what things are bad-for you?

Utilitarianism holds that the answer to this question is pain and pleasure. One's welfare—one's well-being or ill-being—depends solely on one's experiences of pleasure and pain. Since Utilitarianism claims that impersonal value and

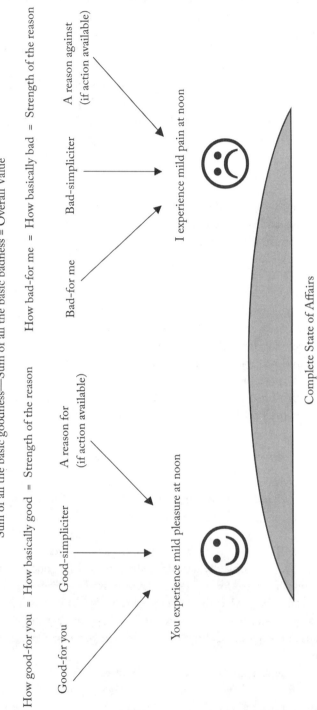

Figure 1.2: *Orderly Ethical Theory*

personal value track the same facts, it also holds that pleasure is not just good-for you; it is also basically good. And pain is not just bad-for you; it is also basically bad. That is to say, put generally, all and only episodes of well-being or ill-being are of Basic Value. Utilitarianism thus answers the Evaluative Version of the Relevance Question by pointing to the descriptive facts involving pain and pleasure.

Utilitarianism offers a similar answer to the Normative Version of the Relevance Question. But, before we spell it out, there is a crucial difference between the evaluative and the normative that we ought to point out. One of the earmarks of evaluative predicates is that they can be used appropriately to talk about circumstances in which there is no agency. For example, no agent was around to influence the circumstances in which the dinosaurs died, but we can still say that it is better that the dinosaurs died quickly and painlessly from a meteorite than if they had died off slowly from disease. By contrast, normative predicates are essentially tied to agency. It only makes sense to talk about reasons for action in contexts in which agency is possible. There can be states of affairs that are good and bad, but because there is no agency, there are no reasons for action.[11] The evaluative outstrips the normative. This difference between these two domains is important. It requires us to make a slight qualification concerning the facts that are reason providing.

The Normative Version of the Relevance Question asks: What descriptive facts are intrinsically reason providing? Given the restricted scope of the normative, we cannot simply answer, being pained and being pleased. Rather, to account for the fact that the normative is linked with action, the relevant properties, according to Utilitarianism, are the property of being an act that brings about pleasure and the property of being an act that brings about pain. The former always is a reason for performing an action. The latter always is a reason against performing an action. The fact that an act would bring about pleasure is necessarily a reason in favor of performing an action; the fact that an act would bring about pain is necessarily a reason against performing an action.[12]

1.3.2 *Utilitarianism's Answer to the Significance Question*

We turn now to the Significance Question: How significant is each relevant descriptive fact? Utilitarianism answers both versions of this question in the same way. Both personal and impersonal value, and the strength of reasons, track the quantity of the pleasure or pain.

Utilitarianism holds that a given pain is bad-for you and a given pleasure is good-for you in direct proportion to its intensity times its duration. And, since Utilitarianism claims that impersonal and personal value treat the significance of pleasure and pain in the same way, it holds that the extent to which a pleasure is good-for you matches the extent to which it is basically good. And the extent to

---

11. This point is due to Dancy (2000: 170–71) and Bykvist (2009).
12. This paragraph draws on Berker (2007: 116–17).

which a pain is bad-for you matches the extent to which it is basically bad. On this view, things are exactly as good-for or bad-for someone as they are basically good or basically bad. That is to say, the basic value of an episode of welfare is strictly proportional to its value-for the subject.

We can now say, in somewhat more detail, how Utilitarianism answers the Significance Question. We'll start with the Evaluative Version: How much Basic Value does a given relevant fact possess? Utilitarianism holds that a pleasure is both personally and impersonally good in proportion to its quantity. And a pain is both personally and impersonally bad in proportion to its quantity. This allows us to represent the significance of these values with integers. We assign, in accordance with their quantity, pleasure positive numbers and pain negative numbers.

We can next answer the Normative Version of the Significance Question: What is the strength of the reason provided by a relevant fact? Utilitarianism answers that, for an act that will bring about some quantity of pleasure, the strength of the reason to perform that act is proportional to the quantity. For an act that will bring about some quantity of pain, the strength of the reason to refrain from performing the act is proportional to the quantity.

1.3.3 *Utilitarianism's Answer to the Combinatorial Question*

We've seen how Utilitarianism answers the Relevance and Significance Questions with reference to the quantity of pain and pleasure. We can now turn to the Combinatorial Question: How do the relevant descriptive facts and their significance get combined? We'll start with the Evaluative Version: How do we arrive at the Overall Value of a Complete State of Affairs?

Utilitarianism holds that the Overall Value of a Complete State of Affairs is arrived at by summing the value of its parts. Put more precisely, the Overall Value of a Complete State of Affairs is determined by the sum of all the basic goodness minus the sum of all the basic badness. The higher the sum total, the better overall is the Complete State of Affairs. We take all the positive numbers representing the quantity of the basic goods—the numbers representing the amounts of pleasure in a Complete State of Affairs—and add them up. We take all the negative numbers representing the quantity of the basic bads—the negative numbers representing the amounts of pain in a Complete State of Affairs—and add them up. Finally, we put them together to get the net sum of goods minus bads.

Utilitarianism's answers to our three evaluative questions thus takes us to

> *Better as the Greater Balance of Pleasure over Pain*: A Complete State of Affairs, S_1, is better overall than a Complete State of Affairs, S_2, if and only if S_1 contains a higher sum total of pleasure minus pain than S_2.

With these claims, we can evaluatively rank every Complete State of Affairs.

We can next turn to the answer to the Normative Version of the Combinatorial Question: How do we arrive at the combined strength of the set of reasons for an action? It should, at this point, come as no surprise that Utilitarianism combines the strength of each reason for and against an action in the same way used to arrive at Overall Value, namely, by sum totaling. Accordingly, an act has the property of having most reason in its favor if and only if the performance of any of the agent's Presently Available Alternatives would not have brought about a Complete State of Affairs that's intrinsically better-simpliciter. And, as we've already seen, the greater the sum total of pleasure minus pain the better-simpliciter the Complete State of Affairs brought about by the performance of this act. Hence, if, of the Presently Available Alternatives, an act brings about the greatest sum total of pleasure minus pain, the set of Intrinsic Reasons for performing this act have a combined strength that is at least as strong as the combined strength of the Intrinsic Reasons for performing any Presently Available Alternative.

1.3.4 *Utilitarianism's Deontic Verdicts*

We've now seen Utilitarianism's answers to the Relevance Question, the Significance Question, and the Combinatorial Question. The upshot from this discussion is that Utilitarianism forges a connection between personal goodness, impersonal goodness, and reasons, such that an action has the property of having most reason in its favor just when it brings about the greatest sum total of pleasure minus pain. Since a world with the greatest sum total of pleasure minus pain is also a world with the greatest sum total of welfare, Utilitarianism holds that an action has the property of having most reason in its favor just when it brings about the greatest sum total of welfare. And since, according to Utilitarianism, a world with the greatest sum total of welfare is also a world that's best overall, the theory holds that an action has the property of having most reason in its favor just when it brings about the Complete State of Affairs that's best-simpliciter.

This last claim—that what you have most reason to do is linked to the best Complete State of Affairs—is worth singling out. It, when combined with the Reasons-Deontic Link, forms the view known as

> *Traditional Consequentialism*: An agent's Presently Available Alternative has the property of being permissible if and only if (and because) the performance of any of her other Presently Available Alternatives would not have brought about a Complete State of Affairs that's better overall.

Traditional Consequentialism is especially important in ethical theory. It receives a great deal of philosophical attention and is regarded by many as tremendously compelling. Indeed, Utilitarianism is often argued for either by assuming, or first arguing for the truth of, Traditional Consequentialism.

We're now well positioned to define Utilitarianism with some precision. It is the view that combines Traditional Consequentialism with Better as the Greater Balance of Pleasure over Pain. We can thus formulate the theory that is the focus of this book as

> *Utilitarianism*: An agent's Presently Available Alternative has the property of being permissible if and only if (and because) the performance of any of her other Presently Available Alternatives would not have brought about a Complete State of Affairs with a higher sum total of pleasure minus pain.

We now see how Utilitarianism makes good on both the enumerative and explanatory aims of an ethical theory. We have a principle that connects being permissible to certain Descriptive Properties—being an act that, were it performed, would bring about the greatest sum total of pleasure minus pain—and it is precisely because an act has (or lacks) this property that it is permissible (or impermissible). So characterized, Utilitarianism takes us from the pleasure and pain brought about by an action to its Deontic Properties in three steps:

> Step 1: Identify your Presently Available Alternatives.

> Step 2: Build an evaluative ranking of the Complete States of Affairs attaching to each of these Alternatives. How does its outcome compare in terms of pleasure and pain to any of your other Presently Available Alternatives? Is the sum total higher or lower?

> Step 3: Use this ranking to assign Deontic Properties to each Alternative. Anything less than the best—having a lower sum total of pleasure minus pain—is impermissible.

With this characterization of the view in hand, we can apply the theory to a schematic case. Consider

> <u>Headache</u>. Your friend has always suffered from a mild headache that, without intervention, will last the rest of her life. You have recently acquired two pills. One is yellow and will completely cure her. The other is pink and will make her headache slightly less painful. The pills together are lethal. You have four Presently Available Alternatives. Cure her with only the yellow pill, provide limited relief with only the pink pill, kill her with both, or do nothing, leaving her with a permanent headache. All else is equal between the outcomes.

By following the three steps above, the results we get for Headache are depicted in Table 1.1.

Table 1.1: *Example of Utilitarianism's Assignment of Deontic Properties*

Presently Available Alternatives	Complete State of Affairs	Deontic Property
Only Yellow	Best (highest sum total)	*Required*
Only Pink	2nd Best (second highest sum total)	*Impermissible*
Nothing	3rd Best (third highest sum total)	*Impermissible*
Both	Worst (lowest sum total)	*Impermissible*

Notice that every act that's less than the best—that would bring about an outcome with a lower sum total of pleasure minus pain—has the property of being impermissible. Utilitarianism is, as this suggests, going to assign a lot of impermissible deontic verdicts. Indeed, in most cases there will be only one permissible action, which will thereby be required. An act will rarely have the property of being optional. An action is optional if and only if so acting would maximize the sum total of pleasure minus pain, but there is some other Presently Available Alternative that ties for best—it too brings about the highest sum total of pleasure minus pain. Undoubtedly, such ties do not happen often.

1.4 *Being a Utilitarian*

You are now in a position to understand the basic architecture of Utilitarianism. Despite its simplicity, however, the view is easily misunderstood. In this section, we head off a pair of common mistakes. The first mistake is to hold that Utilitarianism requires agents to live directly as Utilitarians. Insofar as believing Utilitarianism is true or desiring what Utilitarianism holds to be desirable would fail to maximize the good, Utilitarianism will tell you to cause yourself to come to have different attitudes. The second mistake involves confusing Utilitarianism—an ethical theory—with the practical strategy we might adopt as Utilitarians in light of our various human shortcomings. Making decisions by calculating whether an act would maximize the sum total of pleasure minus pain, for example, would likely end in disaster. Think about how things would turn out if you drove a car by following this procedure. But Utilitarianism is an ethical theory. It should not be confused with the strategy we use, given our psychological makeup and circumstances, to approximate the moral ideal.

1.4.1 *Utilitarianism and Self-Effacement*

Up to this point, most of the examples we've considered focus on bodily movements, like administering a dose of medication. This might be misleading. For, inasmuch as certain attitudes are under our control, Utilitarianism will tell us to adopt the attitudes that bring about the best. That our attitudes can fall under Utilitarianism's jurisdiction has an important implication. It opens up the possibility that the theory tells you not to live your day-to-day life as a Utilitarian. This is important because much of the intuitive resistance to Utilitarianism is animated by the thought that the theory requires too drastic a revision to our moral lives. This resistance weakens if Utilitarianism turns out to be

> *Self-Effacing*: An ethical theory is self-effacing if it requires an agent to possess an attitude whose object falls within the ethical domain; but, if the ethical theory were true, this attitude fails to accurately represent its object.[13]

This definition requires elaboration. What does it mean for an attitude to accurately represent its object?

Here it will be helpful to start with a particular attitude: belief. What a belief is about or directed toward is its object. When you believe that it's raining, the belief is about the weather, in particular, that it is raining. And part of what it is to believe, as opposed to having some other attitude, is to represent the object of the belief as being true. Your belief that it is raining accurately represents its object if and only if it is true that it is raining. Take another attitude: desire. Again, what a desire is about or directed toward is its object. When you desire that you get a coffee, the desire is about coffee, in particular, that you get to drink it. And part of what it is to desire, as opposed to having some other attitude, is to represent the object of the desire as being desirable. Your desire that you get a coffee accurately represents its object if and only if it is desirable that you get a coffee. Similar claims hold for other attitudes. An intention accurately represents its object—an action—just when that action is choice-worthy. Blame accurately represents its object—an agent—just when the agent is blameworthy.[14]

We've seen that beliefs represent their objects as being true, desires represent their objects as desirable, and so forth. Now return to the ethical domain. Suppose that an ethical theory required that you believe a claim that is inconsistent with the theory itself. If the theory is true, then it would require you to form a belief that fails to accurately represent its object. That is, it would tell you to believe something that, if the theory were true, is false. Or suppose that an ethical theory required that you desire something for its own sake that the theory itself takes not to be intrinsically desirable. If the theory is true, then it would require you to form a

---

13. This formulation is inspired by Parfit (1984: §17) and Stocker (1976).
14. This paragraph draws on Rosen (2015) and Portmore (2019: §5.3).

desire that fails to accurately represent its object. That is, it would tell you to desire something that, if the theory were true, is not desirable. In both of these cases, the theory is Self-Effacing. And the same goes for intentions, blame, and the like.

To see why it is possible that Utilitarianism is Self-Effacing, consider

> Demon's Threat. An omniscient and omnipotent evil demon will torture everyone for eternity unless ten years from today you believe that maximizing the sum total of pleasure minus pain is sometimes impermissible.[15]

In this case, Utilitarianism will tell you to do whatever it takes over the next ten years to avoid triggering the demon. Since your beliefs are probably not under your voluntary control, this may require taking a circuitous route. You might hire a hypnotist or a psychotherapist or live by the precepts of some other theory and let cognitive dissonance do its work. But the point is that, in Demon's Threat, Utilitarianism requires you not to be a Utilitarian. It requires you to believe that maximizing the sum total of pleasure minus pain is sometimes impermissible. But, if the theory were true, this belief is false. Utilitarianism is Self-Effacing.

Demon's Threat shows that Utilitarianism can be Self-Effacing. But it's a fanciful case. Self-Effacement only weakens the intuitive resistance to Utilitarianism if we get a large number of similar results in our own lives. Do we? The answer seems to be Yes. A range of everyday circumstances appears to call for self-effacement. A few examples lend support.

Promises facilitate mutually beneficial cooperation. But notice what happens to promises if you conduct yourself as a Utilitarian. It would not be long before those you interacted with discovered your persuasion. And once they did, they would cease to see you as someone capable of entering into a promise with. Promises are useless when both parties know that one believes the following conditional: If this promise does not maximize the sum total of pleasure minus pain, I will break it.[16] Such conditional promises cannot be relied on. They are not worth making. The benefits of promises would be lost if one of the parties were a self-conscious Utilitarian. Assuming that the world would be a worse place without promises, Utilitarianism will tell us to take steps to ensure we can make them, which will entail trying to disbelieve Utilitarianism. The kinds of creatures we are and the nature of promises leads to Self-Effacement. Utilitarianism does not call for as drastic a revision to our beliefs about promises as is sometimes thought.

Close personal relationships are one of the greatest sources of pleasure. But the pleasure afforded by the near and dear quickly evaporates when you desire, say, their health, not for their own sake, but because it would maximize the sum total of pleasure minus pain. This point has long been recognized. Here's Austin:

---

15. This case is modified from Parfit (1984: 43–45).
16. This example is from Markovits (2010: 231–32).

> Of all the pleasures bodily or mental, the pleasures of mutual love, cemented by mutual esteem, are the most enduring and varied. They therefore contribute largely to swell the sum of well-being, or they form an important item in the account of human happiness. And, for that reason, the well-wisher of the general good, or the adherent of the principle of utility, must, in that character, consider them with much complacency. But, though he approves of love because it accords with his principle, he is far from maintaining that the general good ought to be the motive of the lover. It was never contended or conceived by a sound, orthodox utilitarian, that the lover should kiss his mistress with an eye to the common weal. (1954 [1832]: 107–8)

Given their importance in contributing to pleasure production, Utilitarianism will tell us to take steps to secure the benefits of personal relationships, which will involve trying to form intrinsic desires for our loved ones. The kinds of creatures we are and the nature of close personal relationships leads to Self-Effacement. And this point concerning the near and dear can be generalized. Exclusively desiring pleasure and the absence of pain for their own sakes can be self-defeating. That is to say, adopting hedonic maximization as your sole end will almost guarantee that you fail to achieve this end.[17] Utilitarianism thus does not call for as drastic a revision to our desires as might be expected.

Blame is one of the most powerful deterrents to harming others. Not only for those blamed but also for those observing. If you blame a friend for performing some act, then your other friends are alerted that blame is in the offing were they to perform similar acts. Since you have the power to deter others from performing certain acts, you ought to exercise this power when doing so would bring about the best. And, if Utilitarianism is true, the occasions when blaming is called for need not be limited to just those occasions when others fail to maximize the sum total of pleasure minus pain. For instance, on occasion, horribly risky behavior, against the odds, brings about the best. Suppose your friend drinks and drives, but she gets home safely. Though it could have ended in catastrophe, her drinking and driving ended up maximizing the sum total of pleasure minus pain. According to Utilitarianism, she thus acted permissibly. Agents that act permissibly are not blameworthy. Nevertheless, there are strong Utilitarian reasons to treat her as a moral failure. Why? Because having genuine, negative reactive attitudes toward her will be an effective deterrent against those who might emulate her behavior. Utilitarianism is Self-Effacing. It tells you to blame those whom, if the theory is true, are unworthy of blame. The theory does not call for as drastic a revision in our reactive attitudes as might be expected.[18]

That Utilitarianism is Self-Effacing makes it extremely flexible. It is comfortable stepping from the limelight and letting us adopt whatever attitudes would

---

17. For a moving defense of this general point, see Mill (1989 [1873]: 117–18).
18. This paragraph draws on Sidgwick (1907: 221) and Smart (1973: 53).

bring about the best outcome.[19] Accordingly, given the kind of creatures we are and the circumstances we find ourselves in, it may very well turn out that Utilitarianism does not require a massive revision to how we live our day-to-day lives. We thus need to be cautious when assessing the theory's plausibility. It is easy to overlook the possibility that Utilitarianism is Self-Effacing. So it is easy to mistakenly believe that Utilitarianism requires you to live directly as a Utilitarian.

1.4.2 *The Approximation Strategy of a Utilitarian*

Utilitarianism attempts to capture the truth about the normative, the evaluative, and how they relate to one another. If true, the theory explains why, for any act, it has the Deontic Properties that it does. Utilitarianism, as an ethical theory, is thus comparable to a mathematical or scientific theory. Euclidean geometry attempts to capture the truth about plane and solid figures. If true, the theory explains why, for any figure, it has the shape properties that it does. For both theories, however, it could be that human beings, due to certain psychological limitations, are unable to use them in certain cases. Most of us cannot eyeball a perfect circle, but that has never been taken as a strike against Euclidean geometry. Similarly, most of us cannot identify, at the moment of choice, the act that maximizes the sum total of pleasure minus pain, but that should not be taken as a strike against Utilitarianism.[20]

What our human limitations do show is that we need a strategy, independent from the correct ethical theory, that will help us to best approximate the standards set by the theory. But what would this strategy look like? It will prove helpful to get a rough sense of the answer to this question. For it is easy to mistakenly mix up the theoretical role played by Utilitarianism with the practical role played by the

> *Approximation Strategy of a Utilitarian*: The strategy that a Utilitarian agent believes would, if followed, bring about the greatest sum total of pleasure minus pain in the long run, given what she believes about her own psychology and circumstances.

A Utilitarian adopts such a strategy, but not because she believes the acts she will then perform will thereby be permissible. Indeed, she knows she will often fail to bring about the best. Rather she adopts such a strategy because without one the outcome she brings about will likely be far worse.

To get a better sense of what the Approximation Strategy of a Utilitarian might involve, imagine that you knew that Utilitarianism is true. What ought you to do right now? This is a tough question to answer. It only takes a moment of self-reflection to realize the following:

---

19. For a similar point, but cast as a criticism, see Williams (1973: 135).
20. This analogy is controversial. For discussion, see §5.3.

- I lack crucial information. I don't know which action, if performed, would bring about the best state of affairs. My actions have far-reaching implications, and I am simply unable to anticipate them all. Indeed, I am not even aware of all of the acts available to me now.

- I lack the time needed to make informed choices. Gathering information and deliberating about how to proceed are resource intensive. They have opportunity costs.

- I am biased. I favor the near future, my own interests, and the interests of my near and dear. If I try to calculate which outcome would be best, these biases will likely distort my judgment.

- My attitudes and emotions are coarse grained. They often are insensitive to minutia. For example, I recoil from betrayal generally, not from particular instances of betrayal.

- My attitudes and emotions have a kind of inertia. I cannot be utterly opposed to torture on Monday, be content to permit it on Tuesday, and oppose it again on Wednesday.

- My loyalties and projects cannot be easily and often changed. I cannot wholeheartedly be committed to my beloved today and still be capable of dropping her altogether tomorrow.

- I am often weak-willed. I cannot always trust my future self to follow through with a plan.

Given these limitations, you will quickly recognize that you need to give up on the prospect of actually bringing about the best state of affairs available to you. Just as you are going to fail to draw perfect circles, you are going to fail to act morally. But just as there are more and less egregious ways to fail at drawing circles, there are more and less egregious ways to fail morally. An approximation strategy is your attempt, given what you believe about yourself and your circumstances, to minimize the egregiousness of the failure. Put differently, adopting and carrying out an approximation strategy involves acts that, in all likelihood, are impermissible according to Utilitarianism. But you still need a strategy because you will almost certainly fail more catastrophically if you try to go without one.[21]

For our purpose—avoiding a prevalent mistake in assessing Utilitarianism—we can focus on two indispensable parts of any approximation strategy: a useful procedure for making decisions and a corresponding set of motives.

As we've seen, every ethical theory forges a connection between the Descriptive Properties of actions and their Deontic Properties. For Utilitarianism, an act that has the Descriptive Property of maximizing the sum total of pleasure minus pain also, for that reason, has the Deontic Property of being permissible.

---

21. This paragraph draws on Hare (1981: chs. 2–3) and Railton (1984).

Obviously, even if we know we are permitted to perform acts that maximize the sum total of pleasure minus pain, we likely have no idea which of our Presently Available Alternatives has this property. So what's needed is a

> *Decision Procedure*: A set of rules that the agent can use, given her beliefs at the time of action, to identify whether an action is to be performed.

The rules of a Decision Procedure pick out certain properties of acts that are immediately recognizable and then tells you to perform acts with these properties.[22] The rule "do the first thing that comes to mind" could serve as a Decision Procedure. This rule gives you, no matter what your beliefs, a way to arrive at a conclusion about what to do. Of course, "do the first thing that comes to mind" will not be part of the approximation strategy of any sensible Utilitarian. It would obviously do a terrible job at approximating what ultimately matters according to the theory.

We can gesture toward what a sensible Utilitarian might land on as a Decision Procedure by considering

> Tasty Cake. You know that you are required to bake a cake for the party tonight. You also know that the tastier the cake the greater the sum total of pleasure minus pain. But you are uncertain how to bake the tastiest cake.

In this case, assuming the truth of Utilitarianism, the act that has the Descriptive Property of producing the tastiest cake will also have the Deontic Property of being permissible. Now the trouble is that there are lots of cakes you could pursue and lots of different ways to bake them. If you tried to work out what acts you ought to perform, you'd almost surely get it wrong. Worse still, you'd waste precious baking time. What you need is a Decision Procedure for making tasty cakes. Fortunately, successful past chefs have furnished us with cookbooks. What you need to do, rather than try to bake the tastiest cake at each act juncture, is follow a tried and true recipe. Following the steps of a tried and true recipe will not guarantee you make the tastiest cake. But it allows you to act according to immediately identifiable properties of the acts available to you. How do you decide what to do next? Answer: Perform the act with the property of being the next step in the recipe. In acting in accordance with the tried and true recipe, you best approximate the tastiest cake.

In Tasty Cake, the approximation strategy involves using a set of rules—the recipe—that allows you to choose what to do next, given your ignorance and uncertainty. And turning to these rules is sensible because the recipe has generated pretty tasty cakes in the past. Traditionally, Utilitarian's have thought along analogous lines. Here's Mill:

---

22. The formulation of Decision Procedure and this description draw on Bales (1971).

> Defenders of utility often find themselves called upon to reply to such objections as this—that there is not time, previous to action, for calculating and weighing the effects of any line of conduct on the general happiness. The answer to the objection is, that there has been ample time, namely, the whole past duration of the human species. During all that time mankind have been learning by experience the tendencies of actions.... People talk as if the commencement of this course of experience had hitherto been put off, and as if, at the moment when some man feels tempted to meddle with the property or life of another, he had to begin considering for the first time whether murder and theft are [generally] injurious to human happiness. (2003 [1861]: 2.24)

Mill's idea is that the Approximation Strategy of a Utilitarian is going to include a Decision Procedure whose simple rules are familiar from commonsense morality: don't murder, don't steal, don't torture, don't lie, and the like. Your uncertainty, time constraints, and biases suggest that following these rules is the best strategy for approaching the maximization of pleasure minus pain. Just as a cookbook guides us in the production of decently tasty cakes, common sense guides us in the production of decently moral lives.

But here a new issue arises. For, in point of fact, the Decision Procedure will vary from person to person. Not only because of differences in people's beliefs but also because, to be part of an effective approximation strategy, the rules that make up the Decision Procedure for a given agent must be usable by that agent at the time of choice. Return to Tasty Cake. Suppose that you are deeply averse to a certain cookbook. Perhaps you hate the chef. Even if you had the cookbook to hand, you simply wouldn't be motivated to follow it. It would thus be pointless to make following this cookbook part of your Decision Procedure. It's worth noting that you may end up performing the exact same actions as you would have performed had you used the cookbook. In other words, you may conform to a Decision Procedure without acting from it. Yet, to serve as part of your approximation strategy, a Decision Procedure needs to mesh with your motives so that you will actually use it for guidance. Put more precisely, the Decision Procedure must be usable in the sense that the rules involved are such that, at the moment of choice, if you believe that the rules call for the performance of a certain act, you will be sufficiently motivated on that basis to perform this act.[23]

The need for a usable Decision Procedure takes us to the second main part of the Approximation Strategy of a Utilitarian, namely, the cultivation of a

> *Motivational Set*: A set of motives including such things as attitudes, emotions, loyalties, and projects.[24]

---

23. This paragraph draws on Smith (2018: chs. 1–2).
24. This description of a Motivational Set is inspired by Williams (1981: 105).

Many items that make up your Motivational Set are outside of your control. Hunger, for example, simply befalls you. Yet many others are under your control. However, as noted above, it is not easy to quickly adjust our attitudes, emotions, loyalties, projects, and the like. Our immediate, voluntary control over much of our Motivational Set is minimal. To be sure, for most of us our motives are so synchronically inflexible that, at the moment of choice, we are psychologically determined to act in a certain way. Coupled with our ignorance and uncertainty about what the future brings, this synchronic inflexibility means that long before we reach the time of action we need to start cultivating a Motivational Set that works in tandem with our Decision Procedure. If, for example, the rules of commonsense morality are adopted then the accompanying motivations will need to be cultivated: a strong aversion toward doing harm or intending to harm others, a desire to keep one's word, a respect for property rights, and so on.

We've seen that the particular Motivational Set included in your approximation strategy needs to take into account the Decision Procedure you believe you will use at the time of choice. But this is not the only factor that matters in determining which set of motives to cultivate. As we saw in our discussion of Self-Effacement, lacking certain motives would rob us of some of the greatest sources of happiness. For instance, it is reasonable to believe that cultivating a love for one's children will be part of the best set of motives. This fact, and the fact that this love cannot be turned on and off at a moment's notice, will need to be taken into account in the development of one's Motivational Set. In developing your strategy, then, you will need to cultivate the set of motives that you believe fits the best Decision Procedure while itself, in the long run, is productive of good consequences.[25]

We can now take stock. To effectively approximate the moral ideal, given our human limitations, we each need a Decision Procedure: a set of rules that allows the agent to classify actions based on her limited beliefs at the time. But we also need an accompanying Motivational Set. The agent must be motivated to perform acts recommended by the rules of the Decision Procedure precisely because they are so recommended. The strategy of the Utilitarian agent consists of the Decision Procedure and Motivational Set that she thinks together, given what she believes about herself and her circumstances, will best approximate the realization of the greatest sum total of pleasure minus pain.

Since it is easy to muddle the distinction between Utilitarianism as an ethical theory with the Approximation Strategy of a Utilitarian, it is easy to find fault in the wrong place. It would be a mistake to hold that the day-to-day life of a Utilitarian would involve a constant lookout for opportunities to maximize Overall Value. We should not expect Utilitarians to readily contemplate murder, tell strategic lies, steal from the rich, or weigh up the costs and benefits of torture.

---

25. This paragraph draws on Parfit (1984: §14).

The Approximation Strategy of a Utilitarian will likely include defeasible constraints against murder and torture, emphasize parental love and other forms of partiality, and promote the cultivation of strong aversions toward theft and promise breaking.

1.5 Conclusion

The job of an ethical theory is to tell us what we ought to do and why we ought to do it. To complete this task, a theory needs to identify what descriptive facts are normatively and evaluatively relevant. It needs to identify how normatively and evaluatively significant each relevant descriptive fact is. And it needs to identify how normatively and evaluatively relevant descriptive facts and their significance get combined.

Utilitarianism offers a systematic account of what we ought to do and why we ought to do it. It does so by linking Deontic Properties to impersonal value properties, linking impersonal value properties to personal value properties, and linking personal value properties to hedonic properties. The relevant Descriptive Properties are pain and pleasure. They are significant in proportion to their quantity. And they add up by simple summing.

Utilitarianism is one of the leading ethical theories, not only because it provides an elegant account of the ethical domain, but also because its central ideas are plausible. Minimally, you probably believe that Deontic Properties have something to do with the good, that the good has something to do with welfare, and that pleasure and pain have something to do with how well your life goes. In this book, we will explore whether these links hold.

References

Austin, J. 1954 [1832]. *The Province of Jurisprudence Determined*. Edited by H. L. A. Hart. London: Weidenfeld & Nicolson.
Bales, E. R. 1971. "Act-Utilitarianism: Account of Right-Making Characteristics or Decision-Making Procedure?" *American Philosophical Quarterly* 8 (3): 257–65.
Bergström, L. 1966. *The Alternatives and Consequences of Actions*. Stockholm: Almqvist & Wiksell.
Berker, S. 2007. "Particular Reasons." *Ethics* 118 (1): 109–39.
Bykvist, K. 2009. "No Good Fit: Why the Fitting Attitude Analysis of Value Fails." *Mind* 118 (469): 1–30.
*Bykvist, K. 2010. *Utilitarianism: A Guide for the Perplexed*. New York: Continuum.
Dancy, J. 2000. "Should We Pass the Buck?" *Royal Institute of Philosophy Supplement* 47: 159–73.
Feldman, F. 2000. "Basic Intrinsic Value." *Philosophical Studies* 99 (3): 319–46.

Hare, R. M. 1981. *Moral Thinking: Its Levels, Method, and Point*. Oxford: Oxford University Press.
Jackson, F. 1998. *From Metaphysics to Ethics: A Defence of Conceptual Analysis*. Oxford: Oxford University Press.
*Kagan, S. 1998. *Normative Ethics*. Boulder, CO: Westview Press.
Markovits, J. 2010. "Acting for the Right Reasons." *Philosophical Review* 119 (2): 201–42.
Mill, J. S. 1989 [1873]. *Autobiography*. New York: Penguin.
Mill, J.S. 2003 [1861/1859]. Utilitarianism *and* On Liberty*: Including Mill's "Essay on Bentham" and Selections from the Writings of Jeremy Bentham and John Austin*. 2nd ed. Oxford: Blackwell.
Parfit, D. 1984. *Reasons and Persons*. Oxford: Clarendon Press.
Plantinga, A. 2003. *Essays in the Metaphysics of Modality*. Oxford: Oxford University Press.
Portmore, D. W. 2019. *Opting for the Best: Oughts and Options*. Oxford: Oxford University Press.
Railton, P. 1985. "Alienation, Consequentialism, and the Demands of Morality." *Philosophy & Public Affairs* 13 (2): 134–71.
Rosen, G. 2015. "The Alethic Conception of Moral Responsibility." In *The Nature of Moral Responsibility: New Essays*, edited by R. Clarke, M. McKenna, and A. M. Smith, 65–87. Oxford: Oxford University Press.
Schroeder, M. 2015. "What Makes Reasons Sufficent." *American Philosophical Quarterly* 52 (2): 159–70.
Sidgwick, H. 1907. *The Methods of Ethics*. 7th ed. London: Macmillan.
Smart, J. J. C. 1973. "An Outline of a System of Utilitarian Ethics." In *Utilitarianism: For and Against*, 3–67. Cambridge: Cambridge University Press.
*Smith, H. M. 2018. *Making Morality Work*. Oxford: Oxford University Press.
Stocker, M. 1976. "The Schizophrenia of Modern Ethical Theories." *Journal of Philosophy* 73: 453–66.
Streumer, B. 2011. "Are Normative Properties Descriptive Properties?" *Philosophical Studies* 154 (3): 325–48.
Williams, B. 1973. "A Critique of Utilitarianism." In *Utilitarianism: For and Against*, 77–135. Cambridge: Cambridge University Press.
Williams, B. 1981. *Moral Luck: Philosophical Papers, 1973–1980*. Cambridge: Cambridge University Press.
Zimmerman, M. 2001. *The Nature of Intrinsic Value*. Lanham, MD: Rowman & Littlefield.

2

An Argument from the Classical Utilitarians

2.1 *Introduction*

Although there are traces of Utilitarianism throughout the history of philosophy, it wasn't until the eighteenth century that it came to be regarded as a well-formed ethical theory. Three figures feature prominently: Jeremy Bentham (1748–1832), John Stuart Mill (1806–1873), and Henry Sidgwick (1838–1900). While all are aptly described as Classical Utilitarians, each approaches the theory from a distinctive philosophical perspective. Bentham was a British philosopher and social reformer who is considered the father of Utilitarianism. Among the reforms he advocated were the abolition of capital punishment, humane prison conditions, and relief programs for the poor. Mill was the popularizer of Utilitarianism. He received an intense early education from his father—James Mill—who was significantly influenced by Bentham. Like Bentham, Mill thought that Utilitarianism called for significant social reforms, including steps to end the subjugation of women. He is also well known for defending the harm principle, which seriously restricts the scope of a state justified use of coercive power.[1] Sidgwick was Knightbridge Professor of Philosophy at Trinity College, Cambridge. He refined Utilitarianism into its canonical form. *The Methods of Ethics* is considered the first academic book in moral philosophy.[2] The problems that Sidgwick discussed, and in many cases discovered, arguably set the tone for the rest of the twentieth century in both metaethics and ethics.

We should be explicit about just what this chapter will accomplish. While we focus on Classical Utilitarians, we're not aiming for fidelity to the texts and we're not engaged in exegesis. We could not in this chapter, nor even in a book, adequately defend particular interpretations of these figures. Others have competently taken up this task and you may wish to consult their work.[3] Rather, our goal is to introduce you to a way of thinking, not to the thought of a particular thinker.

---

1. The harm principle holds that "The only purpose for which power can be rightfully exercised over any member of a civilized community, against his will, is to prevent harm to others" (Mill 2003 [1861/1859]: L1.9).

2. See Rawls (2007: 378).

3. For Bentham, see Harrison (1983) and Schofield (2009). For Mill, see Crisp (1997) and Brink (2013). For Sidgwick, see Schneewind (1977), Philips (2011), Lazari-Radek and Singer (2014), and Crisp (2015). For an extensive overview of all three, see Schultz (2017).

To this end, we'll pursue a single line of argument that's loosely inspired by the work of Bentham, Mill, and Sidgwick. Very roughly, the argument runs as follows: Your experiences of pleasure and pain are part of what determine your level of welfare. The level of welfare that a complete state of affairs contains is part of what determines its value. The value of a complete state of affairs is part of what determines what you ought to do. And, if you accept this much, then you should accept Utilitarianism. Whether or not this particular argument succeeds is of secondary interest. In this chapter, we're primarily concerned to give some indication of the kind of argument that can be marshaled in favor of Utilitarianism.

2.2 Bentham's Argument from the Burden of Proof

Bentham's defense of Utilitarianism is dialectical. He is trying to convince you to accept Utilitarianism. He holds that you already accept, albeit probably implicitly, that pain and pleasure matter in determining what you ought to do. And he argues that, insofar as you accept this, the onus is on you to justify any departure from Utilitarianism. Finally, he maintains that the prospects of supplying this justification are dim. The focus of his argumentative strategy, then, is less about getting you on the hook—he thinks you are already on it—and more about reeling you in.

This reasoning is discernable in two passages in Bentham's work. The first passage conveys his view about the status of Utilitarianism as the default moral theory. Notice how quickly Bentham moves from the uncontroversial observation made in the first sentence, to a much more significant claim asserted in the second:

> No man will deny but that occasion has place in which the enjoyment and accordingly the pursuit of pleasure in some shape or other, and the endeavour to avoid experiencing pain in some shape or other, are modes and courses of action not exposed to well-grounded reproach. But if this is true in any one case, on any one occasion, it rests upon him who says that there is any occasion on which it is not true to produce this same occasion and say why it is that, on that same occasion it is not true—and so in the case of every exception which he would be for cutting out of the general rule. In a word, on the opponent of the greatest happiness principle . . . lies the burden of proof. (1983 [1829]: 313)

The first sentence is uncontroversial in part because it makes an extremely modest claim. Few would deny that sometimes our actions are justified—"not exposed to well-grounded reproach"—by the prospect of pleasure and the avoidance of pain. Although this observation is consistent with Utilitarianism being true, it doesn't entail that it is true. You probably accept that the fact that you'd feel pain can count against performing an action. And you probably accept that the fact that you'd feel pleasure can count in favor of performing an action. But this doesn't commit you to accepting that the prospects of pain and pleasure are the only things that matter, nor does it entail anything about how much weight you attach to these considerations. In the second sentence, Bentham offers a more substantial assertion. In light of the initial observation, he contends that the burden of proof is on those who would ever depart from the greatest happiness principle (i.e., Utilitarianism).[4]

A similar line of reasoning can be retrieved from Bentham's most famous work: *An Introduction to the Principles of Morals and Legislation*. This passage begins with a claim similar to that which began the first passage. But this line more explicitly asserts that people, at least on some occasions, appeal to Utilitarianism. As before, the passage continues on to assert that this gives Utilitarianism a privileged status. Here's Bentham:

> Not that there is or ever has been that human creature at breathing...who has not on many, perhaps on most occasions of his life, deferred to [the principle of utility]. By the natural constitution of the human frame, on most occasions of their lives men in general embrace this principle, without thinking of it: if not for the ordering of their own actions, yet for the trying of their own actions, as well as of those of other men. There have been, at the same time, not many perhaps, even of the most intelligent, who have been disposed to embrace it purely and without reserve. There are even few who have not taken some occasion or other to quarrel with it, either on account of their not understanding always how to apply it, or on account of some prejudice or other which they were afraid to examine into, or could not bear to part with. For such is the stuff that man is made of: in principle and in practice, in a right track and in a wrong one, the rarest of all human qualities is consistency. (1996 [1789]: 1.XII)

Bentham believes that at least some of your moral thinking is already Utilitarian. But, of course, Utilitarianism is a theory that applies to all cases. What, then, does he mean by saying that you already accept the principle on some occasions?

Here's one plausible answer. When nothing else is at stake, you accept that the balance of pleasure minus pain determines what you ought to do. That is to say, you accept Utilitarianism in qualified form. More precisely, you are committed to

> *Weak Hedonic Maximization*: If two presently available alternatives, X and Y, are identical in every morally relevant respect except that X brings about a greater sum total of pleasure minus pain than Y, then it is impermissible to do Y.[5]

---

4. This way of understanding Bentham's argument draws on Shaver (2013).

5. Here we've construed Bentham as endorsing maximizing. This is controversial. For defense of this construal, see Gustafsson (2018). Again, we should stress that our interest in this chapter is not to get clear about the details of these historical figures' views. Rather, we're interested in a set of arguments that display a way of thinking.

This claim is "weak" on account of the stipulation that, besides the difference in the total amount of pleasure, all else is morally equal between the acts in question. While Bentham recognizes that people commonly deviate from Utilitarianism, and at times challenge it, he nonetheless maintains that when only pain and pleasure are at stake people accept that they ought to maximize happiness. At the end of the passage we arrive at Bentham's crucial move. He claims that, once you've committed to Weak Hedonic Maximization in some cases, the demands of consistency—treating like cases alike—require that you justify any deviation in other cases.

The dialectical force of this argument depends on how you answer the following three questions:

i. Have you, perhaps unwittingly, already committed to Weak Hedonic Maximization?

ii. If you have, is the burden of proof on you to justify any departure from Utilitarianism?

iii. If you do face this burden, can you meet it?

We will take up these questions in turn.

Is it true, as Bentham suggests, that you already accept Weak Hedonic Maximization? To see why you might answer this question affirmatively, consider

> Lunch Break. You work in a skyscraper. You often order a pizza for lunch and eat it on the roof. Today, as you wait for the pizza, you hear a scream. You rush to the side of the building and see a window washer dangling from a rope. The rope is tied near where you stand, and you can see the knot is slipping. If you hold on to the rope for a minute, rescue crews will arrive and pull the window washer to safety. But just then your phone rings. It's the pizza. If you don't answer it immediately, the pizza deliverer will leave and you'll be hungry till dinner.

In Lunch Break you face a choice between holding and not holding the rope. To be clear about what these options entail, note that

- Holding the rope will cause you a little bit of pain, forgoing the pizza will deprive you of a little bit of pleasure, and you'll be pained by hunger until dinner.

- Not holding the rope will result in the window washer's death, depriving her of all future pleasure and causing great pain to her family and friends.

Most people think that if this story ends with you enjoying your pizza, you've not done what you ought. And Bentham thinks that, in light of accepting this verdict, you accept Weak Hedonic Maximization. Notice that, if asked to explain why you held the rope, you might appeal to some or all of the following claims:

- The value of the complete state of affairs, in part, is determined by the amounts of pain and pleasure.

- The complete state of affairs in which the window washer dies is worse than the complete state of affairs in which you are hungry until dinner.

- Your own pain and pleasure do not carry special significance. The pleasure of the pizza does not outweigh the window washer's death.

- The difference in the value of the complete state of affairs that will be brought about by holding the rope as opposed to the complete state of affairs that will be brought about by not holding the rope makes it obvious that you ought to hold the rope.

Now, if you accept the above considerations, then perhaps, as Bentham contends, you are already committed to Weak Hedonic Maximization. We might provisionally answer the first question in the affirmative.

We can next turn to the second question, concerning the burden of proof. If you accept Weak Hedonic Maximization in some cases, must you justify a departure in other cases? Here is one way of understanding what Bentham has in mind. Suppose that your daughter already owns an expensive calculator. It works fine, but she comes asking for a new one. In trying to figure out if she really needs one, you might say, "This calculator was sufficient for last year's math course. Is it not sufficient for this year's course?" Unless there's a reason she needs a new calculator, the old one ought to suffice. If the math problems are relevantly similar and she accepts that the calculator was sufficient for last year's class, then consistency, treating like classes alike, demands that she accept that it is sufficient for this year's class as well. Bentham thinks the same thought applies in the context of moral theory. If you've already accepted Weak Hedonic Maximization, then, unless you can show that it is not up for the task in some cases, you should regard it as sufficient in all cases. A departure requires justification. And if you cannot supply such a justification, then you should accept Utilitarianism. Bentham thus thinks you'll want to answer the second question affirmatively as well.

This takes us to the third question. Can you meet the burden of proof? To do so you would need to identify some morally relevant considerations other than pain and pleasure. That is, you would need to explain how a case could be morally different such that Weak Hedonic Maximization no longer applies. Bentham doubts that you can, and he points to two related reasons any attempt is likely to fail.

First, when you go to identify some purportedly non-Utilitarian considerations, you will draw on reasons that are, in fact, Utilitarian. Suppose you're convinced that, for example, promise keeping is morally important. This idea is firmly placed within commonsense morality, yet may sometimes conflict with the principle of utility. But imagine how you might defend such a principle. Keeping one's promises is obviously important. What explains this? If you are

Chapter 2: An Argument from the Classical Utilitarians

going to supply reasons in support of a principle of fidelity, what sorts of considerations might you appeal to? Bentham thinks that, ultimately, you are going to answer this question by appealing to the goodness of pleasure and the badness of pain. The ability to gain assurance of other people makes cooperation possible in conditions in which it otherwise might not be. And cooperation is incredibly valuable, both as a way of producing good outcomes and as a guard against bad ones. When promises are broken, this frequently causes avoidable pain. The promise broken may have immediate bad consequences and may also weaken, even if slightly, confidence in promises made later. So, the suggestion goes, much of what seems morally relevant about keeping promises is ultimately explained by the utility of doing so. What initially appeared as an independent moral ideal is revealed to be of merely instrumental value. This is why Bentham claims, "When a man attempts to combat the principle of utility, it is with reasons drawn, without his being aware of it, from that very principle itself" (1996 [1789]: 1.XIII). When attempts are made to defend non-Utilitarian factors in deontic assessment it is very hard, when supplying the needed justification, to avoid sounding like a Utilitarian.

Suppose you're unpersuaded by these remarks. You really think that promises ought to be kept, even when this conflicts with the requirements of Utilitarianism. This brings us to Bentham's second point. You will now need to identify how these considerations combine with Weak Hedonic Maximization. That is, you'll need to justify a principle that explains how hedonic considerations and considerations of fidelity interact in determining what we ought to do. And Bentham thinks that you won't be able to justify this interaction principle.

To see why, start with the idea that promises must always be kept. This extreme view is hard to believe. It would require that you ought to keep your promises—no matter how trivial—even if the results are disastrous. A more plausible view would hold that promises trade off against pleasure and pain. In some cases, promise keeping will carry more weight than a certain amount of utility; and in other cases, when the utility at stake is high enough, fidelity will give way. But, on this more plausible view, you'll need to specify the point at which the utility at stake is enough. That is, you'll need an interaction principle with a threshold.

This sounds like a sensible compromise. There is, however, a problem: How do you specify the location of this threshold in a nonarbitrary way? How do you justify locating in one position rather than a slightly different position? To bring out why this problem is pressing, a visualization may help (see Figure 2.1).

The upward-pointing arrow indicates the increasing cost of keeping the promise. The shaded region depicts the range in which a threshold might be located. Any view that posits a threshold can be represented by something like this figure. This is because all such views will have the same structure. Promise keeping will be

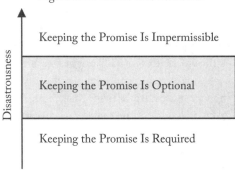

Figure 2.1: *Promises with Thresholds*

required in some range of circumstances. At some point, the sum total of pleasure minus pain will rise to a level at which promise keeping is optional, and then once the results are sufficiently disastrous, it will be impermissible. The location and width of the shaded region may change, but all threshold views will feature one. And you need to be able to justify each transition, from required to optional and then from optional to impermissible. For each of these transitions cries out for explanation. At each, something morally important happens. But how would we justify the precise location of the change? Suppose, for example, we held that keeping a promise is required unless doing so would cause someone 100 hours of agony. How can we be confident that one second less of agony isn't also sufficient to justify breaking a promise? The difference between an act being optional and impermissible is significant. The difference between 100 hours of agony, and 99 hours, 59 minutes, and 59 seconds of agony is insignificant. Wherever the line is placed will look arbitrary. Some explanation is needed, but it's not clear one can be supplied.

We can now see why Bentham maintains that combining non-Utilitarian considerations with Weak Hedonic Maximization appears indefensible. In his words:

> If he should be for compounding the matter, and adopting his own principle in part, and the principle of utility in part, let him say how far he will adopt it? When he has settled with himself where he will stop, then let him ask himself how he justifies to himself the adopting it so far? and why he will not adopt it any farther. (1996 [1789]: 1.XIV)

Adding non-Utilitarian considerations introduces the need for an interaction principle. And if this principle is going to be plausible, then you'll need to appeal to thresholds. But setting these thresholds appears unjustifiable. Wherever you set the threshold will be arbitrary. So once you've taken on Weak Hedonic Maximization, anything short of Utilitarianism looks untenable.

The burden of proof you face when trying to justify a supplement to Weak Hedonic Maximization, Bentham contends, is not easily met. You face two hurdles. You need to justify, without appeal to utility, the moral significance of non-Utilitarian considerations. And, even if you make it over this hurdle, you also need to identify how Weak Hedonic Maximization interacts with these non-Utilitarian considerations, and this looks very hard to pull off in a nonarbitrary fashion.

The forgoing suggests one line of reasoning to the conclusion that you should accept Utilitarianism. We can call this

Bentham's Argument from the Burden of Proof

1. You accept Weak Hedonic Maximization.
2. If you accept Weak Hedonic Maximization, the burden of proof is on you to justify a departure from Utilitarianism.
3. The burden of proof is on you to justify a departure from Utilitarianism.
4. If the burden of proof is on you to justify a departure from Utilitarianism and you cannot meet this burden, then you should accept Utilitarianism.
5. You cannot meet the burden of proof needed to justify a departure from Utilitarianism.
6. Hence, you should accept Utilitarianism.

> *Weak Hedonic Maximization*: If two presently available alternative actions, X and Y, are identical in every morally relevant respect except that X brings about a greater sum total of pleasure minus pain than Y, then it is impermissible to do Y.

Premise 1 is supported by cases like Lunch Break. Premise 2 is supported by the idea that we should not add to the materials we've already committed to unless they are inadequate. Premise 5 is supported by the thought that it is hard to avoid appealing to Utilitarian considerations and the thought that a principle that combines Utilitarian and non-Utilitarian elements will be hopelessly arbitrary.

While each of the substantive premises can be challenged, the main problem with Bentham's argument lies with the idea that you accept Weak Hedonic Maximization. We've presented Lunch Break as suggesting this. But, in point of fact, claiming that you accept Weak Hedonic Maximization in this case is a stretch. Indeed, you may not even accept the verdict that you ought to grab the rope and forfeit your lunch. Perhaps you are an egoist. Perhaps you believe that your pleasure and pain matters, but no one else's does. You might then think that what you ought to do is answer the phone and let the caller know you'll be down to pick up the pizza. Or, you may accept the verdict but deny that it's explained by the balance of pleasure and pain that will result. You may think that you have certain Samaritan duties to lend a hand in cases like this one. Or you may think that you ought to help because that's what a person with the right sort of character would do. What Bentham presented as an uncontroversial observation, on inspection, is revealed to be contentious.

This challenge to Premise 1, we should stress, is not easily remedied. What Bentham needs is a case that shows that you clearly accept Weak Hedonic Maximization. Lunch Break falls short here, but other cases will encounter similar difficulties. Here's the dilemma. If a case is structured such that by accepting the verdict you must accept Weak Hedonic Maximization, then you will probably be able to reasonably reject the verdict. But if the case is such that you must accept the verdict, then you will probably not have to accept Weak Hedonic Maximization as the explanation. Success on one front makes failure on the other front hard to avoid. The support for Premise 1 is thin.

2.3 *Mill's Argument from Desire as Sole Evidence*

Bentham's argument falters at the first step. He doesn't supply adequate reason to think that you already accept Weak Hedonic Maximization. Here we can present Mill as taking up this task. If the argument we reconstruct from Mill is successful, then it could serve as a defense of Premise 1 in Bentham's Argument from the Burden of Proof.

The passage of interest is complex. We'll begin with the first few lines:

> The only proof capable of being given that an object is visible is that people actually see it. The only proof that a sound is audible is that people hear it; and so of the other sources of our experience. In like manner, I apprehend, the sole evidence it is possible to produce that anything is desirable is that people do actually desire it. If the end which the utilitarian doctrine proposes to itself were not, in theory and in practice, acknowledged to be an end, nothing could ever convince any person that it was so. (Mill 2003 [1861/1859]: U 4.3)

Mill's claim is about the kind of evidence one could marshal in support of an evaluative judgment. To get a better idea of what this claim amounts to, we should elaborate the analogy he's offered. What evidence do you have for the judgment that this heart - ♥ - is black? Of course, you're looking at it and perceive it to be black, and this provides you with reason to believe that the heart is black. So one obvious reply is that your perceiving it to be black supplies evidence for its being black. Is perceptual evidence the only evidence? Suppose you consult a friend who looks at the heart and concludes, with you, that it is indeed black. This is more evidence, but notice, it is still based on perception. Your friend's testimony is credible only because she's seen the heart. Had she never seen it, you have no reason to count her agreement as increasing your evidence about the heart's color. More generally, then, we might conclude that the only kind of evidence that can support the judgment that the heart is black is ultimately traceable to perception.[6]

---

6. This paragraph and the next draw on West (2006).

In the passage, Mill is inviting us to consider a parallel question in the context of morality. What evidence could you have for an evaluative judgment such as the claim that pleasure is valuable? Clearly, this isn't a matter of perceiving the goodness of pleasure. You don't perceive goodness. Goodness doesn't impinge on any of your sense organs. So what evidence do we have to go on? Just as perception is the only source of evidence concerning the color of the heart above, Mill claims that the fact that someone desires something is the only source of evidence concerning that thing's desirability. To say that something is desirable is to say that it is worthy of being desired; it is valuable. Mill's point is that the only evidence that you can have for evaluative judgments is ultimately traceable to what people desire. There are, to be sure, lots of things that we desire. But some of these desires are instrumental. For example, you might desire money. This is not evidence for the fact that money is itself desirable. You don't intrinsically desire money; you don't desire it for its own sake. Rather you have an instrumental desire for money because it is a means to getting something that you have an intrinsic desire for. And it is this latter thing—what you have an intrinsic desire for—that Mill is interested in. Mill thus holds

> *Desire as Sole Evidence*: The evidence for a judgment that something is intrinsically valuable ultimately comes from, and only from, intrinsic desires.

Apart from the analogy with perceptual evidence, there is another consideration that makes Desire as Sole Evidence attractive. Suppose that having an even number of hairs on your head was of great intrinsic value. But suppose, as is very likely true, that having an even number of hairs is not something anyone has an intrinsic desire for. Given that no one intrinsically desires to have an even number of hairs on her head, it seems we lack any evidence that having an even number of hairs is desirable. Since our desires don't light up, we simply are in the dark. Absent any intrinsic desires, it seems we would forever remain ignorant of this source of value. Desire as Sole Evidence nicely explains our ignorance. This is why Mill concludes the passage above with the thought that, if happiness were not desired for its own sake, then nothing could ever convince any person that it is the ultimate end.

Having explained Mill's view concerning what could serve as evidence for evaluative judgments, we're prepared for the remainder of the passage. He continues:

> No reason can be given why the general happiness is desirable, except that each person, so far as he believes it to be attainable, desires his own happiness. This, however, being a fact, we have not only all the proof which the case admits of, but all which it is possible to require, that happiness is a good, that each person's happiness is a good to that person, and the general happiness, therefore, a good to the aggregate of all persons. Happiness has made out its title as one of the ends of conduct and, consequently, one of the criteria of morality. (Mill 2003 [1861/1859]: U 4.3)

While Mill's reasoning here is opaque, it's clear what the conclusion is supposed to be: you should accept that "the general happiness" is one of the factors relevant to deontic assessment—that is, you should accept Weak Hedonic Maximization.

To see how Mill hopes to secure this conclusion, we can walk through the argument, identifying the main moves along the way. A pair of claims can be extracted from the first sentence and the beginning of the second sentence of the passage:

> *Self-Hedonic Desiring*: Each person desires pleasure for herself (for its own sake) and the absence of pain for herself (for its own sake).

> *Weak Hedonism*: One's welfare is, in part, determined by experiences of pleasure and pain. Pleasure is intrinsically good-for the person experiencing it. Pain is intrinsically bad-for the person experiencing it.

Given Mill's view about what could constitute evidence for an evaluative judgment—Desire as Sole Evidence—Self-Hedonic Desiring makes Weak Hedonism hard to resist.

The next move in the argument is the hardest to understand. Mill seems to suggest that given that pleasure and pain are elements of your welfare—Weak Hedonism—we can infer that "the general happiness [is] a good to the aggregate of all persons." This claim is extremely puzzling. Taken at face value, Mill seems to be making the implausible claim that everyone's happiness added together—aggregate welfare—is good-for you and good-for every other individual. Fortunately, Mill later clarified what he intended to convey, writing:

> When I said the general happiness is a good to the aggregate of all persons I did not mean that every human being's happiness is a good to every other human being.... I merely meant in this particular sentence to argue that since A's happiness is a good, B's a good, C's a good, &c., the sum of all these goods must be a good. (From a Letter to Henry Jones, cited in Crisp 1997: 78)

This passage thus makes a third claim explicit. Notice that Mill, when talking about each person's happiness, holds that it is good-simpliciter, not just good-for the person enjoying it.[7] Accordingly, he accepts that the sum of all these personal goods must also be impersonally good. He thus forwards

> *Weak Welfarism*: Each person's welfare is of basic value such that, all else equal, a complete state of affairs, S_1, is better overall than another complete state of affairs, S_2, if S_1 contains a higher sum total of welfare than S_2.

---

7. For more on the distinction between good-for and good-simpliciter, see §1.2.3.

Chapter 2: An Argument from the Classical Utilitarians

These evaluative claims—Weak Hedonism and Weak Welfarism—put us well on our way to Weak Hedonic Maximization. All that's needed is a claim that links the goodness of outcomes to the deontic status of acts. Mill thinks this link is easily secured. "The doctrine of rational persons of all schools," he writes elsewhere, "[holds that] the morality of actions depends on the consequences which they tend to produce" (Mill 2003 [1861/1859]: 83). He thinks that only rational persons accept Traditional Consequentialism.[8] But that's a more controversial claim than he needs. For we could arrive at Weak Hedonic Maximization from a more modest claim. We need not accept that consequences are all that matter in determining an act's deontic status. We only need to accept that consequences matter at least somewhat. And again, this is a very modest claim. As Rawls writes, "All ethical doctrines worth our attention take consequences into account in judging rightness. One which did not would simply be irrational, crazy" (1999: 26).

Let's take a moment to see how the argument has developed. We can identify three major moves. First, appealing to Desire as Sole Evidence, Mill infers Weak Hedonism from Self-Hedonic Desiring. Second, he moves from Weak Hedonism to Weak Welfarism. Third, he combines these two evaluative claims with Traditional Consequentialism to deliver Weak Hedonic Maximization.

However, the second move—from Weak Hedonism to Weak Welfarism—is somewhat mysterious. It's not clear why Mill thinks that, because you take your own pleasure and pain to figure in your welfare, you are committed to the idea that pleasure and pain are good- and bad-simpliciter. What warrants the transition from something's being personally good to something's being impersonally good? On this question, Mill is silent.

Given this gap in Mill's argument, we should posit what's needed to fill it. We can then ask if what's been posited is plausible. And there is a claim in the vicinity that seems up for the task. We could infer Weak Welfarism from Weak Hedonism by appealing to

> *Personal from Impersonal Value*: Something is intrinsically good-for you (or bad-for you) only if that thing is intrinsically good-simpliciter (or bad-simpliciter).[9]

This link holds that whatever makes your life go better must be something that is in its own right good. This is not a wild idea. It captures the way we typically understand benefits and burdens.

To see this, suppose that you are a contestant on a game show and stand to win some big prizes. You might think to yourself, upon seeing these prizes, "Those

---

8. For more on Traditional Consequentialism, see §1.3.4.

9. We modify this principle, and the idea that Mill implicitly helped himself to it, from Sayre-McCord (2001).

look really great. I hope I win some." The prizes are good. And, because of this, if you came to possess one, it would be good-for you. What seems to be going on here is this: The prizes are good independent of their connection to you. And, if you came to have one, you'd have something that's good, and that would be good-for you. This way of thinking about the relationship between what's good and what's good-for we can call the

> *Possession Model*: When something is good-for you (or bad-for you), that thing is good-simpliciter (or bad-simpliciter) and you have it.

On this model, there is a bunch of impersonally good and bad stuff floating around, and your life is made better or worse depending on whether you get these goods or bads. If the goods come into your possession—if your life has them—you are made better off. If you get the bads, your life is made worse off. This is a natural model for thinking about welfare.

We are now in a position to give

Mill's Argument from Desire as Sole Evidence

1. Desire as Sole Evidence and Self-Hedonic Desiring are both true.
2. If Desire as Sole Evidence and Self-Hedonic Desiring are both true, then you should accept Weak Hedonism.
3. You accept the Possession Model.
4. If you accept the Possession Model, then you should accept Personal from Impersonal Value.
5. If you should accept Weak Hedonism and Personal from Impersonal Value, then you should accept Weak Welfarism.
6. If you should accept Weak Welfarism, then you should accept Weak Hedonic Maximization.
7. Hence, you should accept Weak Hedonic Maximization.

> *Desire as Sole Evidence*: The evidence for a judgment that something is intrinsically valuable ultimately comes from, and only from, intrinsic desires.
>
> *Self-Hedonic Desiring*: Each person desires pleasure for herself (for its own sake) and the absence of pain for herself (for its own sake).
>
> *Weak Hedonism*: One's welfare is, in part, determined by experiences of pleasure and pain. Pleasure is intrinsically good-for the person experiencing it. Pain is intrinsically bad-for the person experiencing it.
>
> *Possession Model*: When something is good-for you (or bad-for you), that thing is good-simpliciter (or bad-simpliciter) and you have it.
>
> *Personal from Impersonal Value*: Something is intrinsically good-for you (or bad-for you) only if that thing is intrinsically good-simpliciter (or bad-simpliciter).
>
> *Weak Welfarism*: Each person's welfare is of basic value such that, all else equal, a complete state of affairs, S_1, is better overall than another complete state of affairs, S_2, if S_1 contains a higher sum total of welfare than S_2.
>
> *Weak Hedonic Maximization*: If two presently available alternative actions, X and Y, are identical in every morally relevant respect except that X brings about a greater sum total of pleasure minus pain than Y, then it is impermissible to do Y.

There are three substantive premises, and all enjoy a measure of support. Premise 1 is supported by Mill's analogy of perception and by the undisputed fact that you desire your own happiness. Premise 3 is supported by the idea that the Possession Model captures our everyday thinking about the relationship between impersonal and personal goods. Premise 6 is supported by the idea that the consequences matter somewhat in determining what ought to be done. If this argument is sound, then Mill has succeeded where Bentham failed. He's provided a defense of Weak Hedonic Maximization.

While each of the substantive premises can be challenged, the main problem with Mill's argument is the move from Weak Hedonism to Weak Welfarism. This move, recall, was left unexplained. To fill the gap, we had to posit Personal from Impersonal Value. And we suggested that Personal from Impersonal Value garners its support from the Possession Model.

Yet the Possession Model is not the only way to think about the relationship between what's good-simpliciter and what's good-for you. What makes this view attractive is its fit with our ordinary language use, and it may be tempting to accept it for that reason. But we should notice that this linguistic evidence is limited. Think back to the game show. There we talked about you and then we talked about the prizes. When we wanted to talk about the potential benefit, we talked about you having or getting the prizes. This lends support to the Possession Model because it looks like there are two independent things—you and the prize—that, when they come together, generate a benefit for you. And since the coming together of you and the prizes didn't generate a new good, we assume it preexisted in the prizes. But notice that we continue to talk like this even when it is clear that the good in question is essentially related to you. Imagine you're back on the game show. It's a special episode reuniting children with their long-lost parents. The host tells you and the other contestants, "One of you will be getting a very special prize. Your long-lost mother has been found and is here to give you a hug." You might be thinking, "I hope I get a hug from my mom." Yet it's surely not the case that a hug from your mother is an impersonal good independent of you and then, when you come to possess it, it becomes a personal good. Your mother's hug is essentially related to you. She's your mother, after all. You don't want a hug from someone else's mother. And you don't think that, if your mother gave a hug to one of the other contestants, it would be good-for them. The benefit you get from your mother's hug does not fit the Possession Model.

The point of this discussion is not to show that the Possession Model is false. It is to show that the evidence in support of the Possession Model is not decisive. You might, for instance, hold that what's good-for you is, like motherly hugs, essentially related to you. It's not merely an impersonal good in your possession. On this alternative, your welfare is understood along the same lines as an egoist might understand what's good-for her. When an egoist thinks about pleasure, she's not thinking that its good-simpliciter and then she comes to possess it. Instead, she is thinking, "Only my pleasure—pleasure I possess—is good." This seems to be a coherent way to think about the relationship between personal and impersonal goodness. And if you favor it, you can reject Personal from Impersonal Value.

2.4 *Sidgwick's Argument from Temporal Insensitivity*

Let's take stock. In §2.2 we investigated Bentham's argument from Weak Hedonic Maximization to Utilitarianism. And we saw that, because his starting point wasn't well supported, he failed to secure his conclusion. What's needed is a defense of Weak Hedonic Maximization. In §2.3 we extracted an argument from Mill that aims to fill this need. While this argument might take us to Weak Hedonism, it falls short of establishing that you should accept Weak Welfarism and so is unable to defend Bentham's starting point. We don't yet have a defense of Utilitarianism. What's needed is an argument that can move us from Weak Hedonism to Weak Hedonic Maximization. Why, if you accept that your own pleasure and pain are good-for you and bad-for you, should you accept that between any two alternatives you ought, when all else is equal, to go in for the one that brings about the greater sum total of everyone's pleasure minus pain? For this, we turn to Sidgwick.

It will be instructive to preview the argument to come. Sidgwick is going to start with a claim about how you ought to treat yourself. Imagine you are the only person in existence. What ought you to do? His answer, which he thinks you'll find obvious, is that you ought to maximize your welfare, not just during some period of your life but over your whole existence. You should be ultimately concerned with how much welfare you have, not when you have it. This is what prudence—the attitude you should have toward your own welfare—requires. He also thinks he can explain why this is so. When it comes to evaluative matters generally, and not just the attitude you should take toward your life, you ought to be ultimately concerned with the quantity of the good on the whole and only derivatively concerned with the parts. This idea, the claim that the good of the whole is of primary importance, has a significant implication. Notice what happens when it is applied to the world you actually live in, which is populated by many people who have their own experiences of pleasure and pain. If you think that anyone's welfare is good-simpliciter (e.g., if you think it's impersonally good that you have a pleasant life) then you should be ultimately concerned with the whole of this good. You ought to be as concerned with everyone else's welfare as you are concerned with your own. You ought to be universally beneficent. Just as it is irrational to favor your welfare at one moment over another, it is, according to Sidgwick, irrational to favor your welfare over someone else's. If he is able to show this—that just as you ought to be indifferent to *when* you experience an episode of pleasure or pain, you ought to be indifferent to *who* experiences an episode of pleasure or pain—then

Chapter 2: An Argument from the Classical Utilitarians

the path to Weak Hedonic Maximization is a short one. With this sketch in place, let's turn to a more detailed account of the argument.

Sidgwick begins with prudence. You're already familiar with this concept. Prudent people do not buy lottery tickets, try heroin, or leave their valuables unattended in public places. They do not procrastinate. Rather they cautiously invest, steer clear of addictive and harmful drugs, buy insurance, and take care of their belongings. They forgo a minor pleasure now for a greater one later. Put generally, to be prudent is to have a special concern for your lifetime welfare. Here is how Sidgwick explains it:

> [A Quantitative Whole] is presented in the common notion of the Good—or, as is sometimes said, "good on the whole"—of any individual human being. ... [The] principle [equal and impartial concern for all parts of our conscious life] we might express it concisely by saying "that Hereafter as such is to be regarded neither less nor more than Now." ... All that the principle affirms is that the mere difference of priority and posteriority in time is not a reasonable ground for having more regard to the consciousness of one moment than to that of another.... [This principle applies to any] interpretation of "one's own good," in which good is conceived as a mathematical whole, of which the integrant parts are realised in different parts or moments of a lifetime. (1907: 381)

Prudence is the attitude you should have toward your own welfare. Because it's about your welfare, and not others' welfare, it involves being personally biased. But your concern should be for the whole of your welfare, not just a part. In this way, it involves being temporally unbiased. You should prefer the life with the most welfare, regardless of how that welfare is distributed. After all, an episode of mild pleasure contributes the same amount to your welfare whether it's experienced now or in a decade. Stated precisely, we can say that prudence involves

Temporal Insensitivity: You ought to be equally concerned for an episode of your welfare, E_1, and another episode of your welfare, E_2, if E_1 and E_2 merely differ with regard to when they occur.

Presumably, you think that you ought to be prudent. And, since prudence is characterized by indifference to time, you ought to accept Temporal Insensitivity.

Sidgwick's next move in the argument is crucial. From this discussion of prudence, he wants you to recognize "the relation which individuals and their particular ends bear as parts to their wholes." That is, he thinks you should accept not only Temporal Insensitivity but also a certain explanation of why it's true. In particular, he wants you to see that, in evaluative contexts, what is of primary importance is the quantity of the good of the whole; the integrant parts matter only derivatively. This is why at both the beginning and the end of the passage he mentions quantitative wholes. In the context of prudence, you should be thinking about your lifetime welfare and, in particular, how much of that good there is: its quantity. Your lifetime welfare is the largest quantitative whole, and, for that reason, it is what you ought to ultimately care about. Thus, the deeper commitment you take on board—what explains Temporal Insensitivity—is

> *Whole Fundamentalism*: For evaluative matters, you ought to be ultimately concerned with the largest quantitative whole and only derivatively concerned with that whole's parts.

For prudence, what ultimately matters is how much welfare your life in its entirety contains. Your episodes of well-being and ill-being matter, but only insofar as they contribute to your lifetime welfare.[10]

Whole Fundamentalism not only explains Temporal Insensitivity but also accounts for certain features of decision making more generally. Consider the role information plays in rational choice. If you're choosing between two lives, A and B, and A has a higher level of total welfare than B, then prudence requires that you select A. You have all the information you need. But suppose you're choosing between two lives, C and D, and all you know is that your welfare on Tuesdays will be higher with life C than D. Here you know how parts of the two whole lives compare. Yet, this is plainly inadequate to justify a choice. You'd need more information. You'd need to know how your life fares at all the other times. Perhaps every other day of the week is far better with life D. Why do you need this information to make a rational choice? Because you're ultimately concerned with the largest quantitative whole. You accept Whole Fundamentalism.

Having argued for Whole Fundamentalism, Sidgwick is positioned to draw a significant conclusion concerning the attitudes we should have toward the welfare of others. He claims that a critical parallel holds between the attitudes you ought to have toward parts of your total welfare and the attitudes you ought to have toward your own welfare as part of the total welfare of all people. He writes:

> So far we have only been considering the "Good on the Whole" of a single individual: but just as this notion is constructed by comparison and integration of the different "goods" that succeed one another in the series of our conscious states, so we have formed the notion of Universal Good by comparison and integration of the goods of all individual human—or sentient—existences. And here again, just as in the former me, by considering the relation of the integrant parts to the whole and to each other, I obtain the self-evident principle that the good of any one individual is of no more importance, from the point of view (if I may say so) of the Universe, than the good of any other; unless, that is, there are special grounds for believing that more good is likely to be realised in the one case than in the other. And it is evident to me that as

---

10. This paragraph draws on Irwin (2009: §1189–90).

> a rational being I am bound to aim at good generally,—so far as it is attainable by my efforts,—not merely at a particular part of it. From these ... we may deduce ... that each one is morally bound to regard the good of any other individual as much as his own, except in so far as he judges it to be less, when impartially viewed. (1907: 382)

In this passage, Sidgwick suggests that Whole Fundamentalism leads us to the idea that we ought to treat our own welfare with equal concern as anyone else's. In outline, it is easy to discern the driving idea. Just as your own welfare at a given time is part of a larger quantitative whole (the sum total of well-being and ill-being over your life), your own welfare is part of an even larger quantitative whole (the sum total of every person's well-being and ill-being). And since you ought to be ultimately concerned with the largest quantitative whole, and only derivatively concerned with that whole's parts, you are committed to

> *Personal Insensitivity*: You ought to be equally concerned for an episode of welfare, E_1, and another episode of welfare, E_2, if E_1 and E_2 merely differ with regard to whose they are.

Presumably, you think that you ought to be benevolent. And benevolence is, given a prior commitment to Whole Fundamentalism, characterized by avoiding personal bias. You ought to accept Personal Insensitivity.

We should here draw attention to one way that Sidgwick's claim about beneficence is importantly limited. Notice, when dealing with prudence, Sidgwick could confidently assume that you would agree that you ought to be prudent. But he cannot similarly assume that you think you ought to be benevolent, even moderately. This explains why, in the passage above, he includes a qualification: "The good of any one individual is of no more importance, *from the point of view (if I may say so) of the Universe*, than the good of any other." This qualification—from the point of view of the universe—is an admission. It's possible to deny Personal Insensitivity. The principle has a conditional form. If you take up the point of view of the universe when thinking about personal value—if you think that any episode of welfare is also impersonally good—then you must accept Personal Insensitivity.[11] But, even if you grant the principle, you may still refuse to take up that point of view. Then you aren't committed to Personal Insensitivity. This is why Sidgwick later notes:

> If the Egoist strictly confines himself to stating his conviction that he ought to take his own happiness or pleasure as his ultimate end, there seems no opening for any line of reasoning to lead him to [Utilitarianism] as a first principle; it cannot be proved that the difference between his own happiness and another's happiness is not for him all-important. (1907: 420)

---

11. In understanding Sidgwick in this way, we follow Shaver (2014).

Sidgwick needs you to admit that your own welfare or the welfare of another is impersonally good. Personal Insensitivity can be resisted.

Still, though the argument for Personal Insensitivity is based on a conditional, many will grant the antecedent. As soon as the egoist admits that her own welfare is impersonally good, which is a tempting position to take, Sidgwick can deploy the argument. Continuing the passage above, he explains:

> When, however, the Egoist puts forward, implicitly or explicitly, the proposition that his happiness or pleasure is Good, not only for him but from the point of view of the Universe . . . it then becomes relevant to point out to him that his happiness cannot be a more important part of Good, taken universally, than the equal happiness of any other person. And thus, starting with his own principle, he may be brought to accept Universal happiness or pleasure as that which is absolutely and without qualification Good or Desirable: as an end, therefore, to which the action of a reasonable agent as such ought to be directed. (1907: 420–21)

Once you acknowledge that your own or another's welfare is not just good-for you but good-simpliciter, Sidgwick can show—via Whole Fundamentalism—that you ought to accept Personal Insensitivity. And chances are you are not the kind of stubborn egoist who is immune to Sidgwick's argument. You already probably agree that someone's pleasure and pain are good- and bad-simpliciter. After all, you probably think your own pleasure and pain are good- and bad-simpliciter. This is all that's needed for Sidgwick's argument to get off the ground. By comparison, Mill needed you to accept that, for all persons, each person's pleasure is good-simpliciter and each person's pain is bad-simpliciter.

To deny Sidgwick's claim would require you to deny that anyone ever has any reason to relieve your pain and promote your pleasure. This would be extremely odd. Anyone who has ever acted to promote your interests would have to be acting irrationally or acting with the expectation that her actions would eventually bring some benefit to herself. Countless ordinary interactions would have to be reinterpreted. Consider what having the attitude of the stubborn egoist would be like. Suppose, upon hearing you are sick, a friend says, "Feel better soon." Why would she say this? Does she need your help with something in the near future and so care that you're healthy enough to lend assistance? Or, suppose, while waiting in line, the stranger ahead of you says, "I hope we get in soon." Why should he care when you get in? Why would he use the first person plural? Will something good happen to him if you get in? If you deny that your own pleasure and pain are good- and bad-simpliciter, you need to adopt a strained view of what others have reason to do. That you are likely to find this view unattractive suggests that you probably are not eager to follow the stubborn egoist in embracing it. Rather, you already see your own pleasure and pain as impersonally good. You think others have reason to relieve your pain and promote your pleasure.[12]

We are thus in a position to give

Sidgwick's Argument from Temporal Insensitivity

1. You accept Temporal Insensitivity.
2. If you accept Temporal Insensitivity, then you (implicitly) accept Whole Fundamentalism.
3. You accept that somebody's welfare is good-simpliciter.
4. If you accept that somebody's welfare is good-simpliciter and you accept Whole Fundamentalism, then you should accept Personal Insensitivity.
5. If you accept Personal Insensitivity and accept Weak Hedonism, then you should accept Weak Hedonic Maximization.
6. Hence, you should accept Weak Hedonic Maximization.

Temporal Insensitivity: You ought to be equally concerned for an episode of your welfare, E_1, and another episode of your welfare, E_2, if E_1 and E_2 merely differ with regard to when they occur.

Whole Fundamentalism: For evaluative matters, you ought to be ultimately concerned with the largest quantitative whole, and only derivatively concerned with that whole's parts.

Personal Insensitivity: You ought to be equally concerned for an episode of welfare, E_1, and another episode of welfare, E_2, if E_1 and E_2 merely differ with regard to whose they are.

Weak Hedonism: One's welfare is, in part, determined by experiences of pleasure and pain. Pleasure is intrinsically good-for the person experiencing it. Pain is intrinsically bad-for the person experiencing it.

Weak Hedonic Maximization: If two presently available alternative actions, X and Y, are identical in every morally relevant respect except that X brings about a greater sum total of pleasure minus pain than Y, then it is impermissible to do Y.

Premise 1 and Premise 2 are supported by what prudence demands and why it demands it. And Premise 3 is supported by the fact that you very likely do not hold the egoist's attitude toward pleasure and pain.

But, for all its ingenuity, this argument faces a serious objection. As we've noted throughout our discussion, Sidgwick's argument turns on Whole Fundamentalism. This principle, as formulated, is a claim about all evaluative matters. However, one might wonder if there is not an important difference between personal and impersonal value. Perhaps Whole Fundamentalism applies to goods within lives, but not goods across lives. To see why this suggestion is a plausible one, consider

> For Her Own Good. Test results reveal that your daughter has a rare condition. If she has a very painful operation now, she will avoid much more suffering in ten years.

Here a burden will be imposed on your child. She'll experience a great deal of pain. But it's for her own good. She'll be compensated. This fact—that her suffering

---

12. This paragraph draws on Nagel (1986: 160).

now prevents even more suffering later—seems relevant to thinking of her good fundamentally as a whole. Applied within a life, Whole Fundamentalism is unobjectionable. For compensation is in the offing. Yet things appear different when burdens and benefits are traded off across lives. Consider

> For Another's Good. Test results reveal that your daughter has a rare condition. If she has a very painful operation now, the patient down the hall will avoid much more suffering in ten years.

Here a burden will be imposed on your child. Again, she'll experience a great deal of pain. But, the operation is not for her own good. She will receive no compensation. And this lack of compensation might give us pause. We may be tempted to conclude that Whole Fundamentalism applies to intrapersonal, but not interpersonal, tradeoffs. Perhaps it's correct for prudence—where compensation occurs—but not for beneficence. If we adopt this narrower interpretation of Whole Fundamentalism, however, then Sidgwick's argument fails.[13]

2.5 Conclusion

In this chapter we've presented an argument that can be extracted from the work of the Classical Utilitarians. Though the argument may ultimately be unsound, it remains instructive. Think about the three claims around which our discussion has turned: Weak Hedonism, Weak Welfarism, and Weak Hedonic Maximization. They are compatible with a wide range of ethical theories. Because they are weak in this way, they are extremely plausible. Each asserts something most people, pretheoretically, would want to affirm. Your pain and pleasure are at least part of what's personally good and bad. People's welfare is at least part of what's impersonally good and bad. And the value of the states of affairs our acts bring about are part of what determines their deontic properties. Of course, these claims do not take us all the way to Utilitarianism. But they do point us in that direction.

From this we can note a distinctive feature of Utilitarianism. You can arrive at the view by assenting to a series of much weaker independently attractive principles. Indeed, most other moral theories end up retaining part of Utilitarianism; and, interestingly, it is rarely the same part. This is why we see the Classical Utilitarians pursuing roughly the same strategy: they try to get you to admit to a set of modest claims that together imply Utilitarianism. The remainder of this book will explore this strategy, but with the benefit of more than a century of additional philosophical investigation.

---

13. This paragraph draws on Rawls (1999: §30). The examples are modified from Parfit (1972: 150).

References

Bentham, J. 1983 [1829]. *Deontology Together with a Table of the Springs of Action and Article on Utilitarianism*. Oxford: Clarendon.

Bentham, J. 1996 [1789]. *An Introduction to the Principles of Morals and Legislation*. Oxford: Clarendon.

Brink, D. O. 2013. *Mill's Progressive Principles*. Oxford: Oxford University Press.

Crisp, R. 1997. *Routledge Philosophy Guidebook to Mill on Utilitarianism*. London: Routledge.

Crisp, R. 2015. *The Cosmos of Duty*. Oxford: Oxford University Press.

Gustafsson, J. E. 2018. "Bentham's Binary Form of Maximizing Utilitarianism." *British Journal for the History of Philosophy* 26 (1): 87–109.

Harrison, R. 1983. *Bentham: The Arguments of Philosophers*. London: Routledge.

*Irwin, T. 2009. *The Development of Ethics: A Historical and Critical Study. Vol. III: From Kant to Rawls*. Oxford: Oxford University Press.

Lazari-Radek, K., and P. Singer. 2014. *The Point of View of the Universe: Sidgwick and Contemporary Ethics*. Oxford: Oxford University Press.

Mill, J. S. 2003 [1861/1859]. Utilitarianism *and* On Liberty*: Including Mill's 'Essay on Bentham' and Selections from the Writings of Jeremy Bentham and John Austin*. 2nd ed. Oxford: Blackwell.

Nagel, T. 1986. *The View from Nowhere*. Oxford: Oxford University Press.

Parfit, D. 1972. "Later Selves and Moral Principles." In *Philosophy and Personal Relations*, edited by A. Montefiore, 137–69. London: Routledge.

Philips, D. 2011. *Sidgwickian Ethics*. Oxford: Oxford University Press.

Rawls, J. 1999. *A Theory of Justice*. Rev. ed. Cambridge, MA: Harvard University Press.

Rawls, J. 2007. *Lectures on the History of Political Philosophy*. Cambridge, MA: Harvard University Press.

*Sayre-McCord, G. 2001. "Mill's 'Proof' of the Principle of Utility: A More Than Half-Hearted Defense." *Social Philosophy and Policy* 18 (2): 330–60.

Schneewind, J. B. 1977. *Sidgwick's Ethics and Victorian Moral Philosophy*. Oxford: Oxford University Press.

Schofield, S. 2009. *Bentham: A Guide for the Perplexed*. London: Continuum.

Schultz, B. 2017. *The Happiness Philosopher: The Lives and Works of The Great Utilitarians*. Princeton, NJ: Princeton University Press.

*Shaver, R. 2013. "Utilitarianism: Bentham and Rashdall." In *The Oxford Handbook of the History of Ethics*, edited by R. Crisp, 292–311. Oxford: Oxford University Press.

Shaver, R. 2014. "Sidgwick's Axioms and Consequentialism." *Philosophical Review* 123 (2): 173–204.

Sidgwick, H. 1907. *The Methods of Ethics*. 7th ed. London: Macmillan.

West, H. R. 2006. "Mill's 'Proof' of the Principle of Utility." In *The Blackwell Guide to Mill's Utilitarianism*, edited by H. R. West. Malden, MA: Blackwell.

PART II
Normative Principles

3

Maximizing Is Sufficient and Constraints

3.1 *Introduction*

Start with whatever you take to be good-simpliciter.[1] Now conjure a choice situation in which you have two identical alternatives, except that one contains more of this good than the other. Intuitively, it seems like it can never be a mistake to go in for the better of these two. Here we've arrived at the question we're concerned with in this chapter:

> Is it always permissible to bring about the best?

It is tempting to answer Yes. This takes us to one of the members of the set of principles examined in this book that together imply Utilitarianism, namely:

> MAXIMIZING IS SUFFICIENT: An agent's presently available alternative has the property of being permissible if the performance of any of her other presently available alternatives would not have brought about a complete state of affairs that's better overall.

This principle is half—it's the sufficient condition—of the deontic theory known as Traditional Consequentialism.[2]

Maximizing Is Sufficient, we should stress, makes a modest claim. It says, of the action that brings about the best complete state of affairs, that it is permissible. It does not say that the action is required. Nor does it say anything about the deontic status of any other action. Moreover, the principle, as formulated, is extremely flexible. First, it places no limitations on what qualifies one state of affairs as better or worse than another. It doesn't say anything substantive about what is good or bad. Second, the notion of "a complete state of affairs" it employs is capacious. It is not merely what causally follows from an act's performance. The complete state of affairs is the entire way things will go, including the performance of the act itself.

Given this flexibility, Maximizing Is Sufficient is hard to deny, for most disagreements about which acts are permissible can instead be construed as

---

1. For an overview of good-simpliciter, see §1.2.3.
2. For more on Traditional Consequentialism, see §1.3.4.

disagreements over which states of affairs are best. Suppose you judge that some act, because it will bring about the greatest balance of pleasure over pain, is permissible. But in performing this act you'll ensure that the distribution of pleasure and pain among people is wildly unequal. Nonetheless, you perform it. Further suppose there was an alternative act that would have brought about the same balance of pleasure over pain but would have maintained equality. Someone might think you should have performed this alternative. There's disagreement. But notice what it is that the disagreement is about. It is not that you brought about the best state of affairs but by impermissible means; it's a disagreement over which state of affairs is best. If you are convinced that equality matters, this does not force you to give up Maximizing Is Sufficient. It merely forces you to adjust the set of evaluative claims you accept. You should now hold that, in addition to pleasure and pain, equality contributes to the value of a state of affairs.

Most apparent counterexamples to Maximizing Is Sufficient can be handled similarly. Most anything thought to render an act impermissible can simply be incorporated into the evaluation of the states of affairs. This pattern of reasoning is deployed so frequently by consequentialists it has come to be known as

> *Consequentializing*: Take whatever consideration might lead to a break with consequentialism's deontic verdicts, and reinterpret it as part of what makes a complete state of affairs better or worse.[3]

Even when the evaluation is made from an impersonal point of view, Consequentializing makes it possible to incorporate an extremely wide range of normative considerations into the framework of consequentialism.

Maximizing Is Sufficient, because both modest and flexible, is compelling. Indeed, it is sometimes referred to as Consequentialism's Compelling Idea.[4] Yet it's not free from objections. In this chapter, we present and evaluate what is perhaps the most serious.

3.2 *One for Two*

As we have suggested, Maximizing Is Sufficient is not easily resisted. Consequentializing shields the principle from many challenges. But this strategy has its limits. Not every consideration can simply be baked into the evaluation of the state of affairs, impersonally assessed. Intuitively, what morality requires of you—a particular agent—may not always bring about the best outcome. Consider, for example:

---

3. Modified from Portmore (2011: 85).
4. The name is due to Foot (1985).

One for Two. The head of the mafia is going to trial. To get a conviction, the state needs testimony from one major witness and one minor witness. Fortunately, a major witness has already agreed to testify and is waiting in a secure location. A pair of minor witnesses are also prepared to testify. Unfortunately, the mafia, who will not allow their leader to go to trial, know that you have access to the major witness. They credibly threaten that, unless you murder the major witness, an assassin will murder the two minor witnesses. If you agree, they'll give you a poison that will allow you to murder the witness without being detected and a pill that will erase your memory of the whole ordeal.[5]

Here either you commit one murder, or two comparable murders will be committed. It is worth taking a moment to explain what "comparable murders" means. Two murders are comparable when, apart from the person who performs them, they are identical in all morally relevant respects. So, for example, they will cause equal amounts of suffering, however much that is. To keep things simple, we can stipulate that each murder directly brings about only effects that are bad-simpliciter and the rest of each world balances out in all morally relevant respects. The choice you face in One for Two is represented, from the impersonal point of view, in Table 3.1.

Table 3.1: *One for Two from an Impersonal Point of View*

Presently Available Alternatives	Complete State of Affairs
Murder	One murder + the bad effects + rest of the world
Don't Murder	Two murders + twice the bad effects + rest of the world

With a clear view of your options we can ask: What ought you to do? Despite how things stand impersonally assessed, many confidently believe that you should keep your hands clean. You ought not to murder. This is true even though the inevitable result will be that two comparable murders will be committed by someone else. This conviction—that you ought not to murder in cases like One for Two—is widely shared.

The intuitive verdict in One for Two suggests something more general, namely, the existence of a

Constraint: A requirement to refrain from performing a certain familiar act-type (e.g., murder) even though performing such an act would minimize the

---

5. This case is modified from Thomson (1997: 274).

total number of act-tokens of this act-type and have no other morally relevant implications.[6]

The definition of a Constraint invokes the distinction between act-types and act-tokens. To get a handle on the difference between types and tokens, consider the question: How many letters are in the word "book"? This question is instructively ambiguous. We might answer: four—counting each instance of a letter. Or we might answer: three—counting each kind of letter, and so counting "o" only once. If we answer four, we took the question to be asking about letter tokens. If we answer three, we took the question to be asking about letter types. The same distinction applies to acts. Constraints require one to refrain from performing certain act-types even when performing them would result in fewer tokens of those types.

We can now start to see why the normative relevance of Constraints is quite different from that of things like equality. From the impersonal point of view, we can plausibly treat all comparable equality disruptions similarly. That is why, for the defender of Maximizing Is Sufficient, Consequentializing equality is possible. Constraints, however, cannot be accommodated in this way. To get the result that you are required to refrain from murder, we cannot treat, as the impersonal perspective would have us, all comparable murders alike. A murder you commit must matter morally to you in a way that a murder someone else commits does not. A Constraint on murdering thus cannot be reinterpreted as part of what makes a state of affairs impersonally better or worse.

In the next section, we'll explain more precisely why Consequentializing is of no help in accommodating the intuitive verdict in One for Two. This will position us to mount a powerful argument against Maximizing Is Sufficient.

3.3 *The Argument from One for Two*

In One for Two, we stipulated that, apart from the number of murders and the bad effects of each, all else is equal. Given this, Maximizing Is Sufficient will unavoidably deliver the result that it is permissible for you to murder.

To see this, consider the following dilemma. Murder is impersonally bad or it is not. Either way, however, Maximizing Is Sufficient will permit your murdering. Consulting Table 3.1, we see that the difference between the world where you murder and the one where you don't is that the former contains an additional murder and an additional set of bad effects. Suppose first we say that murder is

---

6. This formulation is modified from Scheffler (1985: 409). We've added "familiar" to rule out certain act-types that create problems for Scheffler's original formulation, e.g., the act-type, "murdering to prevent more murders."

impersonally bad. Since each murder is comparable, we need to add in the same amount of badness for each. Now perform some basic algebra. For each world, we can cancel out the badness of one murder, the badness of one set of bad effects from murder, and the value of the rest of the world. That leaves the complete state of affairs where you murder worse to the extent of one murder and one set of bad effects. The result is clear. The world where you murder is better overall than the world where you refrain. Thus, if Maximizing Is Sufficient is true and murders are impersonally bad, then, in a case like One for Two, you are permitted to murder. Next suppose that murder is not bad. It makes no evaluative difference from the impersonal point of view. Were this so, the difference in value of each world would hinge exclusively on the bad effects of each murder. The murders make no difference from the impersonal point of view, and the value of the rest of each world washes out. Here too the result is clear. The world where you refrain and the assassin kills two, is worse overall by the magnitude of one set of bad effects. Thus, if Maximizing Is Sufficient is true and murders are not impersonally bad, then, in a case like One for Two, you are permitted to murder. Either way—whether murders are impersonally bad or not—Maximizing Is Sufficient permits your murdering in One for Two.

This reasoning applies, of course, not just to murder but to a wide range of acts. Wherever there are Constraints against acting in certain ways (e.g., torturing, stealing, and lying), Maximizing Is Sufficient will offer unintuitive verdicts. And given that they cannot be captured from the impersonal point of view, Consequentializing is of no help.

From here we are positioned to articulate

The Argument from One for Two

1. There is at least one Constraint.
2. If there is at least one Constraint, then Maximizing Is Sufficient is false.
3. Hence, Maximizing Is Sufficient is false.

The only controversial claim is Premise 1. That there is a Constraint against murder is supported by our intuitive judgments in cases like One for Two. But, even if that case is unpersuasive, other plausible examples are easily generated. And, if even just one Constraint survives critical scrutiny, then Maximizing Is Sufficient must be rejected. The central question then, which we'll take up over the next few sections, is this: Are there any Constraints?

Maximizing Is Sufficient: An agent's presently available alternative has the property of being permissible if the performance of any of the agent's other presently available alternatives would not have brought about a complete state of affairs that's better overall.

Constraint: A requirement to refrain from performing a certain familiar act-type (e.g., murder) even though performing such an act would minimize the total number of act-tokens of this act-type and have no other morally relevant implications.

3.4 *Why Are Constraints Puzzling*

Whatever their initial intuitive appeal, Constraints, on reflection, are thought by many to be paradoxical. Here's Nozick:

> Isn't it *irrational* to accept a side constraint C, rather than a view that directs minimizing the violations of C? . . . If nonviolation of C is so important, shouldn't that be the goal? How can a concern for the nonviolation of C lead to the refusal to violate C even when this would prevent other more extensive violations of C? (1974: 30)

What makes Constraints puzzling is that they conflict with our ordinary way of reasoning about what to do. In everyday choice situations, we think about what matters and then try to bring about as much of it as is possible. Consider a variation on the example that kicked off this chapter. If, when all else is equal, you face a choice between bringing about something impersonally morally problematic or bringing about something much more impersonally morally problematic, to go in for the latter verges on incomprehensible. That is why Nozick begins his line of questioning by asking whether Constraints are irrational. In Scheffler's words, "How can the minimization of morally objectionable conduct itself be morally unacceptable?" (1985: 413). Constraints do not fit into a model of thinking about what to do that has all requirements focus exclusively on bringing about certain states of affairs and evaluates them impersonally.

So, to accommodate Constraints, we must reject part of this model. We can either hold that requirements attach to something other than making a certain state of affairs obtain, or we can retain the focus on states of affairs but introduce normative considerations relative to individual agents. But both of these proposals have their own unwelcome implications. On the one hand, it's puzzling to think that requirements relate agents to something other than propositions (i.e., bringing about certain states of affairs). When we claim that an agent ought to act in a certain way, we are usually claiming that this agent ought to see to it that she acts in this way. As Portmore writes:

> If our actions are the means by which we affect the way the world goes, and if our intentional actions necessarily aim at making the world go a certain way, then it is only natural to suppose that what we have most reason to do is determined by which way we have most reason to want the world to go. (2011: 56)[7]

---

7. For a similar suggestion, see Mill (2003 [1861]: U 1.2).

On the other hand, it is puzzling to think that states of affairs are to be evaluated differently for different agents, as this entails that agents face different requirements. As Schroeder writes, "Surely it would be simpler to think that moral obligations are the same for everyone rather than different—'neutral' rather than 'relative'" (2011: 38).

This explains why many have found Constraints so stubbornly paradoxical. It seems that, as One for Two makes vivid, morality includes Constraints. But, to accommodate them, we have to either deny the focus on states of affairs or deny that the same things are required of all agents. Neither of these options is attractive. Both are puzzling. Of course, many things that initially seem puzzling, upon investigation, turn out not to be. So we'll next look at each of these approaches in more detail.

3.5 *The Standard Story of Action Argument against Non-Consequentialism*

On the first of these approaches, we account for Constraints by holding that some of your requirements relate you to something other than bringing about certain states of affairs. And the most obvious candidate is that some of your requirements relate you to actions. That there is a distinction between these two kinds of requirements is suggested by ordinary language. In English, we use "ought"—which is a synonym for "required"—to make claims both about the way things ought to be but also about what someone ought to do. For example, we say, "You ought not to murder," but we also say, "It ought to be that you not murder." We'll refer to the requirements corresponding to this distinction as

> *Requirements for Actions*: Requirements that relate an agent to an action (e.g., you ought not to murder).
>
> *Requirements for States of Affairs*: Requirements that relate an agent to a state of affairs (e.g., it ought to be that you not murder).

Although these two kinds of requirements are grammatically different, many philosophers have thought that all requirements are fundamentally Requirements for States of Affairs.[8] After all, "You ought not to murder" and "It ought to be that you not murder" seem, if you do as you ought, to amount to the same thing: a world in which you don't murder. But this treatment generates a strong presumption against Constraints. For, if Requirements for States of Affairs are fundamental, then a theory that includes Constraints implies that morality demands different

---

8. See, for example, Chisholm (1964).

things of different agents. In One for Two, what's required of you is that you bring about a certain state of affairs: that you not murder. And what's required of the assassin is that she bring about a certain state of affairs: that she not murder. That's puzzling. Why would morality make different demands on different people?

Yet, if we deny that Requirements for Actions are fundamentally Requirements for States of Affairs, this puzzling feature of Constraints can be avoided. Constraints may be understood as requiring the same thing—a certain type of act—of every agent. In One for Two, we can claim that what's required of you is an action: not murdering. And what's required of the assassin is the action: not murdering. Since not murdering is the same action, these are the same requirements. Let's call the view that makes room for Constraints in this way the

> *Non-Consequentialist Approach*: Constraints are possible because it is not the case that all requirements are Requirements for States of Affairs. Some requirements are Requirements for Actions.

On this approach, there is no mystery as to why you are required to refrain from murder even though the result is that two comparable murders are committed.[9]

Yet, if the Non-Consequentialist Approach is to be viable, there must be a fundamental—not merely verbal—difference between Requirements for Actions and Requirements for States of Affairs. The requirement that one perform an action must amount to something other than a requirement that one bring about a state of affairs. However, a widely accepted and independently plausible theory of action implies that there is no such distinction. As we'll explain, on this account of action, to require a specific action of an agent is just to relate that agent—via her psychology—to a certain state of affairs. As a result, Requirements for Actions collapses into Requirements for States of Affairs.

Not every movement of your body is an action. Many times throughout the day your body moves—your hair and nails grow, you stumble, blink, and shift in your sleep. These are things that happen to you. At other times you play a more active role—you walk around, carry on conversations, stand up, and lie down. These are things that you do. But what distinguishes these actions from mere bodily movements? A theory of action answers this question.

According to the prevailing theory, we distinguish mere movements from actions, not by reference to what happens in the world when the movements are initiated but by their causes. This popular view is known as the

> *Standard Story of Action*: [A] subject's actions are those of his bodily movements that are done because he wants certain things and because he believes that he can achieve those things by moving his body in the ways he does. (Smith 2013: 51)

---

9. The last two paragraphs draw heavily on Schroeder (2011).

When you roll while awake your movement flows from certain features of your psychology. You are acting on a desire (that you be more comfortable) and a belief (that shifting your position will be more comfortable). Your action in this way is rationalized. If asked, you could explain why you acted as you did by citing this belief-desire pair. By contrast, the movement of your body while sleeping involves no similar rationalization. Because asleep, you don't have any thoughts about the world, and you didn't have any conscious desire that it be a certain way. So, according to the Standard Story of Action, what you do is suitably caused by features of your psychology—your desires and beliefs—while what happens to you is not so caused.[10]

If this story is correct, then Requirements for Action relate agents to certain movements caused and rationalized by a certain belief-desire pair. This does not yet impugn the Non-Consequentialist Approach. But notice what happens when we elaborate the concepts of desire and belief. As Stalnaker explains:

> To desire that P is to be disposed to act in ways that would tend to bring it about that P in a world in which one's beliefs, whatever they are, were true. To believe that P is to be disposed to act in ways that would tend to satisfy one's desires, whatever they are, in a world in which P (together with one's other beliefs) were true. (1984: 15)

Desires and beliefs are propositional attitudes. They take as their objects "that clauses," picking out some state of the world. This is why Stalnaker uses "that P" in the passage above. When we believe, we try to get our minds to conform to the world; when we achieve this fit our beliefs are true. When you believe that aspirin will relieve your headache, you want this to accurately depict the world. Beliefs, for this reason, are attitudes with mind-to-world direction of fit. When we desire, we try to get the world to conform to our minds; when we are successful our desires are satisfied. When you desire that your headache end, you want the world to conform. Desires, for this reason, are attitudes with world-to-mind direction of fit.

The upshot, then, is this: actions are distinguished from mere movements by how the agent is related to the bringing about of a certain state of affairs. One's movements are actions when a certain state of affairs is the object of one's desires and beliefs. This is why we can, without loss, say either "you took aspirin" or "you made it the case (ensured, brought it about) that you took aspirin."[11]

The problem for the Non-Consequentialist Approach should now be in view. Recall, to accommodate Constraints, there must be a fundamental difference

---

10. This paragraph draws on Davidson (1980).

11. This last point is due to Hammerton (2018).

between Requirements for Actions and Requirements for States of Affairs. But, if the Standard Story of Action is correct, this distinction marks a merely superficial difference.[12]

We are now in a position to forward

The Standard Story of Action Argument against the Non-Consequentialist Approach

1. If the Standard Story of Action is true, the Non-Consequentialist Approach fails.
2. The Standard Story of Action is true.
3. Hence, the Non-Consequentialist Approach fails.

The central claim of the argument is that of Premise 2. The Non-Consequentialist Approach depends crucially on this theory of action being mistaken. Yet the Standard Story of Action has earned its appellation. It's the standard account because it's the best we've come up with.

> *Standard Story of Action*: A subject's actions are those of his bodily movements that are done because he wants certain things and because he believes that he can achieve those things by moving his body in the ways he does.
>
> *Non-Consequentialist Approach*: Constraints are possible because it is not the case that all requirements are Requirements for States of Affairs. Some requirements are Requirements for Actions.

3.6 *The Collective Self-Defeat Argument against Agent-Relative Consequentialism*

We turn now to consider the second way of accommodating Constraints. This approach retains the idea that all requirements are Requirements for States of Affairs but expands the Consequentializing program beyond its traditional, impersonal limits. As a result, states of affairs are ranked differently for different agents, and so moral requirements are different for different agents. On this suggestion, morality may require that agents be especially concerned about their own agential involvement and close personal ties. To allow for this we need to introduce a notion of goodness that is sensitive to partial concerns. In addition to what is good-simpliciter (or bad-simpliciter) and what is good-for you (or bad-for you), we also recognize what is good-relative-to-you (or bad-relative-to-you).[13]

But what exactly is agent-relative value? To get a grip on this notion, consider

---

12. Our discussion of the relation between the Standard Story of Action and Requirements for States of Affairs follows Hurley (2018).
13. For an overview of these evaluative notions, see §1.2.3.

> Good News. Ryan's work makes the world a better place. Were he to stop, many people would be worse off. Unfortunately, yesterday, Ryan learned that either he or his daughter has a debilitating illness. Today he's waiting for the test results. When the doctor calls, it's revealed that it is Ryan, and not his daughter, who is afflicted. Upon hearing the news Ryan says, "That's good."[14]

It's easy to understand where Ryan is coming from. But we should be clear about what he's saying. He isn't saying that the news of his diagnosis is personally or impersonally good. His diagnosis is personally bad. It's bad-for him; he's going to be miserable. And his diagnosis is impersonally bad. It's bad-simpliciter; when Ryan stops working many people will be worse off. Nonetheless, Ryan's expression—that's good—is perfectly intelligible. It's what we might expect from any parent. Proponents of agent-relative goodness claim that what Ryan is talking about is good-relative-to-him, as the father of his daughter. From Ryan's evaluative perspective, it's good news that he, and not his daughter, is the one to be afflicted. Ryan's reaction in Good News suggests a rough idea of the concept of agent-relative goodness.

The foregoing is enough to convey the contours of agent-relative value. And once this notion of goodness is incorporated into the evaluation of states of affairs, the rankings of the states of affairs will vary across agents. What makes a state of affairs better or worse will be partly determined by what's good-relative-to-you. The same state of affairs may thus be evaluated differently by different people. Let's call this strategy for accommodating Constraints the

> *Agent-Relative Consequentialist Approach*: Constraints are possible because it is not the case that the evaluative ranking of states of affairs is the same for everyone. The complete state of affairs that is best-relative-to-you might diverge from the complete state of affairs that is best-relative-to-someone else.

On this approach, we can claim that your violating a Constraint is worse-relative-to-you than the alternative state of affairs in which two comparable Constraints are violated by someone else. We can then make sense of the verdict in One for Two. The state of affairs in which you refrain from murdering one and the assassin murders two will be better-relative-to-you than the state of affairs in which you murder one and the assassin does nothing. And so, since you are required to bring about the state of affairs that's best-relative-to-you, you are required to refrain from murder. We have made room for Constraints.

---

14. This example, and the discussion that follows, draws on Dreier (2011).

Chapter 3: Maximizing Is Sufficient and Constraints

Yet a troubling feature of the Agent-Relative Consequentialist Approach is readily apparent. Because the ranking of states of affairs will vary across individuals, and all requirements relate agents to states of affairs, morality will require different things of different agents. It was already suggested that a theory of this sort departs significantly from the simplicity of a neutral theory. And in what follows we'll canvass what seems a less forgivable defect.

Whatever else we expect of a consequentialist theory, we can reasonably insist that if no one is compliant (i.e., if everyone fails to do what's required) the state of affairs thereby produced shouldn't be better than that which would arise if everyone were compliant. Indeed, if a consequentialist theory, whose central idea is maximizing the good, yields the result that universal noncompliance is better than universal compliance, then the theory seems to condemn itself. Let's call such consequentialist theories

> *Collectively Self-Defeating*: When a consequentialist theory is such that when everyone fails to act as the theory requires the complete state of affairs brought about is better (impersonally or relative-to-each) than the complete state of affairs that would have been brought about had everyone instead acted as the theory requires.

To be Collectively Self-Defeating appears to be a devastating defect. As Parfit explains, "Moral principles or theories are intended to answer questions about what all of us ought to do. So, such principles or theories clearly fail, and condemn themselves, when they are directly self-defeating at the collective level" (2011: 306).

A theory that takes the Agent-Relative Consequentialist Approach is, as we will now show, Collectively Self-Defeating. Recall, this approach, because it incorporates agent-relative goodness, allows that agents may evaluate states of affairs differently. Yet, even though each agent has her own ranking of states of affairs, the states of affairs that are in fact brought about will be the product of everyone's choices. And, in some cases, the actions of multiple agents, taken together, interact in depressing ways. In particular, each agent, acting as required, may bring about a state of affairs that is worse-relative-to-each than that which would have resulted had each agent been noncompliant. By way of demonstration, consider

> <u>Worse Together</u>. Alf and Betty, who are the only moral agents who exist, both have homicidal desires. Absent intervention, each will freely murder three young children (who are not yet moral agents). Fortunately, Alf has a drug. If he treats himself, his murders will be reduced by one. If instead he treats Betty, her murders will be reduced by two. Betty also has a drug. If she treats herself, her murders will be reduced by one. If instead she treats Alf, his murders will

be reduced by two. Taken together, the drugs completely eliminate homicidal desires.[15]

Adopting the Agent-Relative Consequentialist Approach, Alf's evaluative ranking of the states of affairs is determined by what's best-relative-to-Alf; while Betty's evaluative ranking is determined by what's best-relative-to-Betty. And, to accommodate the idea that there is a Constraint against murder, we know that the fewer murders Alf commits the better-relative-to-him, and the fewer murders Betty commits the better-relative-to-her. Table 3.2 represents the rankings of the available states of affairs in Worse Together.

Table 3.2: *Payoff Matrix for Worse Together*

		Betty	
		Treats self	Treats Alf
Alf	Treats self	• Third-best-relative-to-Alf • Third-best-relative-to-Betty	• Best-relative-to-Alf • Worst-relative-to-Betty
	Treats Betty	• Worst-relative-to-Alf • Best-relative-to-Betty	• Second-best-relative-to-Alf • Second-best-relative-to-Betty

Neither Alf nor Betty alone chooses the state of affairs that will obtain. Each chooses only between two pairs. Which of the pair is realized depends on the other's choice. Given Alf's and Betty's options, regardless of what the other does, each individually is required to treat themselves. Whether Betty treats herself or Alf, the state of affairs that is better-relative-to-Alf will be brought about if he treats himself. Whether Alf treats himself or Betty, the state of affairs that's better-relative-to-Betty will be brought about if she treats herself. This result is depressing. For, if they do what they are required to do, their acts, taken together, bring about the state of affairs that is third-best-relative-to-each. Yet, there exists an act available to each, which, if taken, would produce a state of affairs that is better-relative-to-each: treating the other person. Of course, Alf and Betty could medicate each other and so bring about what both regard as the second-best state of affairs. But, in so doing, they would each fail to bring about what's best-relative-to-each. They would, by the lights of the Agent-Relative Consequentialist Approach, be acting impermissibly.

The upshot of Worse Together should now be clear. Both agents, in doing what is required, bring about a state of affairs that is less good-relative-to-each than

---

15. This case, and the discussion of Collectively Self-Defeating theories that follows, draws on Parfit (1984: ch. 4).

is possible. It would be better-relative-to-each if neither did what's required. The Agent-Relative Consequentialist Approach, because it gives different agents different requirements, is Collectively Self-Defeating.

We can now mount

The Collective Self-Defeat Argument against Agent-Relative Consequentialism

1. If the Agent-Relative Consequentialist Approach is Collectively Self-Defeating, then it fails.
2. The Agent-Relative Consequentialist Approach is Collectively Self-Defeating.
3. Hence, the Agent-Relative Consequentialist Approach fails.

> *Agent-Relative Consequentialist Approach*: Constraints are possible because it is not the case that the evaluative ranking of states of affairs is the same for everyone. The complete state of affairs that is best-relative-to-you might diverge from the complete state of affairs that is best-relative-to-someone else.
>
> *Collectively Self-Defeating*: When a consequentialist theory is such that when everyone fails to act as the theory requires the complete state of affairs brought about is better (impersonally or relative-to-each) than the complete state of affairs that would have been brought about had everyone instead acted as the theory requires.

The only controversial claim is Premise 1. But it's well supported. Collectively Self-Defeating theories fail on their own terms.

3.7 The No Approach Succeeds Argument against Constraints

Over the previous two sections, we've discussed the two ways one might accommodate Constraints. We've organized these options around two questions, as depicted in Table 3.3.

Table 3.3: *Approaches to Vindicating Constraints*

	Are all requirements Requirements for States of Affairs?	Does every agent face the same requirements?
Non-Consequentialist Approach	No	Yes
Agent-Relative Consequentialist Approach	Yes	No

Traditional Consequentialism, of course, answers Yes to both questions. Each alternative makes a crucial departure, answering No to one of the questions. Yet it is noteworthy that both still want to retain part of the traditional view.

The Non-Consequentialist Approach maintains that all agents face the same requirements. The Agent-Relative Consequentialist Approach maintains that all requirements are Requirements for States of Affairs. Evidently, there's something attractive about Traditional Consequentialism.

We are now in a position to see why. The Non-Consequentialist Approach conflicts with the Standard Story of Action. That story implies that all requirements, even what appear to be Requirements for Actions, relate agents to states of affairs. The Agent-Relative Consequentialist Approach is Collectively Self-Defeating. By giving different agents different requirements, we are put at moral odds with one another. This conflict permits choice situations in which everyone, acting as required, brings about a state of affairs that is worse (relative-to-each) than the state of affairs that would have resulted if everyone had failed to act as required.

Given that these two approaches appear to be the only plausible ways to accommodate Constraints, and that both fail, we can now offer

The No Approach Succeeds Argument against Constraints

1. If there are Constraints, then either the Non-Consequentialist Approach or Agent-Relative Consequentialist Approach must succeed.
2. Neither the Non-Consequentialist Approach nor the Agent-Relative Consequentialist Approach succeeds.
3. Hence, it is not the case that there are Constraints.

The crux of the argument is Premise 2. But, as we've seen, both approaches appear to be deficient. If this argument is sound, then the chief objection to Maximizing Is Sufficient is rebuffed.

Constraint: A requirement to refrain from performing a certain familiar act-type (e.g., murder) even though performing such an act would minimize the total number of act-tokens of this act-type and have no other morally relevant implications.

Non-Consequentialist Approach: Constraints are possible because it is not the case that all requirements are Requirements for States of Affairs. Some requirements are Requirements for Actions.

Agent-Relative Consequentialist Approach: Constraints are possible because it is not the case that the evaluative ranking of states of affairs is the same for everyone. The complete state of affairs that is best-relative-to-you might diverge from the complete state of affairs that is best-relative-to-someone else.

3.8 *Decision-Deontic Confusion*

Regardless of how congenial one finds the foregoing argument, the feeling that there are Constraints can be hard to shake. It may be tempting to regard this as a strike against Maximizing Is Sufficient. But this temptation is misplaced. For it is unsurprising, given our moral educations and typical psychological development, that we regard Constraints as inviolable, endowing them with a significance they lack. If this is correct—if there's a good explanation as to why this conviction

Chapter 3: Maximizing Is Sufficient and Constraints

is so persistent—then its intuitive force will be diminished. This is the possibility we investigate in this section.

Consider how children are morally educated. They are not taught ethical theory. They lack the cognitive sophistication. This places certain limits on how their behavior can be managed. For example, consider

> Lying Child. Your four-year-old has just told a blatant lie. Though she does not know it, the lie is, in point of fact, innocuous. You are the only one around.

Even though you recognize the sometimes subtle difference between morally objectionable deception and that which is unobjectionable, you are quite sure your child does not. She lacks what's necessary to appreciate the nuance. You are then likely to respond to her deception as if it were the objectionable sort. Her behavior should be corrected. You tell her that lying is wrong. You do not tell her that lying is wrong when certain conditions obtain. Such qualifications would not only be lost on a child; they would invite potential wickedness. Given their stage of psychological development, children need a simple set of rules that helps them approximate the moral ideal. What they are taught is a

> *Decision Procedure*: A set of rules that the agent can use, given her beliefs at the time of action, to identify whether an action is to be performed.[16]

A categorical prohibition on lying is part of the Decision Procedure that you believe is best for your child, given her current abilities and knowledge.

In addition to cognitive sophistication, children also lack the emotional dispositions needed for true moral compliance. To ensure that they are able to later act as morality requires, you must inculcate suitable attitudes. They should find compliance easy and be resistant to any violation of the rules. When you praise compliance and punish violation of the rules, you are instilling the kinds of attitudes that make them easier to follow in the future. You want her to have a reverence for these rules, showing them the same respect she would show for the moral law. It is then utterly unsurprising when the child grows up thinking these rules—the content of the Decision Procedure—are of fundamental importance. Because these rules have been presented to children during their moral education in this way, it is entirely predictable that they take on the status of what is actually the correct

> *Deontic Theory*: The theory that assigns deontic properties to acts.[17]

---

16. For further discussion of Decision Procedures, see §1.4.2.

17. It is worth stressing that almost all plausible ethical theories will rely on a Decision Procedure that diverges from its Deontic Theory. For an example of how Kant's view might diverge in this way, see Timmons (1997).

Because so many of one's encounters with morally complex situations involve reliance only on Decision Procedures, and because moral education places such heavy emphasis on these rules, people reasonably treat them as giving the insight of a Deontic Theory.

This is an entirely sensible way to proceed with moral education. Even if you believe Maximizing Is Sufficient is true, you still ought to provide your children with a Decision Procedure that contains Constraints. As Hare writes:

> I have been brought up to think that one ought not to tell lies, as most of us have been. And suppose that I get into a situation in which I decide that I ought, in the circumstances, to tell a lie. It does not follow in the least that I shall be able to tell the lie without compunction. That is how lie-detectors work (on people who have been to this minimal extent well brought up). Even if I do not blush, something happens to the electrical properties of my skin. And for my part, I am very glad that this happens to my skin; for if it did not I should be a morally worse educated person. When we bring up our children ... one of the things we are trying to do is to cause them to have reactions of this kind: "to like and dislike the things they ought to like and dislike." It is not by any means the whole of moral education.... But there is no doubt that most of us have, during our upbringing, acquired these sentiments, and not much doubt that this is, on the whole, a good thing. (1981: 30–31)

Putting these points together, you want your child to desire to be moral and to feel guilt when she fails to do so. But you, given her stage of development, cannot actually tell her what you take to be the truth about morality. At this point, she can only handle a Decision Procedure. So you pretend, in order to cultivate the corresponding emotions and attitudes, that the Decision Procedure is the correct Deontic Theory.

This sketch of moral education should sound familiar. What you would do to your child is what your moral educators did to you. Yet this sensible way of proceeding with moral education courts a confusion. From the beginning, the moral judgments you are taught are actually the rules of a Decision Procedure. But they are, in order to ensure you have the correct motivational set, being treated as if they were the correct Deontic Theory. We are all encouraged as children to believe that these useful rules have the status of moral bedrock. So it is no surprise that we are all prone to

> *Decision-Deontic Confusion*: Mistakenly treating what is part of a Decision Procedure as if it were part of a Deontic Theory.

Few of us have occasion to think systematically about why acts have the deontic properties they do. Most of us get along fine with a Decision Procedure. It is then very easy for the Decision Procedure you were given as a child to take on an exalted status. Most grown-ups, for example, still treat playground rules—first come first serve, finders keepers, no cutting, and so on—as if they were handed down from on high. Similarly, we should expect that people are apt to judge Constraints—which are part of the best Decision Procedure—as if they are part of a Deontic Theory. This Decision-Deontic Confusion is the predictable result of our moral educations.

We are now well positioned to see how a debunking explanation of our persistent belief in the existence of Constraints might go. Constraints such as don't lie, don't murder, don't steal, and the like probably featured prominently in your moral education. And hence, like Hare, you cannot think of violating them without compunction. Further, you may not be altogether clear about the classification of your normative judgments. Chances are you've not sat down and thought carefully as to whether a particular normative judgment is part of your Decision Procedure or part of your Deontic Theory. In a word, our moral education sets us up to fetishize Constraints, mistakenly bestowing the rules of our Decision Procedure with the status of Deontic Theory.

Reflection on our moral education thus seems to call into question the reliability of our belief in Constraints. Their intuitive appeal may not be the product of our tracking the moral truth. Rather this appeal may simply be the residue of effective childhood scolding.

3.9 *Conclusion*

In this chapter, we've investigated the challenge that Constraints pose to Maximizing Is Sufficient. We've tried to show why defending the existence of Constraints proves difficult. Which of the arguments is the weakest?

There is a good case to be made that it's the Argument against the Non-Consequentialist Approach. Recall, this argument hinges on the truth of the Standard Story of Action. This story, as usually told, treats the relevant attitudes—desire and belief—as relating an agent to a state of affairs. But this crucial claim may be denied. Perhaps, at least in cases of intentional action, we should think of desires, not as propositional but as performative attitudes. Desires, on this alternative view, do relate agents to actions. And this is precisely what the Non-Consequentialist Approach needs.

Ordinary language expressions lend support to the idea that desires are performative attitudes. As Thompson explains:

> Suppose that I am walking to school intentionally. It follows, we have supposed, that I want to walk to school—that's why I'm taking this step, for example. What, on a propositional construction, will the object of this wanting be? Presumably this: that I walk to school. And when philosophers do manage to fill in the blank in the omnipresent "I want that p," we inevitably

find just this sort of substitution. The trouble, of course, is that the requisite proposition doesn't exist; the bit of English we use here . . . in fact expresses a habitual sense, which is nothing like what we had in mind. (2008: 127–28)

So, at least in English, in some cases the descriptions of actions tell against treating desires as propositional attitudes. If desires are indeed performative attitudes, then the Standard Story of Action poses no threat to the Non-Consequentialist Approach. There may be a way to make sense of Constraints after all. But can English usage bear the weight of such a substantial conclusion?

References

Chisholm, R. M. 1964. "The Ethics of Requirement." *American Philosophical Quarterly* 1 (2): 147–53.
Davidson, D. 1980. *Essays on Actions and Events*. Oxford: Oxford University Press.
*Dreier, J. 2011. "In Defense of Consequentializing." In *Oxford Studies in Normative Ethics*, edited by M. Timmons, 97–118. Oxford: Oxford University Press.
*Foot, P. 1985. "Utilitarianism and the Virtues." *Mind* 94 (374): 196–209.
Hammerton, M. 2018. "Distinguishing Agent-Relativity from Agent-Neutrality." *Australasian Journal of Philosophy*: 1–12.
Hare, R. M. 1981. *Moral Thinking: Its Levels, Method, and Point*. Oxford: Oxford University Press.
Hurley, P. 2018. "Consequentialism and the Standard Story of Action." *The Journal of Ethics* 22 (1): 25–44.
Mill, J. S. 2003 [1861/1859]. Utilitarianism *and* On Liberty: *Including Mill's "Essay on Bentham" and Selections from the Writings of Jeremy Bentham and John Austin*. 2nd ed. Oxford: Blackwell.
Nozick, R. 1974. *Anarchy, State, and Utopia*. New York: Basic Books.
Parfit, D. 1984. *Reasons and Persons*. Oxford: Clarendon Press.
Parfit, D. 2011. *On What Matters*. Vol. 1. Oxford: Oxford University Press.
Portmore, D. W. 2011. *Commonsense Consequentialism: Wherein Morality Meets Rationality*. Oxford: Oxford University Press.
*Scheffler, S. 1985. "Agent-Centred Restrictions, Rationality, and the Virtues." *Mind* 94: 409–19.
Schroeder, M. 2011. "Ought, Agents, and Actions." *Philosophical Review* 120 (1): 1–41.
Smith, M. 2013. "The Ideal of Orthonomous Action, or the How and Why of Buck-Passing." In *Thinking about Reasons: Themes from the Philosophy of Jonathan Dancy*, edited by D. Bakhurst, M. O. Little, and B. Hooker, 51–74. Oxford: Oxford University Press.
Stalnaker, R. 1984. *Inquiry*. Cambridge, MA: MIT Press.
Thompson, M. 2008. *Life and Action: Elementary Structures of Practice and Practical Thought*. Cambridge, MA: Harvard University Press.
Thomson, J. J. 1997. "The Right and the Good." *The Journal of Philosophy* 94 (6): 273–98.
Timmons, M. 1997. "Decision Procedures, Moral Criteria, and the Problem of Relevant Descriptions in Kant's Ethics." *Annual Review of Law and Ethics* (5): 389–417.

4

Maximizing Is Necessary and Demandingness

4.1 *Introduction*

Start with whatever you take to be good-simpliciter.[1] Now conjure a choice situation in which you have two identical alternatives, except that one contains more of this good than the other. Intuitively, it is always a mistake to go in for the worse of the two. To make this vivid, consider

> Healing Gaze. You've just discovered that you have an extraordinary ability. You can, by simply gazing into a child's eyes, cure her ailments. Before you are two morally decent children, both of whom are terminally ill. You can, by shifting your gaze toward each, cure both.

It's obvious what's morally required. To do nothing, letting both wither and die, would be monstrous. To cure only one, though better, would still be impermissible. You ought to cure both. You are required to gaze into the eyes of the first child, and then gaze into the eyes of the second. But should we generalize this idea? Here we've arrived at the question we're concerned with in this chapter:

> Is it always impermissible to bring about less than the best?

It is tempting to answer Yes. This takes us to one of the members of the set of principles examined in this book that together imply Utilitarianism, namely:

> MAXIMIZING IS NECESSARY: An agent's presently available alternative has the property of being permissible only if the performance of any of her other presently available alternatives would not have brought about a complete state of affairs that's better overall.

This principle is half—it's the necessary condition—of the deontic theory known as Traditional Consequentialism.[2]

Maximizing Is Necessary is in certain respects flexible. It makes no substantive claims about what makes one complete state of affairs better than another.

---

1. For an overview of good-simpliciter, see §1.2.3.
2. For more on Traditional Consequentialism, see §1.3 and §3.

And the notion of "a complete state of affairs" it makes use of is broad. It includes the entire way things might go.[3]

However, Maximizing Is Necessary is, in other respects, inflexible. The act attaching to the uniquely best state of affairs is not merely permissible; it's required. While this seems correct in cases like Healing Gaze, in many other contexts insisting on only the best appears misguided. To ask so much from agents is to ask too much. In this chapter, we develop and assess this challenge.

4.2 *Endless Self-Sacrifice*

If Maximizing Is Necessary is correct, it is never permissible to do less than the best. This is a tremendous demand for agents to shoulder. To feel its full force, consider

> Endless Gazing. Things are just as described in Healing Gaze, except that, having got wind of your extraordinary ability, sick children have flocked to you. If you always perform the optimal act, the remainder of your life will be organized around maximizing the number of children at which you gaze.[4]

Are you really required to spend your remaining years gazing into the eyes of children? Maximizing Is Necessary says Yes. You are permitted to attend to your basic needs—you can sleep and nourish your body—but only to the extent that is needed to maximize the number of children you can cure.

Obviously, you would do nothing wrong if you choose to use your extraordinary ability to maximize the good. That would be permissible. Yet, even in Endless Gazing you are not required to always bring about the best. You are not morally required to rearrange your life to be a full-time human panacea. Morality affords you some measure of leeway. You have the option, at least sometimes, to perform acts that make things worse overall, but better for you. Reflection on ordinary moral thinking thus suggests that, in this and other cases, there exist

> *Agent-Favoring Options*: Situations in which it is morally permissible for you to perform a certain act that brings about the best complete state of affairs; but it is also morally permissible for you to refrain from the performance of this act, thereby bringing about a complete state of affairs that is worse overall but better for yourself.

Absent Agent-Favoring Options, our lives would be swallowed up by the unrelenting requirement to maximize the good. Even if you can't cure the sick by

---

3. For a longer version of these remarks, see §3.1.
4. This case is inspired by Timmerman (2015).

gazing into their eyes, you can, at great cost to yourself, dedicate your life to helping others. And, if you accept Maximizing Is Necessary, then this is what you must do. But this, it seems, is not something a moral theory could sensibly ask of you.

In the next section, we'll explain precisely why, by excluding Agent-Favoring Options, Maximizing Is Necessary is thought unreasonably demanding.

4.3 *The Argument from Endless Self-Sacrifice*

Any plausible moral theory will require agents, under certain circumstances, to make sacrifices. This much is unsurprising. We're familiar with the idea that to comply with a moral theory we need to adjust our behavior. And sometimes we must bear the costs of these adjustments. What, then, about Maximizing Is Necessary makes it unacceptably demanding? The answer is that Maximizing Is Necessary is thought to make unreasonable demands. To understand exactly what's being claimed here, a pair of related issues call for clarification: what it means to have a reason, and the connection that holds between moral requirements and reasons.

Reasons are considerations that count in favor or against acting in a certain way. It might be useful to imagine yourself at the crossroads of action with reasons as forces pulling in favor or against your performance, like tug-of-war. Suppose, for example, you're deliberating about getting a vaccination. The fact that the shot will cause mild pain counts against getting it. The fact that it will inoculate you counts in favor of getting it. Judging this latter reason to be of greater strength, you conclude that you have decisive reason to get the vaccination. Of course, in arriving at this conclusion you do not deny the reasons you have to refrain from the shot. It will still hurt and that still counts against getting it. It's just that your reason to get the shot is stronger.[5]

With this brief sketch of reasons in hand, we can next turn to what seems an eminently sensible claim about the relationship between reasons and morality, namely:

> *Moral Rationalism*: Necessarily, if an agent is morally required to perform some act, then she has decisive reason, all things considered, to perform this act.

Moral Rationalism claims that you always have exclusively the most reason, everything taken into account, to do what morality demands. Complying with your moral requirements is always rational; noncompliance is always irrational.

The special connection Moral Rationalism posits between the moral requirements one faces and the reasons one has is hard to deny. Indeed, many take it to hold as a matter of conceptual necessity. As Smith writes:

---

5. For a more detailed overview of reasons, see §1.2.2.

> Moral requirements apply to rational agents as such. But it is a conceptual truth that if rational agents are morally required to act in a certain way then we expect them to act in that way. Being rational, as such, must therefore suffice to ground our expectation that rational agents will do what they are morally required to do. But how could this be so? It could be so only if we think of the moral requirements that apply to agents as themselves categorical requirements of rationality or reason. For the only thing we can legitimately expect of rational agents as such is that they do what they are rationally required to do. (1994: 85)

To see what Smith is driving at here, contrast etiquette with morality. Start with etiquette. It would be perfectly intelligible for a rational agent to say, "I know that etiquette requires me to refrain from putting my elbows on the table, but I nonetheless deny that I have decisive reason to act in that way." We can see how someone might recognize that there is such a requirement yet maintain that they have decisive reason to act otherwise. Now, try to imagine a rational agent sincerely saying, "I know that morality requires me to donate to this charity, but I nonetheless believe that I lack decisive reason to donate." This is hard to make sense of. To suppose that one can flout moral requirements, while remaining on the side of reason, suggests a failure to understand their peculiar force. We expect rational agents to do what they take morality to require of them. When agents don't meet this expectation, we question their rationality. This suggests that we take there to be an unbreakable connection between moral requirements and what one has decisive reason to do.

We are now in a position, by appealing to Moral Rationalism, to say when a moral theory is unacceptably demanding. A moral theory is unacceptably demanding when it imposes unreasonable requirements: requirements that an agent does not have decisive reason to satisfy. Our inquiry now shifts. We need to determine what reasons agents have. If we can show—by some principled means—that agents lack decisive reason to comply with Maximizing Is Necessary, then we can reject it as unreasonably demanding.

The most popular account of reasons provides exactly what we need. On this account, an agent's reasons depend on her psychology. If, say, you want a drink of water, and there's water in the kitchen, then it seems you have reason to head there. Yet if you lost the desire, then you'd surely lose the reason. Since the existence of reasons is tied to something within the agent, this account of reasons is known as

> *Existence Internalism*: If there is a reason for an agent to act in a certain way, then her acting in this way promotes the object of one of her desires.[6]

---

6. For the canonical formulation and defense of Existence Internalism, see Williams (1981).

Why accept Existence Internalism? One powerful argument starts with the observation that at least some of our reasons are internal. It is obvious that, in many cases, different agents have different reasons. One natural explanation for this is the fact that different agents have different desires. For example, if you want a drink of water, and there's water in the kitchen, then you have a reason to head there. If your friend is not at all thirsty, then the fact that there's water in the kitchen provides her with no reason to go there. The issue, then, is not whether some reasons are internal—clearly some are—but whether all reasons are internal. And here offering a unified and simple account of reasons pushes us to accept Existence Internalism. If we accept that some reasons are internal, we should accept that all reasons are. As Schroeder (2007: 201) notes, it would be very surprising if our use of the term "reason" in "You have a reason to gaze in Healing Gaze" and "You have a reason to go to the kitchen" were homonymous. The best explanation is the unified one offered by Existence Internalism.

Combining Moral Rationalism and Existence Internalism provides a principled means of assessing the demandingness of a theory. And Maximizing Is Necessary does not fare well. It requires agents to perform acts that, given their motivational sets, they lack reason to perform. It imposes unreasonable demands.

To see why, return to Endless Gazing. We should not expect that you have the desires needed to have decisive reason to spend the bulk of your life gazing into people's eyes. It's not that you don't care about others' welfare. It's just that you care about many other things. Your motivational set is likely to include a range of partial concerns, concerns that reflect your attachments, projects, commitments, and the like. But Maximizing Is Necessary implies that you are morally required to perform every optimific gaze. It thus imposes an unreasonable demand. Williams articulates this line of reasoning in a now famous passage:

> It is absurd to demand of such a man, when the sums come in from the utility network which the projects of others have in part determined, that he should just step aside from his own project and decision and acknowledge the decision which utilitarian calculation requires. It is to alienate him in a real sense from his actions and the source of his action in his own convictions. It is to make him into a channel between the input of everyone's projects, including his own, and an output of optimific decision; but this is to neglect the extent to which his actions and his decisions have to be seen as the actions and decisions which flow from the projects and attitudes with which he is most closely identified. (1973: 116–17)

If Moral Rationalism and Existence Internalism are both true, then acceptable moral demands will be those agents have reason to comply with. But, given our psychologies and the world we live in, compliance with Maximizing Is Necessary will require agents to perform acts that they lack reason to perform. And hence, it is unreasonably demanding.

The foregoing reasoning delivers

The Unreasonable Demands Argument against Maximizing Is Necessary

1. Both Moral Rationalism and Existence Internalism are true.
2. If both Moral Rationalism and Existence Internalism are true, then Maximizing Is Necessary is false.
3. Hence, Maximizing Is Necessary is false.

Premise 1 is the only controversial claim. But it's well supported. Moral Rationalism is regarded by many as a conceptual truth. Proponents of Traditional Consequentialism are unlikely to dispute it.[7] And Existence Internalism, although more contentious, offers an appealing and unified account of reasons. If these claims are accepted, Maximizing Is Necessary must be rejected.

> *Moral Rationalism*: Necessarily, if an agent is morally required to perform some act, then she has decisive reason, all things considered, to perform this act.
>
> *Existence Internalism*: If there is a reason for an agent to act in a certain way, then her acting in this way promotes the object of one of her desires.
>
> *Maximizing Is Necessary*: An agent's presently available alternative has the property of being permissible only if the performance of any of the agent's other presently available alternatives would not have brought about a complete state of affairs that's better overall.

4.4 *The Minimal Beneficence Argument against Existence Internalism*

The reasoning of the previous section shows that Moral Rationalism, Existence Internalism, and Maximizing Is Necessary form an inconsistent triad. The argument developed there concludes that, of the three, Maximizing Is Necessary is the commitment to reject. Yet, as we'll show in this section, the inconsistency arises even when something much weaker than Maximizing Is Necessary is assumed. And if Maximizing Is Necessary can be replaced with something far weaker and yet the inconsistency persists, then perhaps it is one of the other two commitments that should go. This is precisely what we'll suggest below. Given the plausibility of Moral Rationalism, this puts immense pressure on Existence Internalism.

Recall, in Healing Gaze, you could save the lives of two people at almost no cost to yourself. Intuitively, you are morally required to save these lives. But notice, we need not accept Maximizing Is Necessary to arrive at this verdict. A much weaker claim will do. All that's needed is

> *Minimal Beneficence*: In situations when one can act to secure an enormous benefit for others at a negligible cost to oneself, one is morally required to do so.

---

7. Although some have suggested that they should, see Dorsey (2015).

Minimal Beneficence would require that you help in the one-off case, Healing Gaze. But importantly, it would not require that you help everyone in the iterated case, Endless Gazing. In that case, as you continue gazing, the costs to you accrue. At some point they no longer qualify as "negligible" and Minimal Beneficence ceases to require that you gaze. In this way, unlike Maximizing Is Necessary, Minimal Beneficence accommodates Agent-Favoring Options. It imposes a moral requirement, but it's comparatively weak.

Minimal Beneficence is hard to deny. A moral theory without it would properly be rejected as intolerably callous. Yet, once this modest claim is combined with Moral Rationalism, we get the result that, in situations when one can act to secure an enormous benefit for others at a negligible cost to oneself, one has decisive reason to do so. This seems like the right result. In cases like Healing Gaze, the demand that you help is perfectly reasonable. Yet, we cannot accept this very modest claim and affirm Existence Internalism. For, if Existence Internalism is correct, then there is no guarantee that the moral requirement in Healing Gaze will be reasonable for every agent. Existence Internalism and Moral Rationalism, once combined, make morality hostage to the desires of agents.

Suppose in Healing Gaze that the extraordinary ability was acquired, not by you but by a jerk—someone whose motivational set is exclusively self-regarding. According to Existence Internalism, for this jerk to have a reason to cure the sick, this act must in some way hook up to her motivational set. But it doesn't. Given her idiosyncratic psychological makeup, she doesn't have a reason—let alone a decisive reason—to help anyone. What Minimal Beneficence requires of this agent, if we accept Existence Internalism, is unreasonable. We should not accept this result. We should insist that any agent has a reason to help in Healing Gaze. The action required there should be regarded as nonnegotiable.

Thus, Moral Rationalism, Existence Internalism, and Minimal Beneficence also form an inconsistent triad. Given the credibility of Moral Rationalism, we must choose between rejecting Existence Internalism or Minimal Beneficence.

We can now offer

The Minimal Beneficence Argument against Existence Internalism

1. If both Moral Rationalism and Minimal Beneficence are true, then Existence Internalism is false.
2. Both Moral Rationalism and Minimal Beneficence are true.
3. Hence, Existence Internalism is false.

> *Moral Rationalism*: Necessarily, if an agent is morally required to perform some act, then she has decisive reason, all things considered, to perform this act.
>
> *Minimal Beneficence*: In situations when one can act to secure an enormous benefit for others, at a negligible cost to oneself, one is morally required to do so.
>
> *Existence Internalism*: If there is a reason for an agent to act in a certain way, then her acting in this way promotes the object of one of her desires.

The argument hinges on Premise 2. Moral Rationalism is not disputed. After all, the charge that a theory is unreasonably demanding itself presupposes Moral Rationalism. What matters then is the credibility of Minimal Beneficence. Given its overwhelming plausibility, due to the modesty of the claim it makes, it's difficult to deny. We're thus left to reject Existence Internalism.

4.5 The Moral Reasons Ubiquity Argument against Rational Options Abound

Even if Existence Internalism is false, Maximizing Is Necessary is not yet in the clear. For it may be argued that, because it precludes Agent-Favoring Options, Maximizing Is Necessary is still unreasonably demanding. Rather than appealing to a theory about the reasons agents have, we appeal to the idea that

> *Rational Options Abound*: For most choice situations, an agent's reasons do not require the performance of any particular act among the alternatives; rather an agent's reasons permit the performance or nonperformance of many of the acts available.[8]

The judgment that agents have an abundance of rational options is intuitive. To be sure, Raz refers to it as a "basic belief" because he thinks it is so plausible that we should hold it to be true "unless it can be shown to be incoherent or inconsistent with some of our rightly entrenched views" (1999: 100).

Rational Options Abound leads to yet another inconsistent triad. Given the world we live in, Maximizing Is Necessary, Moral Rationalism, and Rational Options Abound cannot all be true. If Maximizing Is Necessary is true, then apart from those rare cases in which two or more states of affairs are tied for best, there is only one permissible course of action. And, if Moral Rationalism is true, we have decisive reason to perform this required action. But this result is flatly incompatible with Rational Options Abound. For, if that claim is true, then in most situations we choose from a range of rationally permissible options. So, one of the three claims must be rejected. In this section, we'll present the case for rejecting Rational Options Abound by showing that it is inconsistent with some of our rightly entrenched views.

In point of fact, having already introduced Moral Rationalism, we are well on our way to seeing how this case might be made. Of course, the idea that, if an act is morally required, it is necessarily supported by decisive reason, does not alone impugn Rational Options Abound. If in many choice situations there are no moral requirements, then one may be permitted to select among a range of

---

8. This principle is inspired by Raz (1999: 100).

options. To come into conflict with Rational Options Abound, Moral Rationalism needs to be supplemented. To this end, we turn now to an argument that seeks to establish that agents confront moral requirements at virtually every choice juncture. If this argument is sound, then among an agent's available acts there will almost always be one supported by decisive reason. And this delivers the result that rational options are scarce.

To get this result, we need a pair of claims. The first is

> *Moral Unreasonableness Is Morally Impermissible*: If you have decisive moral reason to perform some act, then it is morally impermissible to refrain from this act.

This claim combines two independently plausible ideas. The first holds that moral requirements are exclusively determined by moral reasons. If you thought a friend failed to act as morality requires, you might cite some moral considerations that favored the act she failed to perform. If she replied that she has done nothing impermissible, and then cited nonmoral reasons—legal reasons or reasons of etiquette, for example—you would rightly conclude that she was missing the point. As Kagan writes, "[When] we are concerned with what is required by *morality*, the relevant reasons—whether decisive or not—must be moral ones" (1989: 66). The second idea is that it is morally impermissible, when choosing between two acts, to perform the one that is less well supported by moral reason. As Dreier argues, "It is hard to see how it could be permissible, from the moral point of view, to refrain from doing something that you have an undefeated reason (from that very point of view) to do" (2004: 148). Combining these two ideas, we arrive at the sensible suggestion that you must perform those acts that are decisively favored by moral reasons.

We've suggested that Moral Unreasonableness Is Morally Impermissible is supported on theoretical grounds. But it garners further support from the fact that it nicely explains certain features of our responses to specific cases. Consider

> Save All or None. Waiting at a stoplight, you spot a runaway car heading for two children. If you dart across the street, you can push either one or both out of harm's way. Whether you save one or both children, your legs will be seriously, permanently injured.[9]

There are a few uncontroversial things to say about this case, and they are exactly what we should expect if Moral Unreasonableness Is Morally Impermissible is true. While you may be breaking the law in running across the street, we are not at all tempted to consider the legal reason this provides as relevant to what you are morally required to do. Next, you are morally required to save none or all. If,

---

9. This case and subsequent discussion draws on Horton (2017).

despite the injury you'll sustain, there is sufficient moral reason for you to save one child, then there is even more moral reason to save both children. To save only one would be morally unreasonable and hence immoral. But, notice further, if you have sufficient moral reason to save your legs rather than save the two children, then you also have more reason to save your legs rather than save just one child. Saving the one, on this assumption, is morally unreasonable and hence immoral. Moral Unreasonableness Is Morally Impermissible thus aligns well with our thinking about this case.

We can now turn to the second claim, namely:

> *Moral Reasons Ubiquity*: For most choice situations, an agent has a moral reason to perform at least one of her alternatives.

The idea here is that, whatever act alternatives you're choosing among, at least one of them is supported by at least some moral reason. To establish Moral Reasons Ubiquity, it is nearly enough to point to the fact that at almost every moment of your life you are in a position to help others or to take the requisite steps to position yourself to do so. For example, right now you could stop reading and send some money to the distant needy. Obviously, the moral reasons favoring donating right now may be overpowered. But an overpowered reason is still a reason. There are thus moral reasons for or against nearly everything we could do. And this is all that's needed to secure Moral Reasons Ubiquity.

Now, notice what happens when Moral Unreasonableness Is Morally Impermissible is combined with Moral Reasons Ubiquity. Given the latter, we know that moral reasons will figure in practically every choice we make. Given the former, we know that if this moral reason is decisive, then the act it favors is morally required. We also know that, if this reason is overpowered, then the act this overpowering moral reason favors is morally required. The key claim is that whether the moral reason is overpowered or not, the result is a moral requirement. As Kagan explains:

> If, in some particular case, the balance of morally relevant reasons did not favor promoting the overall good but favored instead promoting the agent's own interests—then it seems that these reasons would still go on to generate a moral requirement. Admittedly, the agent would not be morally required to promote the overall good, but she would be morally required to promote her interests. Yet . . . what we were looking for was a defense of a moral option, according to which the agent would still be morally permitted (although not required) to do the act with the best results overall. (1994: 338–39)

It might be noted here that in rare cases two acts may be equally well supported by moral reasons. But this offers little comfort for defenders of Rational Options Abound. For such ties are exceedingly rare. And, when they do arise, they accommodate options in only an attenuated sense.

We are now in a position to forward

The Moral Reasons Ubiquity Argument against Rational Options Abound

1. If Moral Unreasonableness Is Morally Impermissible, Moral Reasons Ubiquity, and Moral Rationalism are all true, then Rational Options Abound is false.
2. Moral Unreasonableness Is Morally Impermissible, Moral Reasons Ubiquity, and Moral Rationalism are all true.
3. Hence, Rational Options Abound is false.

Premise 2 is the crucial one. More precisely, the argument hinges on the two claims—Moral Unreasonableness Is Morally Impermissible and Moral Reasons Ubiquity—that have been the focus of this section. And, as we've seen, both of these claims are well entrenched in common thinking. Thus, we're invited to reject Rational Options Abound.

> *Moral Unreasonableness Is Morally Impermissible*: If you have decisive moral reason to perform some act, then it is morally impermissible to refrain from this act.
>
> *Moral Reasons Ubiquity*: For most choice situations, an agent has a moral reason to perform at least one of her alternatives.
>
> *Moral Rationalism*: Necessarily, if an agent is morally required to perform some act, then she has decisive reason, all things considered, to perform this act.
>
> *Rational Options Abound*: For most choice situations, an agent's reasons do not require the performance of any particular act among the alternatives; rather an agent's reasons permit the performance or nonperformance of many of the acts available.

4.6 *Impermissibility-Blame Confusion*

Up to this point we've been focusing on the idea that Maximizing Is Necessary, because incompatible with Moral Rationalism, is unreasonably demanding. Now, in point of fact, this is a rather philosophical way of articulating a rather ordinary concern. Many people—people who have never thought about Moral Rationalism—regard the demands imposed by Maximizing Is Necessary as excessive. The charge of overdemandingness seems correct even in the absence of sound supporting arguments. This takes us to a pair of questions that are the focus of this section: What accounts for the pull of the overdemandingness objection? And should we embrace or resist this pull?

A plausible answer to the first question points to the levels of blame thought to accompany Maximizing Is Necessary. If Maximizing Is Necessary is true, then the standard for morally acceptable behavior is extremely high. Most people most of the time will act impermissibly. They will freely and knowingly fail to do what's required of them. And, according to our folk theory of moral responsibility, when people fail to satisfy their other-regarding moral requirements, they are appropriately blamed. They become the target of a range of potent reactive attitudes. Compare the reaction you would likely receive for squandering your retirement savings and for squandering your children's college fund. If it's your retirement that you've wasted, then you may be thought foolish and imprudent. If, instead, it's your children's college fund, then you are blamed. Maximizing Is Necessary, because it imposes onerous other-regarding requirements that we likely will not meet, appears to open the floodgates of anger, resentment, and indignation from others as well as shame and guilt toward yourself. Yet, most people are, unsurprisingly, extremely averse to being subject to negative reactive attitudes. The prospect of being constantly blamed for one's shortcomings is deeply unappealing. Daunted by the possibility, we're inclined to push back. The foregoing suggests the

> *Blame Conjecture*: The intuitive force of the demandingness objection rests in large part on the belief that, were Maximizing Is Necessary true, most people would constantly be subject to negative reactive attitudes such as anger and resentment.[10]

This conjecture holds that people regard Maximizing Is Necessary as too demanding because they believe that, in accepting it, we would radically increase the scope of behaviors for which we are blamed. Such levels of blame strike us as excessive, draconian, and unwarranted. Indeed, because we loathe to be blamed, we're viscerally opposed to it. The charge of demandingness resonates with this visceral aversion.

The Blame Conjecture is initially plausible. But more can be said in its favor. If the conjecture is correct, then our judgment that a theory is excessively demanding tracks, not the stringency of its demands but the amount of blame associated with it. This suggests a testable prediction. A theory that is extremely stringent in its requirements but that involves little or no blame will not be regarded as excessively demanding. A familiar theory can help us test this prediction:

> *Ethical Egoism*: An agent's presently available alternative has the property of being permissible if and only if the performance of any of her other presently available alternatives would not have brought about a greater sum total of well-being minus ill-being for her.

Ethical Egoism is relevantly similar to Maximizing Is Necessary. For both, doing anything less than the best (overall or for oneself) is impermissible. Ethical Egoism is thus also very stringent in its requirements. This might come as a surprise. But notice, it is hard to do almost anything perfectly, and perfect selfishness is no exception. If Ethical Egoism is true, you thus often act immorally. Nevertheless the theory raises no concerns about excessive blame. We are not tempted by our folk theory of moral responsibility to take negative reactive attitudes toward

---

10. This conjecture is also suggested by Morris (2017).

people that fail to be maximally selfish. And, just as the Blame Conjecture predicts, we do not regard Ethical Egoism as excessively demanding.

We have an answer to our first question. The intuitive draw of the demandingness objection is explained by the Blame Conjecture. Now for the second question. Is our concern about constantly being subject to negative reactive attitudes to be taken seriously or is it the product of some confusion? It is predicated on a mistake. It assumes that those who perform impermissible other-regarding actions thereby ought to be blamed. Our concern is the product of

> *Impermissibility-Blame Confusion*: Mistakenly assuming that an agent who freely and knowingly fails to satisfy an other-regarding moral requirement is thereby to be blamed.

It is perfectly understandable that we suppose there to be such a tight connection between impermissible acts and blame. This accords with our folk theory of moral responsibility. But, were Maximizing Is Necessary true, then our folk theory is mistaken. Impermissible acts aren't always properly met with blame.

To explain: If Maximizing Is Necessary is true, then freely and knowingly acting impermissibly and blame are only contingently related. To blame someone is to perform an act of a specific kind. Like all acts, acts of blame can be assessed by the value of the states of affairs they produce. A blaming act would be morally permissible when it produced a state of affairs at least as good as that which would be produced by any alternative act. This forward-looking justification for blame is insensitive to what's happened in the past. On this view, our ordinary notion of responsibility, as Smart writes, "should be replaced by 'Whom would it be useful to blame?'" (1973: 53). Given this understanding of blame, we should not assume that levels of blame will radically increase with the number of impermissible acts performed.[11]

We can start with a very general point. The only blaming acts that will be permitted are those that maximize the good. And it's easy to imagine circumstances in which blaming an impermissible act wouldn't have that effect. After all, the experience of being blamed is an unpleasant one. For it to be justifiable, it must be instrumental in bringing about the best state of affairs. If blaming isn't a necessary means for securing that outcome, it ought not to be engaged in. Beyond this general claim we can point to a few more specific circumstances in which blame would be misplaced.

Blame is an imprecise tool. Sometimes, blame directed at an undesirable behavior has an unwelcome influence on other desirable behaviors. To blame in such cases would be an error. For example, consider

---

11. For more on how Utilitarianism is self-effacing and how this bears on blame, see §1.4.1.

Good Motives. When faced with a choice to either secure a moderate benefit for your child or a slightly larger benefit for a stranger, you benefit your child.[12]

We can assume that by benefiting your child you fail to maximize the good. According to Maximizing Is Necessary, you thus act impermissibly. But should you be blamed? Probably not. You act from a disposition that should be encouraged. Deep affection between parents and children as a general social practice is a great source of value. This love is not compatible with an equal regard for strangers. Nor is it easily overridden. So, while your disposition led you to an impermissible act, we would not want to discourage you or others from adopting such a disposition. Were we to blame you, we would fail to maximize the good. And, we should emphasize, there's nothing peculiar about Good Motives. It's an everyday case. Often, a general practice or set of motives would, if adopted, help approximate the best. It would be counterproductive to blame in specific instances yielding suboptimal results.[13]

Blame is a powerful motivator. It's morality's razor wire. The prospect of being subject to reactive attitudes such as resentment is a strong disincentive. But, by overuse, it can be dulled. If every action were met with blame, then blame would cease to ward off future breaches of morality's demands. There is thus a limit to how much an agent's behavior can be improved through sanctions. Those who are relentlessly blamed will, at some point, cease to work toward improvement. If blame is practically unavoidable, then why strive to avoid it? Further, in a world in which everyone is nearly always failing morally, no one will be in a position of authority. Anyone who acts to blame anyone else will lack the needed moral standing. People generally do not welcome corrective action undertaken by someone whose behavior is equally defective. Under these conditions, when our blaming practices are greatly increased, blame will be even less effective as a means of shaping behavior. So here too blaming would be counterproductive.[14]

We focused our discussion in this section on two questions. The first asked why the demandingness objection strikes a chord with us. Our answer was the Blame Conjecture. If that is correct, then it's perceived levels of blame, and not the stringency of a theory's requirements, that make a theory seem unacceptably demanding. The second question asked whether our intuitive resistance should be taken seriously. Our answer was No. We claimed that Impermissibility-Blame Confusion is common and leads people to mistakenly link impermissible acts with blame. These answers together go some distance to weakening the intuitive grip of the demandingness objection. When we see that much of our opposition is

---

12. This case and subsequent discussion loosely follow Parfit (1984: §14).

13. For more on how the approximation strategy of a Utilitarian will include a set of motives like those in the case above, see §1.4.2 and §3.8.

14. The ideas in this paragraph are suggested by Kagan (1989: 397).

animated by concerns about blame, and not the stringency of a theory's requirements, and when we appreciate that compliance with Maximizing Is Necessary may not radically increase levels of blame, our intuitive resistance is diminished.

4.7 Conclusion

In this chapter, we've evaluated the charge that Maximizing Is Necessary is unreasonably demanding. We've explored a number of arguments in an attempt to rebuff this charge. Which of the arguments is the weakest?

There is a good case to be made that it's the Argument against Rational Options Abound. That argument rests on a controversial assumption about reasons, namely, that they all function in the same way. Recall the metaphor—tug-of-war—introduced earlier. On this model, all reasons play the same role: their strength counts in favor or against a course of action. But perhaps this is overly simplistic. Perhaps some reasons serve merely as counteracting forces—they count in favor of the action being permissible—but no more. On this suggestion, some reasons are

> *Permissibility Makers*: Facts that make it permissible to perform an act that otherwise would be impermissible to perform.[15]

But not all reasons play this role. Others are

> *Requirement Makers*: Facts that make it impermissible to refrain from performing an action that otherwise would be permissible to refrain from performing.

The Argument against Rational Options Abound assumes that all reasons are Requirement Makers. But commonsense seems to support the existence of Permissibility Makers. For example, commonsense holds that it is impermissible to intentionally kill people without their consent. If someone is trying to kill you, however, then you may be permitted to kill in self-defense. But here it seems, while you're permitted to kill, you're not required to.

With the distinction between Requirement Makers and Permissibility Makers in place, the following position is available. We can hold that reasons to favor yourself are Permissibility Makers. And, when these reasons are strong enough, they grant a permission for you to perform some action, without also generating

---

15. The definition for Requirement Makers and Permissibility Makers is modified from Portmore (2011: 121), who is following Gert (2004), and so uses the terms "requiring strength" and "justifying strength." A similar distinction is found in Dancy (2006), who calls them "peremptory reasons" and "enticing reasons."

a requirement that you perform it. So, for example, if you could save a life by donating a dollar, you may be morally required to donate. Here, the Permissibility Maker is of insufficient strength. But suppose instead of a dollar, you had to donate your life savings. Here the Permissibility Maker to keep your savings may be of sufficient strength to block the reason you have to save the life from making the act of donation morally required.

While the proposed distinction between Requirement Makers and Permissibility Makers is initially plausible, the question is whether it can be given adequate defense.

References

Dancy, J. 2006. "Enticing Reasons." In *Reason and Value: Themes from the Moral Philosophy of Joseph Raz*, edited by J. R. Wallace, P. Pettit, S. Scheffler, and M. Smith, 91–118. Oxford: Oxford University Press.
Dorsey, D. 2015. "How Not to Argue against Consequentialism." *Philosophy and Phenomenological Research* 90 (1): 20–48.
Dreier, J. 2004. "Why Ethical Satisficing Makes Sense and Rational Satisficing Doesn't." In *Satisficing and Maximizing: Moral Theorists on Practical Reason*, edited by M. Byron, 131–54. Cambridge: Cambridge University Press.
Gert, J. 2004. *Brute Rationality: Normativity and Human Action*. Cambridge: Cambridge University Press.
Horton, J. 2017. "The All or Nothing Problem." *The Journal of Philosophy* 114 (2): 94–104.
*Kagan, S. 1989. *The Limits of Morality*. Oxford: Oxford University Press.
Kagan, S. 1994. "Defending Options." *Ethics* 104 (2): 333–51.
Morris, R. 2017. "Praise, Blame, and Demandingness." *Philosophical Studies* 174 (7): 1857–69.
Parfit, D. 1984. *Reasons and Persons*. Oxford: Clarendon Press.
*Portmore, D. W. 2011. *Commonsense Consequentialism: Wherein Morality Meets Rationality*. Oxford: Oxford University Press.
Raz, J. 1999. *Engaging Reason: On the Theory of Value and Action*. Oxford: Oxford University Press.
Schroeder, M. 2007. "The Humean Theory of Reasons." In *Oxford Studies in Metaethics*, edited by R. Shafer-Landau, 195–219. Oxford: Oxford University Press.
Smart, J. J. C. 1973. "An Outline of a System of Utilitarian Ethics." In *Utilitarianism: For and Against*, 3–67. Cambridge: Cambridge University Press.
Smith, M. 1994. *The Moral Problem*. Oxford: Blackwell.
Timmerman, T. 2015. "Sometimes There Is Nothing Wrong with Letting a Child Drown." *Analysis* 75 (2): 204–12.
*Williams, B. 1973. "A Critique of Utilitarianism." In *Utilitarianism: For and Against*, 77–135. Cambridge: Cambridge University Press.
Williams, B. 1981. *Moral Luck: Philosophical Papers, 1973–1980*. Cambridge: Cambridge University Press.

5

Objectivism and Action Guidance

5.1 *Introduction*

When thinking about whether or not an act is permissible, we usually attend to what would happen if the act were performed, not to what the agent was thinking at the time. We focus on the state of affairs that would be brought about by the action, not on what the agent foresees or expects. Of course, you might wonder if what we usually think is what we should think. And this brings us to the question we're concerned with in this chapter:

> Do deontic properties depend on the facts, independent of the agent's perspective on them?

The roles that moral advice, new information, and hindsight play in our thinking about what we ought to do suggest that it's the facts, not what the agent takes the facts to be, that determine the deontic properties of actions.

We can start with

> <u>Advice.</u> A doctor's patient is suffering from frequent headaches. She can treat him with either Drug X or Drug Y, but she is uncertain which to give. Seeking advice, she calls you. You've recently completed research that strongly indicates that patients like the one she's treating will respond best to Drug X. You tell her that's what she ought to administer.

When advising the doctor, you don't merely tell her what, given her perspective, she ought to do. Rather, you draw on what you know. The course of action you suggest thus reflects a perspective that outstrips hers.[1]

Having received quality advice, the doctor has strong reason to believe that Drug X is what she ought to give her patient. But consider how new information bears on this case:

> <u>New Information.</u> The doctor is about to administer Drug X. But just before she does, a nurse informs her that the patient has a rare allergy. For anyone with this allergy, Drug X will prove lethal.

---

1. Our discussion of advice draws on Thomson (2008: 187–91).

The doctor now regards her previous judgment as mistaken. Given its lethal effects, it was never the case that she ought to administer Drug X. New information does not change, but only reveals, what ought to be done.[2]

Lastly, notice how what actually happens factors in our judgments. Consider

> Hindsight. The doctor's best evidence indicates that Drug Y is best for her patient. She administers that drug. Unbeknownst to her, the batch of Drug Y she used had been laced with poison. Her patient dies.

Although she took all necessary precautions, and acted in light of her best evidence, the doctor regrets what she has done. She thinks, "I ought not to have administered Drug Y. My patient would still be alive." To be clear, in assessing the act as impermissible we are not also assessing the agent. The doctor is not to be blamed.[3] But, nonetheless, she has failed to do what she ought to have done.[4]

The roles that moral advice, new information, and hindsight play in our thinking about what we ought to do takes us to one of the members of the set of principles examined in this book that together imply Utilitarianism, namely:

> OBJECTIVISM: The deontic properties of an agent's presently available alternatives depend solely on the complete states of affairs they would bring about if performed, not her perspective on these states of affairs.

Theories that accept Objectivism—which we'll call Objective—hold that what you ought to do is determined by the facts, independent of your perspective on them. In previous chapters, we've taken it for granted that Traditional Consequentialism accepts Objectivism.[5] As formulated, it holds that an act is permissible because it brings about the best outcome available, not the outcome you believe to be best, have evidence for being best, know to be best, or the like. We can now make this assumption explicit by referring to the view as Objective Consequentialism.

Objective Consequentialism can explain the nature of moral advice. It can explain why new information seems to change your beliefs, but not what you ought to do. And it can explain why doing what's best from your perspective can, in hindsight, seem like a moral mistake. Despite these virtues, Objective Consequentialism also faces a serious problem. Even the most careful calculations leave us uncertain about the future. We simply do not know which act, if performed, would bring about the best state of affairs. As nonomniscient agents, we cannot

---

2. Our discussion of new evidence draws on Graham (2010: 91–92).

3. This point is explored in detail in Driver (2012) and Moore (2005 [1912]: 98–100). For more on the relationship between impermissibility and blame, see §1.4 and §4.6.

4. Our discussion of hindsight draws on Broome (2013: 40).

5. For more on Traditional Consequentialism, see §1.3, §3, and §4.

act on the facts; we can only act on what we take them to be. Objective Consequentialism thus ensures that nearly all of our moral requirements are inaccessible to us. As a result, it appears unsuited to guide action. In this chapter, we will explore this challenge.

5.2 *Mineshafts*

Objective Consequentialism tells us that moral requirements are not the product of the perspective of the agents to whom they apply. To see why this presents a problem, consider

> Mineshafts. You are in charge of emergency services at the local mine. A nearby reservoir has ruptured and water is heading toward the mine's two shafts, Blue-Shaft and Red-Shaft. Both shafts have the same volume, and the amount of water coming is equal to it. A hundred miners are in one of the shafts, but you don't know which one. You have three options. You can direct the water to flood Blue-Shaft, killing its occupants but saving anyone in Red-Shaft. You can direct the water to flood Red-Shaft, killing its occupants but saving anyone in Blue-Shaft. Or, you can distribute the water, partially filling both shafts. This will guarantee that ninety miners are saved and that ten drown.[6]

Your available alternatives and what will happen depending on the location of the minors are depicted in Table 5.1.

Table 5.1: *Conditional Outcomes in Mineshafts*

	If Miners in Red-Shaft	If Miners in Blue-Shaft
Flood Blue-Shaft	100 Saved	0 Saved
Flood Red-Shaft	0 Saved	100 Saved
Distribute	90 Saved	90 Saved

Let us stipulate that the miners are in fact in Blue-Shaft. Given this, Objective Consequentialism requires that you flood Red-Shaft. This verdict is puzzling in two ways.

First, since you have no idea which shaft the miners are actually in, it would be a matter of sheer luck if you flooded the correct shaft. Each shaft has, by your lights, a fifty-fifty chance of being occupied. Even if you do what, according to Objective Consequentialism, you ought to do, and you flood Red-Shaft, you can't

---

6. This case and the chart below are modified from Parfit (2011: 159–60).

perform this act on the basis of the fact that it will bring about the best state of affairs. The fact that generates the requirement—the reason—cannot be the fact you act on because you don't know that flooding Red-Shaft is best. That fact is not within your perspective. Objective Consequentialism faces what we'll call the

> *Action Problem*: The problem of requiring agents to perform actions on the basis of facts that they, at the time of action, are incapable of acting on.

This problem is serious. It is deeply counterintuitive for the very facts that Objective Consequentialism claims generate moral demands to be inaccessible to the agents to whom they are addressed.

Second, since flooding either shaft is the moral equivalent of a coin flip with one hundred lives at stake, it would be reckless not to play it safe and distribute the floodwaters. Sensible people will go in for the known outcome of saving ninety lives rather than take their chances. However, while distributing seems like the intuitively correct course of action, according to Objective Consequentialism it is also certainly impermissible. But is it not irrational to intend to perform an act that one knows to be impermissible? This in turn suggests that Objective Consequentialism does not capture the "ought" that is central to practical deliberation. Thus, it faces what we'll call the

> *Centrality Problem*: The problem of offering an account of ought that is not what rational agents are concerned with when reasoning practically.

This problem is serious. It is deeply counterintuitive for a theory to claim that it is perfectly rational to think you ought not to distribute but then intend to do so.

Mineshafts thus highlights a pair of worries—the Action Problem and the Centrality Problem—that both suggest Objective Consequentialism is unsuited as a guide for moral action. We turn now to present these problems in detail.

5.3 *The Action Problem Argument against Objective Consequentialism*

We can start with the Action Problem. The worry driving this objection is put forcefully by Jackson:

> The fact that a course of action would have the best results is not in itself a guide to action, for a guide to action must in some appropriate sense be present to the agent's mind. We need, if you like, a story from the inside of an agent to be part of any theory which is properly a theory in ethics, and having the best consequences is a story from the outside. It is fine for a theory in physics to tell us about its central notions in a way which leaves it obscure

how to move from those notions to action, for that passage can be left to something which is not physics; but the passage to action is the very business of ethics. (1991: 466–67)

There are two points in this passage worth stressing. First, a moral theory must tell us how to get from its main ideas to action. Second, to get to action, we need a story from the inside. Objective Consequentialism faces the Action Problem because it cannot provide such a story. We'll take each of these points in turn.[7]

Why think a moral theory must get from its main ideas to action? One attractive way of answering this question appeals to the thought that a moral theory is not merely an account of which states of affairs would be better or worse. It's not a solely evaluative enterprise. A moral theory must be normative, telling agents what to do and why to do it. These two notions—the evaluative and the normative—are distinct. And there is a test we can run to see if a purported moral theory includes both. If it does, it should be able to distinguish between the "oughts" in the following two cases.

> Avalanche. An avalanche is headed down a mountain. If it goes left, it'll plow into some people. If it goes right, it'll slow to a stop in an empty field. It ought to be that it turns right.
>
> Driver. You're driving down a mountain and your brakes go out. If you turn left, you'll plow into some people. If you turn right, you'll slow to a stop in an empty field. It ought to be that you turn right.[8]

Despite surface similarities, there is a clear difference between the ought-statements in these two cases. The ought in Avalanche is not normative. It is a disguised evaluative claim. That ought captures the idea that it would be good if things went a certain way. That the avalanche turns right is what ought to happen. By contrast, the ought in Driver conveys something more. It makes a normative claim. It captures the idea that you are morally required to turn right. That's what you ought to do.

The problem facing Objective Consequentialism is that it seems unable to distinguish, in a principled way, between these two ought-statements. For the view seems to hold that the avalanche ought to turn right in the very same sense that you ought to turn right. Here's Gibbons:

> If all we meant when we said that [you have] most objective reason to [perform a certain action] were that [your performing this action] would be for the best, then the avalanche would have an objective reason to go to the right.

---

7. What follows is intended neither as an exegesis of the passage nor as a representation of Jackson's arguments generally.
8. These cases are modified from Gibbons (2013: ch. 6).

> After all, that would be for the best. . . . Even if we were to call the evaluative fact a reason, it just can't get a grip on the avalanche. And here's what that means. Even if the avalanche has a reason to go right, and even if it's possible for the avalanche to go right, it can't go right for that reason. If this is why avalanches don't have reasons, then it looks as though a necessary condition on having a reason is the ability to do things for that reason. And this looks like a general constraint on the notion of a reason. It's not a reason to act if you can't ever act on it. (2013: 134)

The thought here is that you cannot have reasons that you are unable to respond to. The avalanche might go right, and that would be good. But this result is not the product of the avalanche recognizing and going in for what's best. It's just what happens, given the forces of nature. By contrast, it's possible that you go right and do so because you recognize and respond to this being best.

The foregoing suggests a general principle that limits what kinds of facts can make it the case that you ought to do something, namely, the

> *Response Restriction*: An agent ought to perform some action only if the agent has the ability to act on the basis of the fact that generates the ought.[9]

This restriction offers a neat explanation of the difference between Driver and Avalanche. After all, what makes you an agent is that you are, while the avalanche is not, responsive to reasons. You are capable of being moved by the recognition of the very facts that make the act what you ought to do. That you can act on the fact that turning right would be best is what allows the normative ought to stick to you. That the avalanche cannot respond to this fact is what ensures that only the evaluative ought applies. If the Response Restriction is true, then Objective Consequentialism is in serious trouble. The theory fails to satisfy this restriction and so cannot tell us how to get from its main ideas to action.

To see why, we can turn to Jackson's second idea: that a moral theory needs to tell a story from the inside. We can state this more precisely, in a way that links it to the Response Restriction, as follows:

> *Perspective Constrains Response*: An agent has the ability to act on the basis of the fact that generates the ought only if that fact falls within the agent's perspective in the situation.[10]

You cannot act on a fact if, at the time of action, it is not in your head, so to speak. Return to Mineshafts. Because you have no idea that the miners are in Blue-Shaft, you cannot act on that fact. You don't believe it or have any evidence for it. It's not

---

9. Modified from Kiesewetter (2016: 763) and Lord (2015: 33).
10. Modified from Way and Whiting (2017: 364).

within your perspective. You can flood Red-Shaft. That's true. And it would be good if you did, just as it would be good if the avalanche turned right. But you cannot, on the grounds that you would save the miners in Blue-Shaft, flood Red-Shaft. Since you cannot act on this fact, given the Response Restriction, you cannot be required to flood Red-Shaft. Yet this is precisely what Objective Consequentialism requires.

We are now in a position to mount

The Action Problem Argument against Objective Consequentialism

1. Response Restriction is true.
2. Perspective Constrains Response is true.
3. Hence, an agent ought to perform some action only if the fact that generates the ought falls within the agent's perspective in the situation.
4. If an agent ought to perform some action only if the fact that generates the ought falls within the agent's perspective in the situation, then Objective Consequentialism is false.
5. Hence, Objective Consequentialism is false.

Response Restriction: An agent ought to perform some action only if the agent has the ability to act on the basis of the fact that generates the ought.

Perspective Constrains Response: An agent has the ability to act on the basis of the fact that generates the ought only if that fact falls within the agent's perspective in the situation.

Objectivism: The deontic properties of an agent's presently available alternatives depend solely on the complete states of affairs they would bring about if performed, not her perspective on these states of affairs.

The core claims in this argument are in Premise 1 and Premise 2. Both are plausible and enjoy considerable support. If both withstand critical scrutiny, then Objective Consequentialism must be rejected.

In the next section, however, we'll suggest that this argument trades on an ambiguity. And what's needed if the argument is to be valid ensures that it won't be sound.

5.4 *The Argument from Ambiguous Ability*

The Response Restriction and Perspective Constrains Response both make assertions about the abilities of agents. Ability claims, however, are multiply ambiguous. To get a feel for how fraught this territory is, consider just a few of the many different meanings conveyed by ordinary uses of the word "able": Given your stature, you are able to reach the top shelf. "Able" here refers to physical ability. Given your optimistic outlook, you are able to see the silver lining. Here "able" indicates psychological ability. Given that you have consent, you are able to perform the operation. This sense of "able" denotes normative ability.[11] Attending to these and other differences is especially important when attempting to draw conclusions

---

11. These examples draw on Kratzer (1977) and Schwan (2018).

from multiple claims. Truth-preserving inferences depend on sameness of meaning. When an argument treats two different terms as if they were the same, it suffers the defect of equivocation. If the Argument from the Action Problem is to avoid equivocation, the sense of "ability" that features in the Response Restriction must be the same as that in Perspective Constrains Response.

There are two senses of ability relevant to interpreting the core claims of the Argument from the Action Problem. The difference can be brought out with examples. Suppose that your friend can swim one hundred meters. You've seen her do it on many occasions. Clearly, it's true that she's able to swim that distance. But suppose that, at this moment, your friend is undergoing a minor operation. She's been anesthetized and is unconscious. Clearly, it's false that she is able to swim one hundred meters. So it is both true and false that your friend is able to swim one hundred meters.

Obviously, there's no contradiction here. There are two senses of "able" in play. In the first instance, to say that your friend is able to swim one hundred meters is to ascribe to her a

General Ability: The ability to do something in a wide range of situations.

To possess a General Ability, one need not be able to exercise it at all times. Because it is true of your friend that when near a body of water and conscious she can swim one hundred meters, she has the General Ability to do so. By contrast, in the second instance, when your friend is lying unconscious in the hospital she lacks a

Specific Ability: The ability to do something in the present situation.

To possess a Specific Ability to do something one must be able to do that thing in the circumstances as they are at the time of action. Because your friend at this moment is unconscious in the hospital, she lacks the Specific Ability to swim one hundred meters. These two senses of ability, obviously, are not mutually exclusive. For instance, you have the General Ability to read, and since reading this now, you also have the Specific Ability.[12]

Equipped with this distinction, we can now distinguish between two interpretations of Perspective Constrains Response:

Perspective Constrains General Response: An agent has the General Ability to act on the basis of the fact that generates the ought only if that fact falls within the agent's perspective in the situation.

---

12. The distinction between General Ability and Specific Ability is due to Mele (2003).

> *Perspective Constrains Specific Response*: An agent has the Specific Ability to act on the basis of the fact that generates the ought only if that fact falls within the agent's perspective in the situation.

Perspective Constrains Specific Response is plausible. It seems correct that, if one is to act on a particular fact, then that fact must be within one's perspective at the time of action. In Mineshafts, you cannot flood Red-Shaft on the grounds that this act would bring about the best, because you have no idea that this is so in the situation. You lack the Specific Ability. By contrast, the alternative interpretation, Perspective Constrains General Response, is clearly false. While you lack the relevant Specific Ability, it simply does not follow that you lack the corresponding General Ability. We can easily imagine a scenario in which you know flooding Red-Shaft will save all of the miners, and so you act on this fact. And this possibility is sufficient for you to possess a General Ability.

Given this, Premise 2 of the Argument from the Action Problem must be interpreted as Perspective Constrains Specific Response. This has an important implication. For, if the argument is to be valid, we must interpret the Response Restriction as employing the same sense of ability. That is, Premise 1 must be interpreted as

> *Specific Response Restriction*: An agent ought to perform some action only if the agent has the Specific Ability to act on the basis of the fact that generates the ought.

While this interpretation of Premise 1 is necessary to avoid equivocation, it invites a different problem. This claim is vulnerable to counterexample. There are cases in which, intuitively, some fact makes it the case that an agent ought to perform some action, though the agent lacks the Specific Ability to perform the action on the basis of this fact. If this intuition is correct, then the Specific Response Restriction is false and the Argument from the Action Problem is unsound.

To get a sense of how these counterexamples work, consider

> Surprise Party. You are quite pleased by surprise parties, but only when they are truly surprising. Unsurprising parties are agonizing. You are totally unaware, but your friends are now next door waiting to surprise you with a party.[13]

It seems correct to say that you ought to go next door. But the fact that makes this the case—that there is a surprise party there—is not something you can act on. If you were to act on that fact, the party would not be a surprise; and so, instead of being pleased, you'd be in agony.

---

13. This example is modified from Schroeder (2007: 33–34).

This case, although instructive, might be taken to rest on a failure to distinguish what is ultimately generating the ought. Proponents of the Specific Response Restriction are likely to point out that the surprise fact is not what really matters. Rather the surprise merely causes—it's a means—to pleasure. And it is this fact—that you'll be pleased—that generates the ought. If this is correct, and the surprise facts get their normative force from pleasure, then Surprise Party is no longer a counterexample. For you can act on the pleasure fact. Suppose, for example, a friend told you, "If you go through that door over there, you'll be really pleased." You could, acting on the basis of this fact, walk through the door. You'd be both surprised and pleased.[14]

This response to Surprise Party is, however, at best a stopgap measure. It works by relying on a specific feature of the case, namely, that the pleasure is linked to something of merely instrumental relevance—surprises. Accordingly, to show this response to be inadequate, we need only devise a case in which the pleasure is linked to something that is intrinsically relevant. Consider, for example,

> Pleased by Unexpected Pleasure. When an episode of pleasure is unexpected, you gain additional pleasure from reflecting on the fact that it was unexpected. Tonight, you have two options for dinner. You can go to Old Favorite or Grand Opening. If you go to Old Favorite, you'll get the dish you've always liked. And, as usual, you'll be very pleased. If you go to Grand Opening, you'll be unexpectedly pleased by your meal. Not quite as pleased as you would be by your meal at Old Favorite but pretty close. However, reflecting on the fact that this pleasing experience was unexpected will bring you additional pleasure. Combining the pleasure of the meal, and the pleasure of reflecting on the fact that it provided unexpected pleasure, your experience at Grand Opening will be more pleasant than dining at Old Favorite.

Intuitively, you ought to go to Grand Opening, as you'll get more pleasure there than dining at Old Favorite. But this is only possible if you do not act on the fact that generates the ought. If you knew you'd be pleased by the meal there, it wouldn't be unexpected and you wouldn't additionally enjoy reflecting on an unexpected pleasure. This makes the case importantly different than Surprise Party. In Surprise Party, you could separate the pleasure of the party from the fact that it was a surprise. No such separation is possible in Pleased by Unexpected Pleasure. In this case the unexpectedness of the pleasure is essential. To see this, suppose a friend said, "If you go to Grand Opening, you'll be pleased." This would ensure that you are denied the pleasure of being unexpectedly pleased. And, in the absence of that pleasure, going to Grand Opening would no longer be what you ought to do. In this case, you cannot act on the facts that ultimately matter in generating the ought. The verdict—that you ought to go to Grand Opening—thus presents

---

14. This response to Surprise Party draws on Portmore (2019: §1.1.9).

a counterexample to Specific Response Restriction that cannot be deflected by appealing to the distinction between instrumental and intrinsic ought-generating facts.

Here's the upshot. There are circumstances, such as Pleased by Unexpected Pleasure, in which an agent ought to perform some action but lacks the Specific Ability to perform it on the basis of the fact that generates the ought.

In response to the Action Problem Argument against Objectivism, we can now offer

The Argument from Ambiguous Ability

1. If the Action Problem Argument against Objective Consequentialism is valid, then Perspective Constrains Response and Response Restriction are either both put in terms of Specific Ability or both put in terms of General Ability.
2. Perspective Constrains General Response is false.
3. Specific Response Restriction is false.
4. If the Action Problem Argument against Objectivism is valid, it is unsound.

Only Premise 2 and Premise 3 are controversial. Yet both are well supported. Perspective Constrains General Response and Specific Response Restriction are subject to counterexample.

This argument may suffice as a response to the Action Problem. But Objective Consequentialism is not yet in the clear. In the next section, we'll develop the other worry made vivid by Mineshafts: the Centrality Problem.

> *Perspective Constrains Response*: An agent has the ability to act on the basis of the fact that generates the ought only if that fact falls within the agent's perspective in the situation.
>
> *Response Restriction*: An agent ought to perform some action only if the agent has the ability to act on the basis of the fact that generates the ought.
>
> *Specific Ability*: The ability to do something in the present situation.
>
> *General Ability*: The ability to do something in a wide range of situations.
>
> *Perspective Constrains General Response*: An agent has the General Ability to act on the basis of the fact that generates the ought only if that fact falls within the agent's perspective in the situation.
>
> *Perspective Constrains Specific Response*: An agent has the Specific Ability to act on the basis of the fact that generates the ought only if that fact falls within the agent's perspective in the situation.

5.5 *The Centrality Problem Argument against Objective Consequentialism*

Return to Mineshafts. It seems correct to say, "You ought to distribute." It also seems correct to say, "You ought to flood Red-Shaft." This is a problem. It can't be that you ought to do both. Those acts are incompatible. In response, one might observe that the apparent conflict may be avoided by distinguishing between two senses of "ought." We might say that you nonobjectively ought to distribute and that you objectively ought to flood Red-Shaft. This maneuver solves one problem but introduces another. For now we need to determine which of these two oughts is of primary importance. To appreciate why this is an issue, suppose a group is, with full information, discussing the case. Some insist that you ought to distribute. Others, sympathetic to your ignorance, contend that you ought to flood Red-Shaft. Would it help at all if another declared, "There's no need for debate. Everyone is right. There is an objective and nonobjective sense of ought"? Presumably not. Even if true, this leaves the matter unsettled. The disputants might reasonably retort: "Fine, there are two senses of ought, but we want to sort out how to proceed. That distinction leaves our question unanswered." The disputants want to know which ought corresponds to what overall you are required to do. They are after what we might call the

Central Ought: What one is required, all things considered, to do.

In this section, we'll look at an argument that aims to show that Objective Consequentialism does not capture the Central Ought.[15]

How might we determine whether the objective or nonobjective ought is central? One promising way to answer this question appeals to the idea of a perfectly rational agent. Rationality, very broadly, is concerned with the relations (e.g., consistency) among an agent's attitudes. One salient feature often thought to characterize a perfectly rational agent is a necessary connection between her beliefs about what she ought to do and what she intends to do. When fully rational agents engage in practical reasoning, they try to figure out what they ought, all things considered, to do. And, if their reasoning is conclusive—they form a belief—then they will, because rational, intend to act accordingly. For example, suppose you sincerely believe that you ought, all things considered, to exercise now, but instead you intend to take a nap. This weak-willed response is a paradigm case of irrationality. How can one believe that, all things considered, one ought to do something yet not intend to follow through? If the judgment is sincere, then, in failing to intend to act accordingly, we must conclude that you are less than perfectly rational.[16]

How does this help us identify the Central Ought? Because this salient feature—that a rational agent will intend to do what she judges she ought to do—only applies to all things considered normative judgments. It doesn't apply to more circumscribed beliefs about what one ought to do from the perspective of one part of the normative domain. For example, you may believe that, as a matter of etiquette, you ought to attend events for which you've made reservations. But if when the time comes you learn that a friend has been badly injured in a car accident, you

---

15. This paragraph draws on Zimmerman (2008: ch. 1).

16. The ideas in this paragraph and the next are the product of cobbling together ideas from Broome (2013) and Wedgwood (2007: §1.3).

may head to the hospital instead. This is no evidence of irrationality. Rather you've judged that, all things considered, you are required to visit your friend.

If this is correct—that the ought-judgments the perfectly rational agent necessarily intends to conform to are all things considered—then we can understand the Central Ought as that which a perfectly rational agent intends to act on. That is, we should accept the

> *Rationality-Centrality Link*: The perfectly rational agent's practical reasoning is ultimately concerned with the Central Ought.

This link anchors the Central Ought to something we have some pretheoretical grip on: rationality. And this puts us in a better position to determine whether the objective or nonobjective ought is of primary importance.

To make this determination requires only a minor supplement. Specifically, we might claim that a perfectly rational agent will never intend to do what she believes she ought, all things considered, not to do. This, if accepted, suggests that a feature of perfect rationality is

> *Impermissibility Aversion*: Necessarily, if perfectly rational, an agent who believes, "I ought not to perform some act" will not intend to perform this act.[17]

This plausible claim is the mirror image of the claim that the perfectly rational agent always intends to do what she believes is required, everything taken into account. It implies, for example, that if you conclude a bit of practical reasoning sincerely believing that, all things considered, you ought not to take a nap, but you intend to take one, then you aren't perfectly rational. A perfectly rational agent will be averse to intending to do what she believes is impermissible.

Drawing on this pair of ideas—the Rationality-Centrality Link and Impermissibility Aversion—we can show that the ought of Objective Consequentialism is not the Central Ought. We can do this by assuming it is and then deriving a contradiction. Return to Mineshafts. Given the Rationality-Centrality Link, a perfectly rational agent will, if we assume that the objective ought is the Central Ought, be ultimately motivated to act in accordance with this ought. If this agent distributes the water between both shafts, then she is sure to bring about a suboptimal state of affairs and so act impermissibly. Since she believes—indeed knows—this, given Impermissibility Aversion, a perfectly rational agent will not distribute. But everyone, even Objective Consequentialists, accepts that a perfectly rational agent will intend to distribute. Thus, having derived a contradiction, we should reject the assumption we started with: the ought of Objective Consequentialism is the Central Ought.

---

17. Modified from Kiesewetter (2018: 108).

We are now in a position to mount

The Centrality Problem Argument against Objective Consequentialism

1. If the ought of Objective Consequentialism is the Central Ought, the Rationality-Centrality Link holds, and Impermissibility Aversion is a feature of perfect rationality, then, in Mineshafts, if you are perfectly rational, you won't intend to distribute.
2. In Mineshafts, if you are perfectly rational, you will intend to distribute.
3. Hence, it is not the case that the ought of Objective Consequentialism is the Central Ought, the Rationality-Centrality Link holds, and Impermissibility Aversion is a feature of perfect rationality.
4. The Rationality-Centrality Link holds and Impermissibility Aversion is a feature of perfect rationality.
5. Hence, it's not the case that the ought of Objective Consequentialism is the Central Ought.

> *Objectivism*: The deontic properties of an agent's presently available alternatives depend solely on the complete states of affairs they would bring about if performed, not her perspective on these states of affairs.
>
> *Central Ought*: What one is required, all things considered, to do.
>
> *Rationality-Centrality Link*: The perfectly rational agent's practical reasoning is ultimately concerned with the Central Ought.
>
> *Impermissibility Aversion*: Necessarily, if perfectly rational, an agent who believes, "I ought not to perform some act" will not intend to perform this act.

The argument hinges on Premise 4. In particular, given the strength of the case for the Rationality-Centrality Link, the argument stands or falls with Impermissibility Aversion. In the next section, we'll critically examine this claim.

5.6 *The Deontic Force Argument against Impermissibility Aversion*

Impermissibility Aversion asserts something that is, initially, quite plausible. After all, the claim that a perfectly rational agent always intends to do what she believes she ought to do is widely supported, and Impermissibility Aversion appears to be something of a corollary. It may be tempting to think it inherits its credibility from its better-established counterpart. But this reasoning overlooks a significant difference between the two claims. In this section, we offer an argument to the conclusion that Impermissibility Aversion is not a condition of perfect rationality.

In sports, competitors "win," "lose," or "tie" matches. These words convey what is perhaps most important about their performance. Knowing, for example, that a particular team lost is informative. But there's more to an assessment of the performance than the final result. The score provides additional information. It reveals whether the game was close, and so gives you a better sense of how the teams compare. The same thought applies to the assessment of acts. Deontic verdicts—required, impermissible, permissible, and so forth—are helpful because they provide speakers with a short, conclusive assessment of the act in question. But they leave out other important information. Even if two acts are both impermissible, the strength of the reasons for or against performing them can differ greatly. Just as a team can lose by a little or by a lot, an impermissible act may be closer or farther from what's required. To see this, consider

> Torture. You must either cause your friend extreme pain, mild pain, or no pain. All else is equal.

Torturing your friend is impermissible, whether you cause extreme or mild pain. But clearly, there is an important normative difference between these two. You have some reason not to cause mild pain. You have even more reason not to cause extreme pain. While both acts have the same deontic property—they are impermissible—a rational agent would not be indifferent to them. We might capture this by saying that a perfectly rational agent is sensitive to

> *Deontic Force*: An act's deontic force is strictly proportional to the total strength of the set of reasons that bear on the performance of the act.

The notion of Deontic Force reveals differences—differences in the strength of the reasons for and against performing an act—that are masked by deontic properties. This enables us, for example, to properly distinguish between the impermissible act of causing your friend extreme pain and the impermissible act of causing your friend mild pain. The former has a much greater negative Deontic Force than the latter.[18]

Once we recognize that acts vary in Deontic Force, a natural question presents itself. How does this fact feature in the deliberations of a perfectly rational agent? If such an agent is fully informed, we can be confident that she will always intend to perform the action she believes she ought to—the one with the greatest Deontic Force. That case is easy. But what about cases of uncertainty? One plausible answer holds that a feature of perfect rationality is

> *Expected Deontic Force Attraction*: Necessarily, if perfectly rational, an agent who believes, "My performing a certain act will uniquely maximize expected Deontic Force" will intend to perform this act.

To get a grip on this idea, return to Mineshafts. As a simplifying assumption, we can let the number of people saved by each act represent that act's Deontic Force. While saving all one hundred miners has a Deontic Force of one hundred, you

---

18. Graham (2010) and Bykvist (2011) argue for the importance of distinguishing between degrees of impermissibility. Our discussion draws on their work.

do not know whether, in order to perform this act, you should flood Red-Shaft or Blue-Shaft. So, if you flood either, there is a 50 percent subjective probability you'll be correct. Thus, the expected Deontic Force of flooding either is fifty. By contrast, the act of distributing the water has a Deontic Force of ninety. And since this state of affairs is certain, the act has an expected Deontic Force of ninety. These calculations are depicted in Table 5.2.[19]

Table 5.2: *Expected Deontic Force for Mineshafts*

Presently Available Alternatives	Expected Deontic Force
Flood Blue-Shaft	$(0.5 \times 100) + (0.5 \times 0) = 50$
Flood Red-Shaft	$(0.5 \times 0) + (0.5 \times 100) = 50$
Distribute	$(0.5 \times 90) + (0.5 \times 90) = 90$

As this table illustrates, distributing uniquely maximizes expected Deontic Force. Given that you believe this, then, if you are perfectly rational, you'll intend to distribute. This is an important result. In cases of uncertainty, such as Mineshafts, it may be perfectly rational to knowingly commit an impermissible act with less Deontic Force than that of the required act in order to avoid risking the performance of an act with much less Deontic Force.[20]

Having recognized that rational agents will not, under uncertainty, be indifferent to the Deontic Force of alternative impermissible acts, we're positioned to offer the following response to the Centrality Problem Argument against Objective Consequentialism.

The Deontic Force Argument against Impermissibility Aversion

1. If Impermissibility Aversion is true, then it's impossible for a perfectly rational agent to believe, "I ought not to perform a certain act" and yet intend to perform this act.
2. If Expected Deontic Force Attraction is true, then it's possible for a perfectly rational agent to believe, "I ought not to perform a certain act" and yet intend to perform this act.
3. Expected Deontic Force Attraction is true.
4. Hence, Impermissibility Aversion is false.

Impermissibility Aversion: Necessarily, if perfectly rational, an agent who believes, "I ought not to perform some act," will not intend to perform this act.

Expected Deontic Force Attraction: Necessarily, if perfectly rational, an agent who believes, "My performing a certain act will uniquely maximize expected Deontic Force" will intend to perform this act.

Deontic Force: An act's deontic force is strictly proportional to the total strength of the set of reasons that bear on the performance of the act.

---

19. This paragraph and the table are informed by Portmore (2011: ch. 1).
20. For more precise explanation of how to calculate Expected Deontic Force, see Sepielli (2009: 11).

The main claim is that of Premise 3. While Impermissibility Aversion is initially plausible, on inspection it rests on mistakenly treating "oughts" (required acts) and "oughts not" (impermissible acts) in parallel fashion. Expected Deontic Force Attraction corrects this mistake. And, crucially, as shown above, Expected Deontic Force Attraction is consistent with the ought of Objective Consequentialism being the Central Ought.

5.7 Conclusion

In this chapter, we've looked at a pair of challenges—the Action Problem and the Centrality Problem—which both aim to show that Objective Consequentialism is unsuited as a guide to action. We've explored a number of responses offered on behalf of Objective Consequentialism. Which is the weakest?

There's a good case to be made that it's the Argument from Ambiguous Ability. A crucial premise in that argument denies the Specific Response Restriction. To support this denial, we pointed to Pleased by Unexpected Pleasure. This case matters because of its structure: There is an act an agent ought to perform, but it is not possible for the agent to act on the fact that generates the ought. Yet one might deny that this case is a legitimate counterexample. Recall what was initially compelling about the Specific Response Restriction. It provides a principled cut between senses of ought that are evaluative and those that are normative. Defenders of the restriction may hold that cases like Pleased by Unexpected Pleasure simply confuse what would be good to happen (the evaluative ought), with what we ought to do (the normative ought). On this view, it would be good if you went to Grand Opening, but it's not what you ought to do.[21]

We have a stand-off. Some claim that pleasure from unexpected pleasure is good and can be part of what makes it the case that you ought to go to Grand Opening. Others agree that unexpected pleasure is good but disagree that it can provide a reason that figures in what you ought to do. If you went to Grand Opening it would be good, but, they insist, it would be good in the same way that it would be good if no one died because an avalanche turned left rather than right. The question, then, is this: When we think, in Pleased by Unexpected Pleasure, that you ought to go to Grand Opening, are we using ought as it appears in Avalanche or in Driver? To be a genuine counterexample to the Specific Response Restriction, the ought must be that which appears in Driver.

---

21. This response draws on Kiesewetter (2016: §3).

References

Broome, J. 2013. *Rationality through Reasoning*. Oxford: Blackwell.
Bykvist, K. 2011. "How to Do Wrong Knowingly and Get Away with It." In *Neither/Nor: Philosophical Papers Dedicated to Erik Carlson on the Occasion of His Fiftieth Birthday*, 31–47. Uppsala: Uppsala University.
*Driver, J. 2012. "What the Objective Standard Is Good For." In *Oxford Studies in Normative Ethics*, edited by M. Timmons, 28–44. Oxford: Oxford University Press.
Gibbons, J. 2013. *The Norm of Belief*. Oxford: Oxford University Press.
*Graham, P. A. 2010. "In Defense of Objectivism about Moral Obligation." *Ethics* 121 (1): 88–115.
*Jackson, F. 1991. "Decision-Theoretic Consequentialism and the Nearest and Dearest Objection." *Ethics* 101 (3): 461–82.
Kiesewetter, B. 2016. "You Ought to φ Only if You May Believe That You Ought to φ." *The Philosophical Quarterly* 66 (265): 760–82.
Kiesewetter, B. 2018. "How Reasons Are Sensitive to Available Evidence." In *Normativity: Epistemic and Practical*, edited by Conor McHugh, Jonathan Way, and Daniel Whiting, 90–115. Oxford: Oxford University Press.
Kratzer, A. 1977. "What 'Must' and 'Can' Must and Can Mean." *Linguistics and Philosophy* 1 (3): 337–55.
Lord, E. 2015. "Acting for the Right Reasons, Abilities, and Obligation." In *Oxford Studies in Metaethics*, edited by R. Shafer-Landau, 26–52. Oxford: Oxford University Press.
Mele, A. R. 2003. "Agents' Abilities." *Noûs* 37 (3): 447–70.
Moore, G.E. 2005 [1912]. *Ethics*. Edited by W. H. Shaw. Oxford: Oxford University Press.
Parfit, D. 2011. *On What Matters*. Vol. 1. Oxford: Oxford University Press.
Portmore, D. W. 2011. *Commonsense Consequentialism: Wherein Morality Meets Rationality*. Oxford: Oxford University Press.
Portmore, D. W. 2019. *Opting for the Best: Oughts and Options*. Oxford: Oxford University Press.
Schroeder, M. 2007. *Slaves of the Passions*. Oxford: Oxford University Press.
Schwan, B. 2018. "What Ability Can Do." *Philosophical Studies* 175 (3): 703–23.
Sepielli, A. 2009. "What to Do When You Don't Know What to Do." In *Oxford Studies in Metaethics*, edited by R. Shafer-Landau, 5–28. Oxford: Oxford University Press.
Thomson, J. 2008. *Normativity*. Chicago: Open Court.
Way, J., and D. Whiting. 2017. "Perspectivism and the Argument from Guidance." *Ethical Theory and Moral Practice* 20 (2): 361–74.
Wedgwood, R. 2007. *The Nature of Normativity*. Oxford: Oxford University Press.
*Zimmerman, M. J. 2008. *Living with Uncertainty: The Moral Significance of Ignorance*. Cambridge: Cambridge University Press.

6

Actualism and Control Sensitivity

6.1 *Introduction*

When thinking about whether or not an act is permissible, we usually attend to the outcome that would come about if the action were performed. We consider the world that would be brought about by the action and then compare it to the world that would be brought about if some other action were performed instead. Of course, you might wonder if what we usually think is what we should think. And this brings us to the question we're concerned with in this chapter:

> Are the deontic properties of actions determined exclusively by what they would bring about?

That what would happen is what matters in deontic assessment enjoys intuitive support. To see this, consider how your acts combine with events in nature, the acts of others, and your own future acts.

Suppose it's New Year's Eve, and you're looking forward to lighting some fireworks. But what happens after they're lit matters a lot. The sparks that are emitted could land harmlessly on the pavement and be quickly extinguished—no problem. Or the sparks could be carried by the breeze to a nearby patch of dry woods, igniting a disastrous fire—big problem. However, what's possible—what could happen—is one thing, and what would happen is another. Suppose that, if you were to set off the fireworks, the sparks would ignite the fire. Given this, it seems you ought not to set them off. When your acts combine with nature, what would happen, not what could happen, dictates what you ought to do.

No fireworks, but you're still feeling optimistic. When the clock strikes midnight, you're considering kissing a friend you've secretly had a crush on. What happens after you make your move matters a lot. Your crush could kiss back—wonderful. Or your crush could turn away—horrible. Suppose, if you were to make a move, your crush would turn away. Given this, it seems you ought not to go in for the kiss. When your acts combine with the acts of others, just as when they combine with forces of nature, what would happen, not what could happen, dictates what you ought to do.

Neither fireworks nor a kiss is in the cards, so your attention turns to your New Year's resolution. You've resolved to drive less and exercise more. Perhaps you ought to buy a bike. As before, what happens after the purchase matters a lot. You could use it—good purchase. Or you could let it collect dust—waste of money. Suppose, if you were to buy a bike, you would let it collect dust. Given this, it seems you ought not to make the purchase. So just as forces of nature and the actions of others influence what you ought to do, so too do your own actions. What you would later do if you bought a bike is relevant to whether you ought to buy a bike. What would happen, not what could happen, dictates what you ought to do.

These observations suggest one of the members of the set of principles examined in this book that together imply Utilitarianism, namely:

> ACTUALISM: The deontic properties of a presently available action depend solely on the complete state of affairs that would be brought about were the agent to perform it compared to the complete states of affairs that would be brought about if the agent were to perform any of her other presently available actions.[1]

Theories that accept Actualism—which we'll call Actualistic—hold that what you ought to do is determined by what would actually happen were an act performed. In previous chapters, we've taken it for granted that Traditional Consequentialism accepts Actualism. As formulated, it holds, for example, that an agent is required to perform a presently available action if and only if what would happen if she were to perform this action is better than what would happen if she were to perform any of her other presently available actions. We can now make this assumption explicit by referring to the view as Actualistic Consequentialism.

Actualistic Consequentialism has much appeal. Yet the last of the examples above—your bike purchase—might give us pause. You don't control nature or the acts of others. But you do control your own acts. You could buy and use the bike. This is up to you. And this difference in control is morally relevant. Actualistic Consequentialism, however, appears insensitive to it. When it comes to determining your present moral requirements, the view treats your future actions as forces of nature. And, as a result, your future laziness gets you off the hook. In this chapter, we'll explain how this difference in control gives rise to a formidable challenge to Actualistic Consequentialism.

A final note before we begin. Actualism, as formulated above, is in two important respects underspecified. First, it invokes the notion of an agent's "available actions." But what exactly does it take for an action to qualify as available?[2]

---

1. As this formulation's use of "presently available actions" indicates, in this chapter, we drop the simplifying assumption made in §1.2.1, namely, that we need only to supply deontic properties to alternatives—acts whose joint performance is impossible. After this chapter, we'll take this assumption back up.

2. In §1.2.1 we offered a general characterization. Below we'll specify the details.

As will soon be apparent, it matters a great deal how this question is answered. Second, Actualism asserts that what would happen if an act were performed is relevant to determining its deontic properties but does not specify whether this determination is direct (as when an act is assessed by the state of affairs it brings about) or indirect (as when an act inherits its deontic status from some act that is directly assessed). This matter, too, is of great importance. In the following discussion, we'll take up both of these issues.

6.2 Sequential Doses

Our present acts often make sense only in light of what we'll do in the future. You ought, for example, to preheat your oven, but only if you will use it. That action, turning the oven on, is reasonable only when understood as one act in a larger sequence. Yet, when it comes to evaluating how agents ought to act over time, Actualistic Consequentialism can deliver counterintuitive results. Consider, for instance,

> Sequential Doses. Dr. Smith's patient has a virus. Without intervention, he'll soon be paralyzed. There's only one treatment. Dr. Smith must administer a dose of "Nine" at 9:00am and a dose of "Eleven" at 11:00am. Dr. Smith could easily administer both doses as directed. However, if she were to give Nine at 9:00am, then at 11:00am she would freely choose to refrain from giving Eleven. Indeed, she will refrain from giving Eleven whether or not she gives Nine.[3]

Dr. Smith's available alternatives, their outcomes, and their evaluative rankings are as follows:

Table 6.1: *Dr. Smith's Possibilities*

Presently Available Alternatives	Outcome	Ranking
Give Nine, then give Eleven.	Patient is cured.	Best
Refrain from Nine, refrain from Eleven.	Patient is paralyzed.	2nd Best
Give Nine, refrain from Eleven.	Patient dies.	Worst
Refrain from Nine, give Eleven.	Patient dies.	Worst

Dr. Smith is free to perform any of these available actions. However, whether or not she gives Nine at 9:00am, at 11:00am she will freely refrain from giving Eleven. The details of this case can be visually represented with the decision tree in Figure 6.1.

---

3. This case is modified from Feldman (1986: 52) and is structurally similar to Professor Procrastinate (Jackson and Pargetter 1986: 235).

116 Part II: Normative Principles

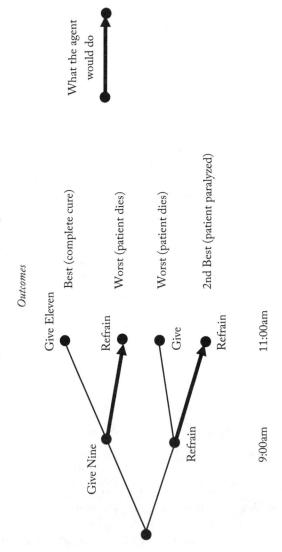

Figure 6.1: *Decision Tree for Sequential Doses*

What's interesting about Sequential Doses is its structure. We'll call cases that share this structure

> *Diachronic Cases*: At t_0 an agent has control over the performance of a certain act at t_1, and at t_2 she has control over the performance of a certain act at t_3. The performance of the act at t_1 is best if and only if the agent performs the act at t_3 ($t_0 < t_1 \leq t_2 < t_3$).

There are three points concerning Diachronic Cases worth emphasizing. First, the agent can freely perform both the act at t_1 and the act at t_3. This is captured by the first sentence in the formulation. Second, the overall value of the outcome of the act at t_1 depends on what the agent does at t_3. This is captured by the second sentence. Finally, t_1 and t_2 may be the identical time. This is captured by the parenthetical.

With a clear view of its structure, we can ask: What ought Dr. Smith do in Sequential Doses? The answer seems obvious. She ought to give both Nine and Eleven. So it might seem equally obvious she ought to give Nine. But this is not what Actualistic Consequentialism requires. For, if Dr. Smith were to give Nine, then when it came time to give Eleven, she would refrain, thereby bringing about the death of her patient. By comparison, if she were to refrain from giving Nine, she would refrain from giving Eleven, and her patient would be paralyzed. Since what would happen if Dr. Smith were to give Nine is worse than if she were to refrain, Actualistic Consequentialism holds that she ought to refrain. This seems to allow her future negligence to shape her present moral requirements. And the surprising result is that she is, in effect, morally required to paralyze her patient. Yet this terrible state of affairs could be avoided. Dr. Smith could easily choose to properly treat her patient. Thus, in Diachronic Cases such as Sequential Doses, Actualistic Consequentialism appears to deliver implausible verdicts. In the next section, we'll explain why this result is troubling.

6.3 *The Argument from Diachronic Identical Control*

In Sequential Doses, Actualistic Consequentialism appears to direct Dr. Smith to engage in avoidable evil. While this result is troubling, it is important to be clear about where exactly Actualistic Consequentialism goes wrong.

To this end, we begin with the moral relevance of control. There are different ways in which one might have control over one's actions. These differences matter. What's troubling about Sequential Doses is that Dr. Smith appears to enjoy a robust kind of control, one that is uninterrupted and enduring. She operates as an agent who can execute a sequence of acts over time. By contrast, we could describe a Diachronic Case in which Dr. Smith does, in some sense, have control over both acts, but intuitively what would happen at 11:00am should influence what she ought to do at 9:00am. Consider

> Shock Treatment. Things are just as described in Sequential Doses except that at 10:00am Dr. Smith will undergo shock treatment. The treatment will leave her psychology entirely intact, except it will wipe out any desires or intentions she formed earlier in the day. If she were to give Nine, then, although she could freely give Eleven, she would choose to refrain. Indeed, she will refrain from giving Eleven whether she gives or refrains from giving Nine.

Dr. Smith has control, at say 8:59am, over what she does at 9:00am. She could give Nine. And she has control, at say 10:59am, over what she does at 11:00am. She could give Eleven. But she lacks, at the beginning of the sequence, control over her acts later in the sequence. She cannot at 8:59am guarantee that she'll follow through—giving both Nine and Eleven—because any psychological adjustment she makes at that time will be wiped out by her later shock treatment. She thus has only a tenuous kind of control. Here it is perfectly reasonable that, prior to 9:00am, she should regard her behavior after the shock treatment as akin to the acts of another agent. She doesn't now control how she'll use her control then. And if she is going to use that control to refrain from giving Eleven, then she ought to refrain from giving Nine.

What does Dr. Smith possess in Sequential Doses that she lacks in Shock Treatment? Only in the former case does she seem to possess

> *Identical Control*: When the agent possesses the sense of control relevant to deontic assessment over a given set of actions starting at t_1, the agent has, at t_0, that same control over all the actions in the set.[4]

Unlike Shock Treatment, in Sequential Doses Dr. Smith appears able to carry out a plan, uninterrupted, to administer both doses. Actualistic Consequentialism nonetheless treats Dr. Smith's later actions as if they were the doings of a hurricane or the work of another agent.

We are now in a position to articulate precisely what's concerning about Actualistic Consequentialism's verdict in Sequential Doses. Given the normative significance of Identical Control, we are led to a condition any adequate consequentialist theory should satisfy. This condition demands that a consequentialist theory be sensitive to the difference in control between cases like Sequential Doses and Shock Treatment. It requires that a theory register the presence of Identical Control. Call this requirement the

---

4. This principle and the subsequent discussion draw on Cohen and Timmerman (2016).

Principle of Control Sensitivity: A consequentialist theory must be such that, if an agent enjoys Identical Control over a set of actions and fails to bring about the best complete state of affairs she could, she has failed to do what she ought.

Actualistic Consequentialism appears to violate this requirement. In Sequential Doses, Dr. Smith seems to enjoy Identical Control over giving Nine and Eleven, she fails to bring about the best state of affairs, and yet Actualistic Consequentialism does not register this crucial fact. Instead of identifying Dr. Smith's negligence as a moral failure, Actualistic Consequentialism modulates her moral requirements. Thus, it violates the Principle of Control Sensitivity.

We can now offer the following challenge to Actualistic Consequentialism.

The Argument from Diachronic Identical Control

1. If Actualistic Consequentialism violates the Principle of Control Sensitivity, then it is false.
2. In some Diachronic Cases, Actualistic Consequentialism violates the Principle of Control Sensitivity.
3. Hence, Actualistic Consequentialism is false.

Both premises are well supported. The central idea in Premise 1—the Principle of Control Sensitivity—expresses an intuitively attractive requirement on consequentialist moral theories. Premise 2 is supported by Actualistic Consequentialism's verdict in Sequential Doses. When bringing about less than the best, Dr. Smith seems to enjoy Identical Control; and yet she is, according to Actualistic Consequentialism, morally faultless. The theory appears to violate the Principle of Control Sensitivity.

> *Actualism*: The deontic properties of a presently available action depend solely on the complete state of affairs that would be brought about were the agent to perform it compared to the complete states of affairs that would be brought about if the agent were to perform any of her other presently available actions.
>
> *Principle of Control Sensitivity*: A consequentialist theory must be such that, if an agent enjoys Identical Control over a set of actions and fails to bring about the best complete state of affairs she could, she has failed to do what she ought.
>
> *Diachronic Cases*: At t_0 an agent has control over the performance of a certain act at t_1, and at t_2 she has control over the performance of a certain act at t_3. The performance of the act at t_1 is best if and only if the agent performs the act at t_3 ($t_0 < t_1 \leq t_2 < t_3$).

In the next section, we will consider an argument that disputes Premise 2.

6.4 *The Ensuring Control Argument against Diachronic Identical Control*

In the previous section, we distinguished between the sense of control Dr. Smith has in Shock Treatment and the more enduring sense of control she enjoys in Sequential Doses. This latter sense of control—Identical Control—is necessary to show that Actualistic Consequentialism violates the Principle of Control Sensitivity in Diachronic Cases. To this point, however, we've said little about what this control consists in. We've worked from the ordinary understanding of control. But ordinary concepts often lack the precision necessary for philosophical purposes. In this section, we present the account in appropriate detail. If the account sketched is correct, then agents cannot exercise Identical Control in Diachronic Cases. Accordingly, the Principle of Control Sensitivity—a requirement concerning contexts in which agents possess Identical Control—has no application in Diachronic Cases. Premise 2 in the Argument from Diachronic Identical Control is false.

There are, of course, many accounts of control. But we need not concern ourselves with all of the options, for the Argument from Diachronic Identical Control invokes control in the context of what an agent ought to do. The relevant kind of control then concerns an agent's ability to satisfy or fail to satisfy a moral requirement. We can thus arrive at an account of control by examining the conditions that must be met if an agent is to do what she ought. By way of preview, the account on offer holds that an agent has control over an act if and only if she possesses a set of properties—you might think of these as amounting to a power or an ability—sufficient to ensure her performance of the act and sufficient to ensure her nonperformance of the act. We arrive at this account in two steps.

First, it follows from the fact that an agent ought to perform some act that she is able to ensure its performance. Morality doesn't demand of you acts that you cannot guarantee are performed. For example, morality cannot require that you spin green on a roulette wheel. This is not an act that you can ensure the performance of. To demand such a thing manifests confusion. You can be morally required to try to spin green on a roulette wheel. This act is one you can guarantee you perform—by, for example, spinning the wheel—and so this is something that morality could require of you. But being required to try to do something and being required to do it are two entirely different things. What explains the fact that you cannot be required to spin green is that you lack the set of properties sufficient to ensure that you do so. That is, you cannot guarantee that the event of your spinning green happens.[5] This takes us to

> *Ought Implies Ensurable Performance*: Necessarily, an agent ought to perform an act only if she possesses the set of properties sufficient to ensure her performance of this act.

The idea is that, absent the ability to ensure that you perform an act, you cannot be morally required to do so.

Second, it follows from the fact that an agent ought to perform some act that she is able to ensure that she refrains from performing it. Morality cannot

---

5. This paragraph draws on Pietroski (2000: ch. 1).

demand of you the performance of acts that you will unavoidably perform. The very notion of a demand presupposes the possibility of failure. Consider, for example, the purported demand that you do or do not donate to charity. Here you cannot fail to comply. Whether you donate or not, you did what you ought. And this reveals that there was really no demand in the first place. About such pseudodemands Lavin writes, "Whatever happens is what ought to happen and that only means that here we can't talk about what ought to happen" (2004: 432). This takes us to

Ought Implies Ensurable Nonperformance: Necessarily, an agent ought to perform an act only if she possesses a set of properties sufficient to ensure the nonperformance of this act.

The idea is that, absent the ability to ensure that you do not perform an act, you cannot be morally required to do so. You'll perform the act of course, but here it makes no sense to also say that in so acting you did what you ought.

Taken together, these two claims—Ought Implies Ensurable Performance and Ought Implies Ensurable Nonperformance—specify the kind of control relevant to deontic assessment. To face a moral demand an agent must have

Ensuring Control: An agent has ensuring control over an act if and only if she possesses a set of properties sufficient to ensure her performance of the act and sufficient to ensure her nonperformance of the act.

This captures the idea that having control over an act entails the ability to dictate the facts concerning the performance of the act. We've arrived at this account of control by considering what must be true of an agent facing a moral requirement. She must be able to ensure her compliance with it as well as ensure her noncompliance with it.

Having offered an argument to the conclusion that Ensuring Control is the proper account of control, we can make a further claim. Ensuring Control is

Single Exercise: Control over an act is single exercise if and only if an agent can exercise it at most once.

If one must possess a set of properties sufficient to ensure that one complies with a requirement or to ensure that one fails to comply with it, and one possesses this control now, then one can't also possess it later. For, if one did, then the control later would render one unable to ensure performance or nonperformance of the act earlier. Why? Because the ability, later, to ensure the performance or nonperformance blocks one from having the ability to ensure this earlier. Similar reasoning explains why if one possesses such an ability now, one could not have possessed it previously.

To see why Ensuring Control Is Single Exercise, it may be instructive to consider another kind of ability. The power of consent is widely understood to be transformative. And this power you exercise at most once. To see this, consider

> Operation. You will undergo an operation tomorrow afternoon. Your consent will be requested once tonight and once tomorrow morning.

If you consent to the operation, it will qualify as surgery. If you don't consent, it will qualify as battery. As the case is described, it appears as though you can exercise the transformative power of consent twice. But this appearance is deceptive. You may be asked to consent twice, but there is only one time at which you exercise the transformative power of consent: the last time you are asked. Whether or not you give consent tonight is irrelevant to determining the status of your operation. This is because you will be asked to consent again in the morning. The answer you offer then will override anything you say tonight.

If, like the transformative power of consent, Ensuring Control can be exercised at most once, then we can draw an important conclusion. It is impossible for an agent to have Identical Control over the sequence of acts in Diachronic Cases. We've seen that the kind of control presupposed by moral demands is Ensuring Control. And we've seen that Ensuring Control Is Single Exercise. Yet, in Diachronic Cases, an agent is claimed to enjoy this control more than once. The agent, at the beginning of the sequence, enjoys Ensuring Control over all of the acts it includes. But she also is claimed to enjoy Ensuring Control immediately prior to the performance of each act throughout the sequence.

This reasoning is worth elaboration. Return to Sequential Doses. To show that Dr. Smith lacks Identical Control, we will assume that she has it and then derive a contradiction. So, to begin, assume that at 8:59am Dr. Smith has Ensuring Control over giving Eleven. If this is true, then at 8:59am she possesses a set of properties to ensure the performance or nonperformance of giving Eleven. Yet it is also claimed that immediately prior to acting, at perhaps 10:59am, Dr. Smith has Ensuring Control over giving Eleven. If this is true, then at 10:59am she possesses a set of properties to ensure the performance or nonperformance of giving Eleven. We have a conflict. The ability to ensure nonperformance at 10:59am precludes the ability to ensure performance at 8:59am. And the ability to ensure performance at 10:59am precludes the ability to ensure nonperformance at 8:59am. If Dr. Smith possesses Ensuring Control over Eleven at 10:59am, then she does not also possess it at 8:59am. Hence it is not possible in Sequential Doses for Dr. Smith to have Identical Control.

If this much is correct, then agents cannot have Identical Control in Diachronic Cases. Ensuring Control is Single Exercise. This is important because the Principle of Control Sensitivity only concerns contexts in which agents do possess Identical Control. The Principle of Control Sensitivity has no bearing on what moral theories say when such control is absent. Properly understood, then, Actualistic Consequentialism cannot violate the Principle of Control Sensitivity in Diachronic Cases.

The problem with Premise 2 in the Argument from Diachronic Identical Control should now be in view. We can forward

The Ensuring Control Argument against Diachronic Identical Control

1. Ensuring Control is the relevant sense of control for deontic assessment and is Single Exercise.
2. If Ensuring Control is the relevant sense of control for deontic assessment and is Single Exercise, then agents do not possess Identical Control in Diachronic Cases.
3. If agents do not possess Identical Control in Diachronic Cases, then the Principle of Control Sensitivity is not relevant to Diachronic Cases.
4. If the Principle of Control Sensitivity is not relevant to Diachronic Cases, then Actualistic Consequentialism cannot violate the Principle of Control Sensitivity in Diachronic Cases.
5. Hence, Actualistic Consequentialism cannot violate the Principle of Control Sensitivity in Diachronic Cases.

Ensuring Control: An agent has ensuring control over an act if and only if she possesses a set of properties sufficient to ensure her performance of the act and sufficient to ensure her nonperformance of the act.

Single Exercise: Control over an act is single exercise if and only if an agent can exercise it at most once.

Identical Control: When the agent possesses the sense of control relevant to deontic assessment over a given set of actions starting at t_1, the agent has, at t_0, that same control over all the actions in the set.

Diachronic Cases: At t_0 an agent has control over the performance of a certain act at t_1, and at t_2 she has control over the performance of a certain act at t_3. The performance of the act at t_1 is best if and only if the agent performs the act at t_3 ($t_0 < t_1 \leq t_2 < t_3$).

Principle of Control Sensitivity: A consequentialist theory must be such that, if an agent enjoys Identical Control over a set of actions and fails to bring about the best complete state of affairs she could, she has failed to do what she ought.

Actualism: The deontic properties of a presently available action depend solely on the complete state of affairs that would be brought about were the agent to perform it compared to the complete states of affairs that would be brought about if the agent were to perform any of her other presently available actions

The argument hinges on the first two premises. Premise 1 is well supported. Reflection on the kind of control presupposed by moral requirements reveals that Ensuring Control is what matters for deontic assessment. And, since having this control at any one time precludes the possibility of having it at any other time, it is Single Exercise. Premise 2 is also well supported. To possess Identical Control in Diachronic Cases, agents must, at more than one time, enjoy the relevant kind of control over their acts. But, because that control is Single Exercise, this is not possible. Actualistic Consequentialism thus cannot mishandle Diachronic Cases where the agent enjoys Identical Control. There are no such cases.

In addition to its role in the argument of this section, Ensuring Control also bears on a further matter. What acts count as available in a choice situation? In the next section, we clarify this question and offer an answer.

6.5 *The Argument for Only Irreversible Actions Are Available*

As noted in the introduction, Actualism, as formulated, invokes the notion of an agent's "available actions" but does not specify what this amounts to. We are now in a position to spell out how this should be understood. To do this, we appeal again to Ensuring Control—the kind of control relevant to deontic assessment. The proposal is straightforward. The set of an agent's available actions at a given time are just those acts over which she possesses Ensuring Control.

Before we begin, we need to introduce a notational convention. The remainder of this chapter requires that we carefully distinguish various acts. To avoid ambiguity, we will use angle brackets to individuate actions. For example, <walk and chew gum> refers to the single act, involving both walking and chewing gum. This, as a single act, has its own deontic status. But this act could be decomposed into, <walk> and <chew gum>. Each of these separate acts have their own deontic status. With this convention in place, we can turn to the proposal.

Most acts—as that word is usually used—are not acts over which the agent has Ensuring Control. In everyday discourse, we talk very loosely about acts. If a friend asked what you did last summer you might say, "I traveled around Japan." But this act itself is a composite of acts. To <travel around Japan> requires that you <book a plane ticket>, <go to the airport>, <check in for your flight>, <board a plane>, and much else. At no point do you have Ensuring Control over the act <travel around Japan>. That's not the kind of act that one ever possesses a set of properties sufficient to ensure the performance or nonperformance of. Even <book a plane ticket> is an act over which you cannot enjoy Ensuring Control. To perform that act you have to <look for a flight>, <select a seat>, <arrange for payment>, and much else. If a problem arises while performing any of these subsidiary acts, you would not have performed the act. For example, your computer could have crashed while your payment was being processed. If this happened, you would not have, at this time, performed the act <book a flight>. This suffices to show that you don't possess Ensuring Control over traveling around Japan.

Eventually, if we continue to decompose <travel around Japan> into its component acts, we'll arrive at those acts over which you do have Ensuring Control. Consider, for example, the first act in the sequence: <form the intention to travel around Japan>. When you form an intention, neither nature nor you can intervene. That act, once started, cannot be stopped. Because at the moment of performance you possessed a set of properties sufficient to ensure whether you performed or refrained from this act, you have Ensuring Control over it. Perhaps the next act in the sequence is <shift your gaze> and the one after that is <lift your index finger> followed by

<click the mouse>. These too are acts over which you have Ensuring Control. Call such actions

> *Irreversible*: An action is irreversible if and only if once begun it cannot physically be stopped short of completion.[6]

Such acts will usually be of short duration, such as <push a button>, but what makes an act Irreversible is not its temporal extension but the kind of control the agent enjoys over its performance. What these acts have in common, and what distinguishes them from other acts, is that, once their performance is initiated, they cannot be stopped. Assuming the agent can start them, they are thus ensurable.

We should pause here to address a potential confusion. There is a sense in which Irreversible actions are unusual. Ordinarily, when we talk about what people do, we stick to larger complex acts like <go to the movies>, <play basketball>, and <travel around Japan>. Because these are not Irreversible actions, but they are the kinds of actions commonly attributed to people, one may be tempted to conclude that most of the time the acts people perform are not Irreversible. This would be a mistake. At any moment an agent is acting, she is performing an Irreversible action. When an agent carries out a complex act over time, this involves the performance of a sequence of Irreversible acts. From this perspective, Irreversible actions are not unusual at all. Quite the opposite. All acts, of any complexity, either themselves are, or are composed of, Irreversible actions.

Having argued in the previous section that Ensuring Control is the kind of control relevant to deontic assessment, and having characterized those acts that correspond to uses of Ensuring Control as Irreversible, we're now in a position to assert

> *Only Irreversible Actions Are Available*: An agent's presently available actions are exclusively Irreversible actions.

And we can offer in its support

The Argument for Only Irreversible Actions Are Available

1. Ensuring Control is the kind of control relevant to deontic assessment.
2. If Ensuring Control is the kind of control relevant to deontic assessment, then Only Irreversible Actions Are Available.
3. Hence, Only Irreversible Actions Are Available.

Both premises are substantive, but both are well supported. Premise 1 was defended in §6.4.

> *Ensuring Control*: An agent has ensuring control over an act if and only if she possesses a set of properties sufficient to ensure her performance of the act and sufficient to ensure her nonperformance of the act.
>
> *Irreversible*: An action is irreversible if and only if once begun it cannot be stopped short of completion.
>
> *Only Irreversible Actions Are Available*: An agent's presently available actions are exclusively Irreversible actions.

---

6. This principle is modified from Sobel (1976: 198). He calls these Minimal Actions.

And once Ensuring Control is accepted, the claim of Premise 2 follows. Agents only have Ensuring Control over Irreversible actions. Accordingly, the acts up for deontic assessment are only Irreversible.

6.6 *The Argument from Synchronic Identical Control*

The foregoing discussion has suggested that Actualistic Consequentialism does not violate the Principle of Control Sensitivity in Diachronic Cases. Actualistic Consequentialism is, however, not yet in the clear. For not only do agents' acts combine over time, they also combine at a time. And the possibility of simultaneous action presents another problem. To make this problem vivid, consider

> Simultaneous Injections. Dr. Miller's patient has a fever. Without intervention, she'll soon suffer mild brain damage. There's only one treatment. Dr. Miller must, at noon, simultaneously administer two injections called "Left" and "Right." To give Left he must use his left hand to press one button, and to give Right he must use his right hand to press another. If he gives only one injection, the patient will die. Dr. Miller could easily give both injections as directed. However, if he were to give Left, he would freely choose to refrain from giving Right. Indeed, he will refrain from giving Right whether he gives Left or refrains from giving Left.[7]

Here are Dr. Miller's available alternatives, their outcomes, and their evaluative rankings:

Table 6.2: *Dr. Miller's Possibilities*

Presently Available Alternatives	Outcome	Ranking
<give Left> and <give Right>	Patient is cured	Best
<refrain from giving Left> and <refrain from giving Right>	Brain damage	2nd Best
<give Left> and <refrain from giving Right>	Patient dies	Worst
<refrain from giving Left> and <give Right>	Patient dies	Worst

Dr. Miller is free to perform any of his available actions. However, regardless of whether he performs <give Left> or <refrain from giving Left>, he's freely going to perform <refrain from giving Right>. The details of this case can be visually represented with the decision tree in Figure 6.2.

---

7. Modified from Goldman (1978: 186).

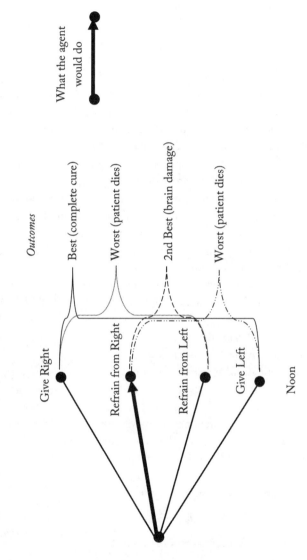

Figure 6.2: *Decision Tree for Simultaneous Injections*

What's interesting about Simultaneous Injections is its structure. We'll call cases that share this structure

> *Synchronic Cases*: At t_0 an agent has control over the performance of multiple acts at t_1. The performance of one of these acts is best if and only if the agent also performs some other of these acts as well.

There are two features of Synchronic Cases worth emphasizing. First, the agent can freely perform any of the acts at t_1. This is captured by the first sentence in the formulation. Second, the value of the outcome of a given act at t_1 depends on what else the agent does at that time. This is captured by the second sentence.

With a clear view of its structure, we can ask, What ought Dr. Miller do in Simultaneous Injections? The answer seems obvious. He ought to <give Left and give Right>. So, it might seem clear that Dr. Miller ought to <give Left>. But Actualistic Consequentialism appears not to require this. For, if Dr. Miller were to <give Left>, he would <refrain from giving Right>, and his patient would die. By comparison, if he were to <refrain from giving Left>, he would <refrain from giving Right>, and his patient would only suffer mild brain damage. So, since what would happen if he were to <give Left> is worse than what would happen if he were to <refrain from giving Left>, Actualistic Consequentialism appears to hold that he ought to <refrain from giving Left>.

Here again we've arrived at a troubling verdict. Unlike in Dr. Smith's case, in Simultaneous Injections Dr. Miller enjoys Ensuring Control over both acts. He has Identical Control over all his presently available actions. Yet, Actualistic Consequentialism appears to require that he bring about a state of affairs that is less than the best he could. And when he does, according to Actualistic Consequentialism, he will not have failed to do what he ought. We thus have an apparent violation of the Principle of Control Sensitivity.

We now are in a position to present

The Argument from Synchronic Identical Control

1. If Actualistic Consequentialism violates the Principle of Control Sensitivity, then it is false.
2. In some Synchronic Cases, Actualistic Consequentialism violates the Principle of Control Sensitivity.
3. Hence, Actualistic Consequentialism is false.

> *Actualism*: The deontic properties of a presently available action depend solely on the complete state of affairs that would be brought about were the agent to perform it compared to the complete states of affairs that would be brought about if the agent were to perform any of her other presently available actions.
>
> *Principle of Control Sensitivity*: A consequentialist theory must be such that, if an agent enjoys Identical Control over a set of actions and fails to bring about the best complete state of affairs she could, she has failed to do what she ought.
>
> *Synchronic Cases*: At t_0 an agent has control over the performance of multiple acts at t_1. The performance of one of these acts is best if and only if the agent also performs some other of these acts as well.

Only Premise 2 is controversial. But Simultaneous Injections lends it support. In that case, when bringing about less than the best, Dr. Miller enjoys Identical Control. If, according to Actualistic Consequentialism, he's done what he ought to do, then this amounts to a violation of the Principle of Control Sensitivity.

In the next section, however, we will question whether Actualistic Consequentialism, properly understood, holds that Dr. Miller ought to <refrain from giving Left>.

6.7 *Actualistic Consequentialism's Response to Synchronic Cases*

There is a crucial assumption operating in the Argument from Synchronic Identical Control. We arrive at Actualistic Consequentialism's verdict that Dr. Miller ought to <refrain from giving Left> by assessing that act directly. That is, we consider the state of affairs that would result if he were to perform that act, consider what state of affairs would result if he were to refrain from performing that act, and then compare the two outcomes. This is the standard approach to deontic assessment. And, taking this approach, Actualistic Consequentialism violates the Principle of Control Sensitivity.

One way to respond to the Argument from Synchronic Identical Control is to deny this assumption, rejecting the idea that all acts are to be assessed directly. If at least some acts are to be assessed indirectly, then we might avoid the troubling verdict in Simultaneous Injections that results in the violation of the Principle of Control Sensitivity. How persuasive this response is, of course, will depend on the strength of the reasons to depart from the standard approach to deontic assessment. Why should we think some acts are to be assessed indirectly? One might worry that such a maneuver deployed by defenders of Actualistic Consequentialism is objectionably ad hoc. That is, one might think that proponents of Actualistic Consequentialism, faced with a serious objection, devise a response lacking independent theoretical motivation.

Fortunately, as we'll explain in the first subsection, there is an independent rationale for departing from the standard approach to deontic assessment. That approach faces a significant problem. In the second subsection, we'll explain how, by assessing some acts indirectly, this problem can be solved. In the final subsection, with this solution in hand, we'll show how Actualistic Consequentialism can avoid the troubling verdict in Simultaneous Injections. It does not violate the Principle of Control Sensitivity in Synchronic Cases.

6.7.1 *The Problem of Act Versions Argument against Every Act Directly*

We just mentioned that there is an important assumption driving the Argument from Synchronic Identical Control. Put precisely, this assumption is

> *Every Act Directly*: Every act is assessed directly. An agent ought to perform such an act if and only if the performance of any of her other presently available actions would have brought about a complete state of affairs that's worse-simpliciter.[8]

Most consequentialist theories assume Every Act Directly. However, despite being widely accepted, it faces a serious challenge. It is incompatible with two other deeply attractive principles. The result is an inconsistent triad. Of the three claims, Every Act Directly is the one to reject.

Before turning to this trilemma, we should introduce what will prove to be a very important concept, namely, performance entailment.[9] Notice, when an agent performs an act, she is in almost every case performing many acts. When we think about acts, we focus only on those that are salient. But what someone has done is actually better thought of as a complex of acts, some of which may be quite trivial. As Brown writes, "Whatever the agent does, she will do not just one act, but many. She will not merely raise her left arm, but will also raise one of her limbs, and move her body, and signal to the taxi driver, and so on. Acts come grouped together as 'package deals'" (2018: 758–59). Rather than performing just one act at a time, it is almost always the case that agents perform many. In these cases, the performance of one act entails the performance of many others. Here are three such examples. First,

> X-ing is logically equivalent to Y-ing.

If two acts differ only in description, then the performance of one will entail the performance of the other. Consider the acts <punching a bachelor> and <punching an unmarried male of marriable age>. If you perform one you necessarily perform the other. This follows from the fact that the two acts are logically equivalent. Hence, the latter performatively entails the former. And, given that the acts are logically equivalent, the former also entails the latter. Second,

> X-ing is a proper part of Y-ing.

The performance of one act may have as parts many subsidiary acts. If you perform the complex act, then you unavoidably perform the acts that are its parts. Consider the act <making a fist>. If you perform this act, you necessarily perform the complex act <curling your index finger, and curling your middle finger, and curling your ring finger, and curling your pinky, and curling your thumb>. Hence, <making a fist> performatively entails each of this act's proper parts—for example, <curling your index finger>. Third,

---

8. Modified from Portmore (2019: §4.1).
9. The following discussion of performance entailment draws heavily on Portmore (2019: §4).

> X-ing is a more specific version of Y-ing.

If one act is a more specific version of another act, then the performance of the former entails the performance of the latter. Consider the acts of <knocking angrily on the door> and <knocking on the door>. If you perform the more specific act, you'll also perform the less specific version. For you can't perform an act in a specific way without performing that act at all. Hence, the performance of a more specific act, like <knocking angrily on the door>, entails the performance of the less specific act, <knocking on the door>.

Equipped with the concept of performance entailment, we're now in a position to spell out the problem facing Every Act Directly. To do so, we need to introduce two principles.

The fact that certain of the agent's presently available actions performatively entail others is obviously relevant for deontic assessment. When we consider acts that ought to be performed, of those presently available, we naturally extend this judgment to the acts they entail. Intuitively, if an agent ought to perform one act, then she also ought to perform those acts it entails. These latter acts inherit their status as "ought to be performed" from the former act. We can call the principle capturing this idea

> *Ought Inheritance*: For any two presently available actions, X and Y, where X-ing entails Y-ing, necessarily, if the agent ought to X, then she ought to Y.[10]

When a required presently available action performatively entails another presently available action, the ought will carry over. For example, if you ought to <make a fist> and performance of this act entails that you <curl your index finger>, then you ought to <curl your index finger>. Not only is Ought Inheritance immediately intuitively plausible, consider what would follow from its denial. Suppose someone held that you ought to <make a fist> but insisted that you ought not to <curl your index finger>. You'd reasonably think this person was confused. Reasoning based on Ought Inheritance is ubiquitous. And by accepting it we can explain why such reasoning is valid.

Whereas Ought Inheritance affirms that deontic status is shared for performatively entailed acts, the second principle of interest denies that evaluative status is similarly shared. It is possible for an act to have one evaluative outcome and yet for acts entailed by it to have different evaluative outcomes. We can call the principle capturing this idea

> *Value Non-Inheritance*: For any two presently available actions, X and Y, where X-ing entails Y-ing, it is not the case that, necessarily, the goodness of the outcome of X-ing is equal to the goodness of the outcome of Y-ing.[11]

---

10. This formulation draws on Portmore (2019: §4.1).
11. This formulation draws on Portmore (2019: §4.1).

This principle is easy to support. Examples that prove it abound. Return to Simultaneous Injections. There, the best state of affairs would obtain if Dr. Miller were to perform the single act <give Left and give Right>. His patient would be cured. And the performance of this act entails the performance of <give Left>. Clearly, however, the goodness of the outcome of <give Left> is not inherited from <give Left and give Right>. For there are ways to <give Left> that do not result in the patient being cured. For example, if Dr. Miller were to <give Left> and to <refrain from giving Right>, then the patient would die. The evaluative status of a presently available action is thus not inherited by the other presently available actions it entails.

Every Act Directly, along with Ought Inheritance and Value Non-Inheritance, are all initially plausible. Yet, they form an inconsistent triad. They can't all be true. Call this the

Problem of Synchronic Act Versions: Every Act Directly, Ought Inheritance, and Value Non-Inheritance are jointly inconsistent.[12]

This problem arises, as we will shortly explain, because Every Act Directly requires that every act be assessed directly; yet, there are many versions of each act. And these versions are importantly different. If we assume that the three claims are true and draw out their implications in a case like Simultaneous Injections, we'll derive a contradiction. And this demonstrates that one of the three must be jettisoned.

Start with the act <give Left and give Right>. If we accept Every Act Directly, then this act is to be assessed, like all others, directly in terms of the goodness of its outcome. Since this act has the best outcome, it is what Dr. Miller ought to do. But <give Left and give Right> performatively entails <give Left>. So, given Ought Inheritance, we must conclude

Yes Left: Dr. Miller ought to <give Left>.

Having reached this conclusion, let's set it aside for a moment.

Start anew with the act <give Left and give Right>. This act, if performed, would bring about the best state of affairs. This act also performatively entails the act <give Left>. But here we have an example of Value Non-Inheritance. The act <give Left>, in light of what Dr. Miller would do were he to perform it, would not bring about the best state of affairs. If Dr. Miller were to <give Left> he would also <refrain from giving Right>, and his patient would die. Now it appears that <give Left> is a terrible option and <refrain from giving Left> is better. So, if we accept Every Act Directly, then we must conclude

---

12. This problem was first discovered by Bergström (1966) and Castañeda (1968). In light of the previous discussion of control, we presented the problem as synchronic. However, different inheritance principles permit diachronic versions of the problem. For discussion, see Feldman (1986: ch. 1) and more recently Gustafsson (2014).

No Left: Dr. Miller ought to <refrain from giving Left>.

We can now see why the fact that there can be different versions of the same act presents a problem. The act <give Left>, when it's part of <give Left and give Right> is great. The act <give Left> when it's part of <give Left and refrain from giving Right> is terrible. This pair of claims is unobjectionable. We can accept them and accept both Ought Inheritance and Value Non-Inheritance. Yet, if we also accept Every Act Directly, we're forced to accept a contradiction. The two conclusions we've drawn, Yes Left and No Left, are flatly incompatible.

We're now positioned to offer

The Problem of Act Versions Argument against Every Act Directly

1. Every Act Directly, Ought Inheritance, and Value Non-Inheritance cannot all be true.
2. Ought Inheritance and Value Non-Inheritance are both true.
3. Hence, Every Act Directly is false.

Both premises make substantive but well-supported claims. The incompatibility of the three commitments asserted in Premise 1 is supported by consideration of their implications in Simultaneous Injections. The pair of principles affirmed in Premise 2 are both extremely plausible. We should thus conclude that Every Act Directly is false.

In the next subsection, we present an alternative approach to deontic assessment that avoids the Problem of Synchronic Act Versions. It also supplies Actualistic Consequentialism with the material needed to mount a response to the Argument from Synchronic Identical Control.

> *Every Act Directly*: Every act is assessed directly. An agent ought to perform such an act if and only if the performance of any of her other available actions would have brought about a complete state of affairs that's worse-simpliciter.
>
> *Ought Inheritance*: For any two presently available actions, X and Y, where X-ing entails Y-ing, necessarily, if the agent ought to X, then she ought to Y.
>
> *Value Non-Inheritance*: For any two presently available actions, X and Y, where X-ing entails Y-ing, it is not the case that, necessarily, the goodness of the outcome of X-ing is equal to the goodness of the outcome of Y-ing.

6.7.2 *The Best Solution Argument for Only Non-Entailed Acts Directly*

Recall, the initial formulation of Actualism does not indicate whether all or only some acts are to be directly assessed by their outcomes. The argument of the previous section, if sound, undermines Every Act Directly. In what follows, we will suggest which acts should be assessed directly.

As with much of philosophy, once we see what drives the problem, we're driven to a particular solution. And, as suggested above, what drives the Problem of Synchronic Act Versions is a failure to distinguish between two very different kinds of acts. We can start with actions that are

> *Non-Entailed*: An action is non-entailed if and only if it is among an agent's presently available actions and its performance is not entailed by the performance of any of her other presently available actions.[13]

Non-Entailed acts are maximally specific among those over which the agent presently has control. They can be performed in only one way. Thus, it is not possible to perform one version of a Non-Entailed act or a different version of the same Non-Entailed act. Non-Entailed acts, because maximally specific, admit of only one version. All other actions are

> *Entailed*: An action is entailed if and only if it is among an agent's presently available actions and its performance is entailed by the performance of some of her other presently available actions.

Entailed acts are not maximally specific. They can be performed in more than one way. Thus, it is possible to perform an Entailed act one way, or to perform that same act a different way. For example, Dr. Miller could perform <give Left> either as <give Left and give Right> or as <give Left and refrain from giving Right>.[14]

Notice, if we directly assess both Non-Entailed and Entailed actions, then given Ought Inheritance and Value Non-Inheritance, we'll generate contradictions. Given Ought Inheritance, our assessments of Non-Entailed actions will carry over to the Entailed actions they entail. But, our assessments of those Entailed actions, given Value Non-Inheritance, will sometimes differ. Since directly assessing both Entailed and Non-Entailed actions is what gives rise to the Problem of Synchronic Act Versions, the solution seems clear: We should directly assess only one of the classes. And the obvious choice is Non-Entailed actions.

On this proposal, only Non-Entailed actions are directly assessed by the goodness of their outcomes, and Entailed actions are assessed indirectly with reference to the Non-Entailed actions that entail them. The resulting view is

> *Only Non-Entailed Acts Directly*: Every Non-Entailed action is assessed directly. An agent ought to perform such an act if and only if the performance of any of her other Non-Entailed acts would have brought about a complete state of affairs that's worse overall. Entailed actions are assessed indirectly. An agent ought to perform such an action if and only if its performance is entailed by a Non-Entailed action that ought to be performed.[15]

---

13. Non-Entailed actions are closely related to what are sometimes known as Maximal actions. They differ in that Non-Entailed actions restrict the scope of the entailment relation. It is limited to the agent's presently available actions. Our formulation draws on Portmore's (2019: §4.2) way of distinguishing Maximal and Nonmaximal actions. The Maximal and Nonmaximal distinction was originally formulated by Goldman (1978: 201).

14. This paragraph draws on Brown (2018: 753–54).

15. This principle is modified from Portmore (2019: §4.2).

This alternative marks a significant departure from Every Act Directly. One set of acts—the Non-Entailed ones—is privileged. Only these are directly assessed. And from these distinctive acts Entailed actions inherit their deontic properties.

A pair of related points are in order. First, we are now able to address the second interpretive issue regarding Actualism. As formulated, Actualism does not commit to any view about whether some or all acts are to be directly assessed. However, having arrived at Only Non-Entailed Acts Directly, the matter is settled. The only acts that are directly assessed are Non-Entailed acts. Second, notice how this commitment combines with Only Irreversible Actions Are Available. Because agents only have Ensuring Control over Irreversible acts, the Non-Entailed acts that Actualism directly assesses will necessarily be Irreversible acts.

The chief virtue of Only Non-Entailed Acts Directly is that it solves the Problem of Synchronic Act Versions. Recall, Every Act Directly, when combined with Ought Inheritance and Value Non-Inheritance, delivered the pair of incompatible conclusions: Yes Left and No Left. By contrast, because it distinguishes between Non-Entailed and Entailed actions, Only Non-Entailed Acts Directly delivers consistent deontic assessments.

We should take a moment to explain how this works. Return to Simultaneous Injections. What does Actualistic Consequentialism, once combined with Only Non-Entailed Acts Directly, tell us Dr. Miller ought to do? As the case is described, the best state of affairs available would obtain from the performance of Non-Entailed act <give Left and give Right>. So Dr. Miller ought to perform this act. It also follows that the Entailed act this entails, <give Left>, is, by virtue of its relation to this Non-Entailed act, also what Dr. Miller ought to do. Thus we can draw the conclusion

> *Inherited Yes Left*: Dr. Miller ought to perform the Entailed act <give Left> as entailed by the Non-Entailed act <give Left and give Right>.

But Actualistic Consequentialism would offer a different assessment of the act <give Left> if its performance were entailed by the performance of a different Non-Entailed act. Suppose, for example, that Dr. Miller were to perform the Non-Entailed act <give Left and refrain from giving Right>. The outcome of this act is the worst—the patient dies. Accordingly, because this Non-Entailed act is impermissible, the Entailed acts it entails are impermissible. So <give Left> is impermissible. Thus we can draw the conclusion

> *Inherited No Left*: Dr. Miller ought not to perform the Entailed act <give Left> as entailed by the Non-Entailed act <give Left and refrain from giving Right>.

While we have arrived at two verdicts concerning <give Left>, there is no contradiction. This is because one of the verdicts applies to <give Left> as entailed by a required Non-Entailed act, and the other applies to <give Left> as entailed by an impermissible Non-Entailed act. While the conclusions of Every Act Directly—Yes Left and No Left—contradict each other, their inherited counterparts delivered by Only Non-Entailed Acts Directly do not.

As should now be apparent, Only Non-Entailed Acts Directly does not deliver a stand-alone deontic verdict for Dr. Miller's act <give Left>. Knowing nothing else, we cannot determine whether this act is morally required. This is because this act's deontic status is inherited from the Non-Entailed acts that entail it. And different Non-Entailed acts can entail <give Left>.

Performance entailment is inescapable. If any version of consequentialism is to avoid contradictory deontic assessments, we need a principled way to distinguish the privilege class of acts that are to be directly assessed from the rest. Here is where Every Act Directly fails and Only Non-Entailed Acts Directly succeeds. We can avoid the Problem of Synchronic Act Versions while retaining both Ought Inheritance and Value Non-Inheritance. If the foregoing is correct, and no better alternative is forthcoming, then there is a strong case in favor of Only Non-Entailed Acts Directly.

We can now give

The Best Solution Argument for Only Non-Entailed Acts Directly

1. If Only Non-Entailed Acts Directly is the best solution to the Problem of Synchronic Act Versions, then it should be accepted.

2. Only Non-Entailed Acts Directly is the best solution to the Problem of Synchronic Act Versions.

3. Only Non-Entailed Acts Directly should be accepted.

The important claim in this argument is Premise 2. It asserts that the proposal on offer—Only Non-Entailed Acts Directly—is the best solution to the Problem of Synchronic Act Versions. This claim garners support from the fact that the proposed solution is a natural response to the problem. Perhaps there is a better solution yet to be discovered. But given what drives the Problem of Synchronic Act Versions, the prospects of finding a better alternative are dim.

> *Non-Entailed*: An action is non-entailed if and only if it is among an agent's presently available actions and its performance is not entailed by the performance of any of her other presently available actions.
>
> *Entailed*: An action is entailed if and only if it is among an agent's presently available actions and its performance is entailed by the performance of some of her other presently available actions.
>
> *Only Non-Entailed Acts Directly*: Every Non-Entailed action is assessed directly. An agent ought to perform such an act if and only if the performance of any of her other Non-Entailed acts would have brought about a complete state of affairs that's worse overall. Entailed actions are assessed indirectly. An agent ought to perform such an action if and only if its performance is entailed by a Non-Entailed action that ought to be performed.
>
> *Problem of Synchronic Act Versions*: Every Act Directly, Ought Inheritance, and Value Non-Inheritance are jointly inconsistent.

6.7.3 The Only Non-Entailed Acts Directly Argument against Synchronic Control Insensitivity

We're now in a position to respond directly to the Argument from Synchronic Identical Control. The challenge posed there, recall, held that Actualistic Consequentialism violates the Principle of Control Sensitivity in Synchronic Cases like Simultaneous Injections. It was suggested that, according to Actualistic Consequentialism, because, if Dr. Miller were to <give Left> he would <refrain from giving Right>, thereby bringing about the death of his patient, he ought not to <refrain from giving Left>. As a result, Dr. Miller would bring about a state of affairs less than the best he could—his patient would suffer brain damage when she could have been cured—and Actualistic Consequentialism would fail to register this.

The crux of this argument is the claim that, according to Actualistic Consequentialism, Dr. Miller ought to <refrain from giving Left>. But this is false. In fact, Actualistic Consequentialism holds that Dr. Miller ought to perform the Entailed act <give Left> as entailed by the Non-Entailed act <give Left and give Right>. This is the conclusion—Inherited Yes Left—arrived at above. Of course, as the case is described, if Dr. Miller were to <give Left> he would <refrain from giving Right>. Thus, he will not perform the required act, <give Left and give Right>. He will surely fail morally, and Actualistic Consequentialism, combined with Only Non-Entailed Acts Directly, will appropriately condemn his action. Actualistic Consequentialism does not violate the Principle of Control Sensitivity.

We are now in a position to forward

> *Only Non-Entailed Acts Directly*: Every Non-Entailed action is assessed directly. An agent ought to perform such an act if and only if the performance of any of her other Non-Entailed acts would have brought about a complete state of affairs that's worse overall. Entailed actions are assessed indirectly. An agent ought to perform such an action if and only if its performance is entailed by a Non-Entailed action that ought to be performed.
>
> *Actualism*: The deontic properties of a presently available action depend solely on the complete state of affairs that would be brought about were the agent to perform it compared to the complete states of affairs that would be brought about if the agent were to perform any of her other presently available actions.
>
> *Principle of Control Sensitivity*: A moral theory must be such that, if an agent enjoys Identical Control over a set of actions and fails to bring about the best complete state of affairs she could, she has failed to do what she ought.
>
> *Synchronic Cases*: At t_0 an agent has control over the performance of multiple acts at t_1. The performance of one of these acts is best if and only if the agent also performs some other of these acts as well.

The Only Non-Entailed Acts Directly Argument against Synchronic Control Insensitivity

1. If Only Non-Entailed Acts Directly is true, then Actualistic Consequentialism satisfies the Principle of Control Sensitivity in Synchronic Cases.

2. Only Non-Entailed Acts Directly is true.

3. Hence, Actualistic Consequentialism satisfies the Principle of Control Sensitivity in Synchronic Cases.

The argument hinges on Premise 2. But this premise is well supported. If the arguments of the previous two subsections are sound, then we should accept Only Non-Entailed Actions Directly. The result is that Actualistic Consequentialism is appropriately sensitive to Irreversible actions over which the agent exercises Identical Control.

6.8 *Conclusion*

In this chapter, we've considered an important challenge to Actualistic Consequentialism. It was claimed that, in both Diachronic and Synchronic Cases, Actualistic Consequentialism licenses avoidable evil. It, more precisely, violates the Principle of Control Sensitivity. In responding to these objections we've further clarified two parts of the formulation of Actualism. First, an agent's available actions are Irreversible. For only these acts are those over which she enjoys Ensuring Control. Second, only Non-Entailed acts are directly assessed, and Entailed acts are indirectly assessed, inheriting their deontic properties from the Non-Entailed acts that entail them.

To complete its enumerative task, an ethical theory needs to assign deontic properties to every member of every set of presently available actions for every agent. The formulation of Utilitarianism we use throughout the book, because it focuses on alternatives, is in this sense incomplete. But, with the clarifications made in this chapter, we are in a position to offer

> *Utilitarianism (complete formulation)*: An agent's Non-Entailed action has the property of being permissible if and only if (and because) the performance of any of her other Non-Entailed actions would not have brought about a complete state of affairs with a higher sum total of pleasure minus pain. An agent's Entailed action has the property of being permissible if and only if its performance is entailed by a permissible Non-Entailed action.

As its name suggest, this formulation of Utilitarianism accomplishes its enumerative task. For any Irreversible action, it is either Entailed or Non-Entailed. If the former, the theory assesses it directly. If the latter, the theory assesses it indirectly. In this way, it assigns deontic properties to every member of every set of presently available actions for every agent.

Yet are the arguments that have taken us to Only Irreversible Actions Are Available and Only Non-Entailed Acts Directly sound? One potential liability is their persistent reliance on Ensuring Control. As we've seen, Ensuring Control is Single Exercise. It precludes the possibility that you have control over an act at more than one time. But many will reject this claim. The motivation for this rejection is supplied by reflection on one's experience as an agent. It certainly seems, from one's own perspective, that control is not limited in the way Ensuring Control implies. It seems, for example, that an agent can now be required to perform an act later, even if she now is unable to ensure that she'll do so then. Consider

> Crosswalk. You are standing at the curb waiting for the light to change. Just ahead, a child tumbles into the busy intersection. Cars are approaching quickly, but you have plenty of time to rescue the child before she is hit.

Ensuring Control implies that, strictly speaking, the sentence, "You now ought to save the child," when uttered while you are standing at the curb, is false. For, at that time, you cannot save the child. To make the save you would have to perform a sequence of acts, and at that moment, you cannot ensure that you'll perform them all. At most, you can ensure that you perform the first in the sequence, <try to step off the curb> or perhaps <form the intention to save the child>. So if Ensuring Control is the correct sense of control for deontic assessment, then, standing at the curb, you don't face the requirement to save the child. But that seems like a mistake. It seems true, now, that you ought to save the child, even if at present you cannot ensure the performance of that act. If this is correct, then Ensuring Control is not the correct account of control for deontic assessment.

There are a number of alternatives to Ensuring Control that avoid this counterintuitive implication. One might hold that your control consists in the fact that the world where you save the child is accessible to you.[16] Or, that there is a sequence of decisions, which starts now, that you can take that ends with the child being saved.[17] Or that you can, now, form a schedule of intentions and then follow them till the child is saved.[18]

The question, of course, is how much stock we should put in the oddness of saying that, "You now ought to save the child" is false. After all, Ensuring Control is consistent with your being required to <form the intention to save the child>, being required to <try to step off the curb>, and so on, all the way till the child is saved.

---

16. This, roughly, is the account of control relevant to deontic assessment defended in Feldman (1986: 17–24).

17. This, roughly, is the account of control relevant to deontic assessment defended in Zimmerman (1996: 46–50).

18. This account of control is suggested by Ross (2012: 82). Timmerman (2015) offers an argument that depends on the truth of something like this account.

References

Bergström, L. 1966. *The Alternatives and Consequences of Actions*. Stockholm: Almqvist & Wiksell.
Brown, C. 2018. "Maximalism and the Structure of Acts." *Noûs* 52 (4): 753–71.
Castañeda, H-N. 1968. "A Problem for Utilitarianism." *Analysis* 28 (4): 141–42.
*Cohen, Y, and T. Timmerman. 2016. "Actualism Has Control Issues." *Journal of Ethics & Social Philosophy* 10 (3): 1–18.
Feldman, F. 1986. *Doing the Best We Can: An Essay in Informal Deontic Logic*. Dordrecht: D. Reidel.
*Goldman, H. S. 1978. "Doing the Best One Can." In *Values and Morals*, edited by A. I. Goldman and J. Kim, 185–214. Dordrecht: Dordrecht.
Gustafsson, J. E. 2014. "Combinative Consequentialism and the Problem of Act Versions." *Philosophical Studies* 167 (3): 585–96.
*Jackson, F., and R. Pargetter. 1986. "Oughts, Options, and Actualism." *The Philosophical Review* 95 (2): 233–55.
Lavin, D. 2004. "Practical Reason and the Possibility of Error." *Ethics* 114 (3): 424–57.
Pietroski, P. M. 2000. *Causing Actions*. Oxford: Oxford University Press.
Portmore, D. W. 2019. *Opting for the Best: Oughts and Options*. Oxford: Oxford University Press.
*Ross, J. 2012. "Actualism, Possibilism, and Beyond." In *Oxford Studies in Normative Ethics*, edited by M. Timmons, 74–96. Oxford: Oxford University Press.
Sobel, J. H. 1976. "Utilitarianism and Past and Future Mistakes." *Noûs* 10 (2): 195–219.
Timmerman, T. 2015. "Does Scrupulous Securitism Stand-Up to Scrutiny? Two Problems for Moral Securitism and How We Might Fix Them." *Philosophical Studies* 172 (6): 1509–28.
Zimmerman, M. J. 1996. *The Concept of Moral Obligation*. Cambridge: Cambridge University Press.

7

Individualism and Overdetermination

7.1 *Introduction*

Usually, we think that the acts of individuals, not the acts of groups, are subject to deontic assessment. What you do, and what I do, can be assessed as permissible or impermissible. But what we do together cannot. Of course, you might wonder if what we usually think is what we should think. And this brings us to the question we're concerned with in this chapter:

> Are deontic properties assigned exclusively to the acts performable by an individual agent?

Reflection on how the deontic assessment of the acts of individuals can cover the assessment of group acts lends support to answering in the negative.

The performance of certain acts, such as moving a piano, involves others. But when we discuss whether this act—our moving the piano—ought to be done, we appear to be using a convenient shorthand. We are not really discussing the deontic properties of the group acts. Rather we are assessing whether it's permissible for me to lift the right side, whether it's permissible for you to lift the left, and so on. The deontic assessment of our moving of the piano is, without remainder, fully covered by the assessment of the acts of each individual. Moreover, we are spatiotemporally distinct creatures. There is thus no agent who can ensure the performance of the compound act of <lifting the left side and lifting the right side>.[1] So, having assessed the acts of every individual, there's little motivation to assign deontic properties to the act of the group. This thought—that claims about what ought to be done are addressed solely to individuals—takes us to one of the members of the set of principles examined in this book that together imply Utilitarianism, namely:

> INDIVIDUALISM: An action possesses deontic properties if and only if, at some point, it is presently available to a single agent.

---

1. This point is due to Conee (2001: 430) and Smith (1986: 342). For more on why ensuring control is necessary for an action's possessing deontic properties, see §6.4.

Few deny that the acts of individuals are up for deontic assessment. Theories that accept Individualism—which we'll call Individualistic—go one step further to claim that only the acts of individuals are to be assessed. Deontic assessment is exhausted by the assessment of what agents do individually. In previous chapters, we've taken it for granted that Traditional Consequentialism accepts Individualism. We can now make this assumption explicit by referring to the view as Individualistic Consequentialism.

Despite its initial appeal, Individualistic Consequentialism faces a problem. In some circumstances, agents collectively bring about suboptimal states of affairs, yet, when each agent is assessed individually, none appears to have acted impermissibly. This is troubling. For if all agents individually comply with a theory yet collectively bring about a suboptimal outcome, then as a consequentialist theory it appears seriously defective. In this chapter, we'll develop this challenge to Individualistic Consequentialism and examine a response.

7.2 *Asteroid*

Individualistic Consequentialism, as you might expect, is well equipped to assess what agents do when acting alone. And, in many circumstances, it's equally capable of assessing what agents do together. However, cases involving cooperation can generate problems. Consider

> Asteroid. An asteroid is on a collision course with Earth. Without intervention, it will land in a playground and five children will die. Fortunately, there is a one-time opportunity to change its trajectory. At noon, Ms. Vertical can press, or refrain from pressing, a button marked "Move Down" and Mr. Horizontal can press, or refrain from pressing, a button marked "Move Over." If both simultaneously press their respective buttons, then the asteroid will miss Earth and no one will die. If only one of them presses, then the asteroid will crash into a school and twenty children will die. Both Ms. Vertical and Mr. Horizontal are fully informed and rational. Unfortunately, both freely choose to refrain from pressing. Moreover, if Ms. Vertical were to press her button, Mr. Horizontal would still freely refrain from pressing his. Similarly, if Mr. Horizontal were to press his button, Ms. Vertical would still freely refrain from pressing hers.[2]

It is worth walking through the details of this case. We can start by summarizing the available alternatives, their outcomes, and their evaluative rankings:

---

2. This case and Table 7.1 are modified from Regan (1980: 18–19).

Table 7.1: *Possibilities in Asteroid*

Presently Available Alternatives	Outcome	Ranking
Ms. Vertical presses; Mr. Horizontal presses	No one dies	Best
Ms. Vertical refrains; Mr. Horizontal refrains	5 children die	2nd Best
Ms. Vertical presses; Mr. Horizontal refrains	20 children die	Worst
Ms. Vertical refrains; Mr. Horizontal presses	20 children die	Worst

Clearly, what ought to happen, given the circumstances, is that each press their respective button. That would be best. But as the case is described, this is not what happens. Instead, both agents freely choose to refrain from pressing their buttons. The details are as displayed in Table 7.1.

Table 7.2: *Payoff Matrix for Asteroid*

		Mr. Horizontal	
		Refrains from pressing	Presses
Ms. Vertical	**Refrains from pressing**	2nd Best	Worst
	Presses	Worst	Best

Moreover, what would happen under different conditions is also stipulated. Put precisely, each agent is assumed to be

> *Intransigent*: An agent is intransigent in a given situation just when, if all others were to do their part in bringing about the best outcome collectively available, she would freely not do her part.[3]

Accordingly, if Mr. Horizontal were to press, Ms. Vertical would refrain. Similarly, if Ms. Vertical were to press, Mr. Horizontal would refrain.

What's interesting about Asteroid is its structure. We'll say of cases that share this structure that they involve

> *Second-Best Overdetermination*: Situations in which two Intransigent agents each perform an action sufficient to ensure a suboptimal outcome and, if any one agent were to instead perform the act individually needed to bring about the best outcome collectively available, the outcome would be even worse.

---

3. We borrow this term—Intransigent—and the formulation of its definition from Zimmerman (1996: ch. 9).

With a clear view of its structure, we can turn to the crucial features of the case.

There are two features of Asteroid worth making explicit. First, it seems obvious that some moral mistake has been made. Ms. Vertical and Mr. Horizontal together bring about the state of affairs that is second best—five children needlessly die. They could have easily done better. Both could have pressed their respective button; then, the asteroid would be diverted and everyone would be saved. Given that this outcome is so much better, and that it could have been brought about instead, it is very hard to accept that everything is morally as it should be. Second, it nonetheless appears that no individual agent—neither Ms. Vertical nor Mr. Horizontal—alone has acted impermissibly. Each one, individually, seems to be absolved by the other's Intransigence. To see this, consider what Mr. Horizontal ought to do. He can press or refrain. If he presses, Ms. Vertical will refrain, and the result is that twenty children die. This is the worst. We get the state of affairs in the northeast quadrant of the matrix in Table 7.1. If he refrains, Ms. Vertical also refrains, and the result is that five children die. This is second best. We get the state of affairs in the northwest quadrant. So, given Ms. Vertical's Intransigence, Mr. Horizontal ought to refrain. That's the best he, through his own actions, could do. Any other course of action will make things worse. Similar reasoning applies to Ms. Vertical. Given Mr. Horizontal's Intransigence, the best Ms. Vertical could do is refrain.

These two features of Second-Best Overdetermination cases, taken together, present a serious challenge for Individualistic Consequentialism. For, in these cases, it seems that something is morally amiss. But it also seems that no individual has acted impermissibly. In the next section, we'll develop this challenge.

7.3 Individualistic Consequentialism and the Principle of Moral Harmony

If Individualism is correct, only acts performed by individual agents can possess deontic properties. However, the possibility of cases like Asteroid suggests that this is mistaken. A deontic theory must go beyond the acts of individuals to evaluate what's done by a collection of agents. The argument for this conclusion proceeds from a very plausible thought about consequentialist theories, namely, that they must coordinate the actions of the compliant such that together they will bring about the best world available to them. This suggestion is regarded by many philosophers, both historical and contemporary, as imposing a minimal condition of adequacy for a consequentialist theory.[4] This idea is expressed in what is sometimes called the

---

4. For an overview, see Feldman (1980).

> *Principle of Moral Harmony*: A consequentialist theory must be such that the agents who satisfy it are guaranteed to bring about the best complete state of affairs collectively available to them.[5]

This principle seems very difficult for a consequentialist to deny. A theory concerned with bringing about the best should not allow the compliant to leave a better result unrealized. The path of permissible action must determinately direct those following it to the best outcome.

In the next two subsections, we will explain why it is thought that Individualistic Consequentialism violates the Principle of Moral Harmony. The argument, in preview, is this: Individualistic Consequentialism can be further specified as assessing voluntary acts only, or assessing both voluntary acts and some nonvoluntary acts. But, as we shall see, either specification appears unable to satisfy the Principle of Moral Harmony.

7.3.1 *The Argument That Volitional-Focused Individualistic Consequentialism Is Unharmonious*

We can start with the version of Individualistic Consequentialism that limits deontic assessment to those acts over which agents enjoy voluntary control. Voluntary control is the kind of control exercised when you do something at will, at the time of your choosing, and for whatever considerations you deem adequate. You exercise voluntary control, for example, when you utter a sentence, lift one end of a piano, or clap your hands. You can do these things whenever you want, for whatever reason, simply by deciding to do them. Let us call theories that focus exclusively on acts over which you exercise voluntary control

> *Volitional-Focused*: Theories that assign deontic properties to all and only voluntary acts.

By contrast, many other acts are nonvoluntary. For example, upon seeing water fall from the sky, you form the belief that it's raining. This act, because nonvoluntary, is not to be assessed on a Volitional-Focused theory.[6]

Our discussion of Asteroid thus far has assumed that Individualistic Consequentialism is Volitional-Focused. The voluntary acts available to Ms. Vertical and

---

5. This formulation is modified from Regan (1980: 6). As usually presented, this principle is thought to serve as a constraint on all deontic theories, not just consequentialist ones. On the face of it, however, this makes the Principle of Moral Harmony seem to imply that consequentialism is true. This implication can be avoided, but explaining the needed qualifications would take us too far afield. We'll thus stick to the narrower version of the principle. The needed qualifications for the wider version can be found in Portmore (2019: §1.1.5).

6. Our discussion of volitional control draws heavily on Portmore (2018: 325–27).

Mr. Horizontal are restricted to pressing or refraining from pressing their respective buttons. And, as we've seen, if we consider only those acts, and assess only what individuals do, we will be unable to identify any impermissible action. We get this result—that no one acts impermissibly—because both are Intransigent. Given this diagnosis of the problem, one may be tempted here to suggest that this Intransigence is itself impermissible. This is a sensible suggestion. But it will not do. For, as we will now show, being Intransigent is not something a Volitional-Focused theory can assess.

To say that someone is Intransigent is to make a counterfactual claim, that is, a claim about what would happen under conditions that don't actually obtain. For example, we say Ms. Vertical is Intransigent because if a certain thing happened—if Mr. Horizontal pressed his button—then she would act in a certain way. She would refrain from pressing hers. Importantly, being Intransigent does not involve any voluntary action. What makes it true that Ms. Vertical is Intransigent is her attitudes. She has a set of attitudes that dispose her to act in a certain way under certain conditions. The same is true of Mr. Horizontal. What, exactly, are these attitudes? It is a set of preferences, or a preference profile. A preference can be understood as a kind of disposition. To prefer one state of affairs over another just is to be disposed, given your background beliefs, to act in ways that bring about that state of affairs rather than the other. Thus, given that Ms. Vertical refrains when Mr. Horizontal refrains, she prefers the state of affairs in which five children die to that in which twenty children die. And given that she would still refrain if Mr. Horizontal presses, she prefers the state of affairs in which twenty children die to that in which everyone is saved. Putting these together, we can conclude that Ms. Vertical prefers the state of affairs in which five or twenty children die to that in which every child is saved. The same preferences can be attributed to Mr. Horizontal. This preference profile is what renders both Intransigent.

Yet neither Ms. Vertical and Mr. Horizontal, as normal human agents, enjoy voluntary control over their preferences. Preferences are not a kind of attitude that can be changed at will. For example, you cannot, at will, prefer being tortured tomorrow morning over sleeping in. Similarly, Mr. Horizontal and Ms. Vertical cannot, at will, prefer the state of affairs in which no child dies to those in which five or twenty children die. If this much is right, and preferences are beyond voluntary control, then the Intransigence of Mr. Horizontal and Ms. Vertical is ineligible for deontic assessment on a Volitional-Focused theory.

It appears, then, that we have a violation of the Principle of Moral Harmony. Although fully compliant with Individualistic Consequentialism—neither agent performs a voluntary act that's impermissible—Ms. Vertical and Mr. Horizontal fail to bring about the best state of affairs. This delivers

The Argument That Volitional-Focused Individualistic Consequentialism Is Unharmonious

1. Volitional-Focused Individualistic Consequentialism identifies no impermissible acts in Second-Best Overdetermination cases.
2. If Volitional-Focused Individualistic Consequentialism identifies no impermissible acts in Second-Best Overdetermination cases, then it violates the Principle of Moral Harmony.
3. Hence, Volitional-Focused Individualistic Consequentialism violates the Principle of Moral Harmony.

The only substantive claim is Premise 1. But its truth is demonstrated by reflection on cases like Asteroid. Individualistic Volitional-Focused theories thus violate the Principle of Moral Harmony.

7.3.2 *The Argument That Volitional-Rational-Focused Individualistic Consequentialism Is Unharmonious*

> *Individualism*: An action possesses deontic properties if and only if, at some point, it is presently available to a single agent.
>
> *Volitional-Focused*: Theories that assign deontic properties to all and only voluntary acts.
>
> *Second-Best Overdetermination*: Situations in which two Intransigent agents each perform an action sufficient to ensure a suboptimal outcome. And, if any one agent were to instead perform the act individually needed to bring about the best outcome collectively available, the outcome would be even worse.
>
> *Principle of Moral Harmony*: A consequentialist theory must be such that the agents who satisfy it are guaranteed to bring about the best complete state of affairs collectively available to them.

What seems morally troubling about Ms. Vertical and Mr. Horizontal is their Intransigence. Yet, because this is a matter of having certain attitudes, attitudes that are not under either's voluntary control, a Volitional-Focused theory cannot account for this defect. But an alternative is available. Consistent with Individualistic Consequentialism we may require that agents perform certain voluntary acts as well as certain nonvoluntary ones. This will allow us to claim that Ms. Vertical and Mr. Horizontal ought not to be Intransigent.

To be sure, most nonvoluntary events are not under your control. For example, you cannot directly cause your heart to beat or your food to be digested. Assuming that ought implies can, no plausible theory will require you to perform such acts. That said, there is a sense in which "You ought to cause your heart to beat" might be true. You can cause your heart to beat indirectly by, say, attaching a defibrillator. But, properly understood, this ought-statement is really telling you that you ought to do the thing over which you have voluntary control—like getting the defibrillator—to get your heart to beat. Since you cannot directly control whether your heart beats, you cannot be morally required to make it beat.

There is, however, a class of nonvoluntary acts that are under your direct control. We often make assertions about what people ought to do, and in many cases the acts in question are not under agents' voluntary control. Consider the following statements, which appear to assert legitimate requirements. "You ought to believe the conclusions of sound arguments," "You ought to desire to learn," "You ought not to fear bananas," and "You ought to admire Aristotle." These are not things over which you have voluntary control. You cannot form beliefs, desires, or fears at will. You cannot admire on command. Yet it seems obvious that you're required to do such things. In some cases, you ought to have certain attitudes, even if they are not under your voluntary control.[7]

These attitudes are distinctive in that they are responsive to reasons. For example, when you see raindrops on the window and hear the sound of rainfall on the roof, you have reason to believe that it's raining. And, if you take these reasons to be decisive, you directly form the belief that it's raining. You have freedom of thought because you possess the properties sufficient to reason about the evidence and your beliefs are responsive to this reasoning. Beliefs are under your rational control. They belong to the category of

> *Judgment-Sensitive Attitudes*: An attitude is judgment-sensitive if and only if it is one that a rational agent tends to have or lack in response to her taking there to be reasons for or against the attitude.[8]

Beliefs, desires, and fears are just a few examples. These mental states are to be contrasted with such states as being tired, irritable, or hungry. Being hungry is not sensitive to your judgments concerning the reasons there are for or against it. A friend, no matter how persuasive her reasoning, cannot talk you out of being hungry. But she can talk you out of your fear of bananas. She can do so by making apparent to you the reasons that they are innocuous. And that's because fear is a Judgment-Sensitive Attitude.

So, even if Judgment-Sensitive Attitudes are nonvoluntary, agents may be required to have them. We should thus expand the range of acts up for deontic assessment to include those over which we exercise rational control. Let us call such theories

> *Volitional-Rational-Focused*: Theories that assign deontic properties to voluntary acts and to acts over which agents have rational control.

If we accept such a theory we can claim that an agent acts impermissibly when she fails to believe what she ought to believe, fails to desire what she ought to desire, and, generally, fails to have the Judgment-Sensitive Attitudes she ought to have.[9]

Before we can understand how this proposal applies to Asteroid, we need to say a bit more about Judgment-Sensitive Attitudes. Such attitudes are responsive

---

7. This paragraph draws on Hieronymi (2006) and McHugh (2017).
8. This formulation is modified from Scanlon (1998: §1.2) and Portmore (2019: ch. 3).
9. Our discussion of rational control draws heavily on Portmore (2018: 325–27).

to reasons, but not just any reasons. An example may be instructive. Suppose you are offered the following deal. If you believe that you are made of glass you will be paid one million dollars. Now, on the face of it, this is an attractive offer. You have what seems to be a very strong reason to do what is virtually costless. But, sadly for your bank account, this fact—that you'd be paid—is not a reason for you to believe that you are made of glass. To see why, notice just how the promise of payment counts in favor of the belief. It is a reason for you to get yourself into a particular mental state, namely, the mental state of believing that you are made of glass. The promise of payment thus belongs in the category of

> *State-Given Reasons*: A reason is state-given if and only if it is a consideration that counts in favor or against holding a certain attitude in virtue of the state of affairs in which that attitude is held.

Crucially, Judgment-Sensitive Attitudes are not sensitive to State-Given Reasons. Why not? Because such reasons are not suitably related to the content of the attitude. In the case we're considering, the attitude is a belief, and its object is the proposition that you are made of glass. That you would be a million dollars richer is not evidence for this belief. No amount of money will make it true. State-Given Reasons are simply not relevant to the contents of beliefs. These considerations—such as being paid to be in a certain mental state of believing—cannot supply you with a reason to directly form a belief. The best you can do is try to indirectly acquire it. You might, for example, have yourself hypnotized or consume mind-altering drugs. But these are the doxastic equivalent of a defibrillator. You cannot, directly responding to State-Given Reasons, change your Judgment-Sensitive Attitudes.

By contrast, Judgment-Sensitive Attitudes are sensitive to

> *Object-Given Reasons*: A reason is object-given if and only if it is a consideration that counts in favor or against holding an attitude in virtue of the object or the content of that attitude.

Unfortunately, all of your Object-Given Reasons—those that bear on the truth of the proposition that you are made of glass—count against it. Consider the facts. You are a human. Humans are biological organisms composed of such things as blood, bones, and muscle. These things are not glass. These facts are relevant to the truth of the belief that you are made of glass, and they provide overwhelming reason to believe that it is false. Here you can exercise rational control, directly forming the belief that you are not made of glass, by responding to these Object-Given Reasons.[10]

---

10. Our discussion of Object-Given and State-Given reasons, including the formulation of the distinction, follows Parfit (2011: ch. 2.5, Appendix A).

Judgment-Sensitive Attitudes, such as desire, admiration, and fear, appear insensitive to State-Given Reasons. And this has an important implication for Volitional-Rational-Focused theories, namely:

> *No State Given*: The deontic status of having or lacking a Judgment-Sensitive Attitude in no way depends on State-Given Reasons.[11]

If you have decisive Object-Given Reasons to have a certain Judgment-Sensitive Attitude, no State-Given Reason, however powerful, can alter the fact that you ought to have this attitude. In this way, No State Given explains why a million-dollar reward does not, and cannot, make it the case that you ought to believe that you are made of glass.

With No State Given, we are now in a position to see precisely what Volitional-Rational-Focused Individualistic Consequentialism will require of agents in a case like Asteroid. And we can see that Ms. Vertical and Mr. Horizontal act impermissibly. The Judgment-Sensitive Attitude that's relevant is a preference. Stated generally, all agents must have the

> *Object-Given Preference Profile*: The preferences an agent has if she properly responds to all and only her Object-Given Reasons.

An agent properly responds to her reasons just when she forms the attitudes she has most reason to form. The Object-Given Preference Profile is thus the profile of preferences an agent would have if she had the preference ranking her Object-Given Reasons call for. But what would this preference ranking look like?

To arrive at more specific claims about the preferences agents ought to have, the relationship between states of affairs and Object-Given Reasons needs to be made explicit. And the least controversial idea to have about this is that the strength of one's Object-Given Reasons is directly proportional to the value of the state of affairs. We can call this

> *Object-Given Reasons to Prefer*: An agent has more Object-Given Reason to prefer one state of affairs, S_1, to another state of affairs, S_2, if and only if S_1 is better than S_2.

If an agent properly responds to her Object-Given Reasons, then she will prefer better states of affairs to worse ones. Now, comparing the outcomes available to the agents in Asteroid, we see that Ms. Vertical and Mr. Horizontal, if they have the Object-Given Preference Profile, ought to have the

---

11. This principle is inspired by Stratton-Lake (2005) and Portmore (2018: 335).

> *Preference for Saving the Children*: The state of affairs in which none of the children are killed is preferred to those in which five or twenty children are killed.

Yet, given their Intransigence, Ms. Vertical and Mr. Horizontal clearly lack this preference. This is inexcusable. Both agents are fully informed and rational. Because informed, they are aware of what will happen if they push or refrain. Because rational, they will take the necessary means to bring about, of those available, the state of affairs they most prefer. The only explanation of their both refraining is thus that Ms. Vertical and Mr. Horizontal, to put it bluntly, have the preferences of jerks. In particular, they each lack the Preference for Saving the Children. Volitional-Rational-Focused Individualistic Consequentialism can thus condemn each for lacking this preference. The Preference for Saving the Children is part of the Object-Given Preference Profile, and so lacking it is impermissible. By appealing to Judgment-Sensitive Attitudes, Volitional-Rational-Focused Individualistic Consequentialism can identify impermissible acts in Second-Best Overdetermination cases.

So far so good. But trouble is in the offing. To solve the problem in Asteroid we can require that Ms. Vertical and Mr. Horizontal have the Preference for Saving the Children. But this requirement will, in other cases, be a liability. For we can easily imagine cases in which having the required preference leads to disaster. Consider

> Mad Telepath. Things are just as described in Asteroid except that a mad telepath will kill 1,000 adults if either Ms. Vertical or Mr. Horizontal have the Preference for Saving the Children.[12]

This case is like Asteroid in one respect. The Object-Given Reasons that bear on the preferences Ms. Vertical and Mr. Horizontal ought to have are unchanged. They ought to have the Preference for Saving the Children. But, in another respect, the case is unlike Asteroid. Now, a mad telepath threatens to kill 1,000 adults if either has the required preference. This threat introduces overwhelming State-Given Reason for both agents to avoid having this preference. But, just as the promise of money cannot make you believe that you're made of glass, the mad telepath's threat cannot change what Ms. Vertical and Mr. Horizontal ought to prefer. They still ought to have the Preference for Saving the Children. The unfortunate result is that both agents, complying with the theory, will bring about a worse state of affairs than was available to them. Had they lacked the Preference for Saving the Children, the outcome would have been better.

The requirement that agents have certain Judgment-Sensitive Attitudes was invoked to address the problem caused by Intransigence in Asteroid. And, in that case, because agents ought to have the Preference for Saving the Children, we got

---

12. Modified from Regan (1980: 181).

the right result. But, in Mad Telepath, this preference is a problem. Volitional-Rational-Focused Individualistic Consequentialism, precisely because it requires agents to have certain Judgment-Sensitive Attitudes, can be made to violate the Principle of Moral Harmony.

We can now offer

The Argument That Volitional-Rational-Focused Individualistic Consequentialism Is Unharmonious

1. If Volitional-Rational-Focused Individualistic Consequentialism renders Intransigence impermissible, then it must require certain Judgment-Sensitive Attitudes.
2. No State Given is true.
3. If No State Given is true, then in certain cases (e.g., Mad Telepath) the agents who form the appropriate Judgment-Sensitive Attitudes will not bring about the best state of affairs collectively available to them.
4. Hence, Volitional-Rational-Focused Individualistic Consequentialism violates the Principle of Moral Harmony.

Premise 1 simply elaborates the view on offer. Premise 2 makes a plausible claim about the kinds of reasons that are relevant to Judgment-Sensitive Attitudes. A survey of examples lends it intuitive support. Premise 3 states a possibility that's demonstrated by reflection on cases like Mad Telepath. Thus, it seems that Volitional-Rational-Focused Individualistic Consequentialism violates the Principle of Moral Harmony.

> *Volitional-Rational-Focused*: Theories that assign deontic properties to voluntary acts and to acts over which agents have rational control.
>
> *Individualism*: An action possesses deontic properties if and only if, at some point, it is presently available to a single agent.
>
> *Intransigent*: An agent is intransigent in a given situation just when, if all others were to do their part in bringing about the best outcome collectively available, she would freely not do her part.
>
> *Judgment-Sensitive Attitudes*: An attitude is judgment-sensitive if and only if it is one that a rational agent tends to have or lack in response to her taking there to be reasons for or against the attitude.
>
> *No State Given*: The deontic status of having or lacking a Judgment-Sensitive Attitude in no way depends on State-Given Reasons.
>
> *Principle of Moral Harmony*: A consequentialist theory must be such that the agents who satisfy it are guaranteed to bring about the best complete state of affairs collectively available to them.

7.3.3 *The Principle of Moral Harmony Argument against Individualistic Consequentialism*

The previous two subsections support two important conclusions. First, if Individualistic Consequentialism is Volitional-Focused, it will violate the Principle of Moral Harmony in Second-Best Overdetermination cases. This result can be avoided by shifting to a Volitional-Rational-Focused theory that requires certain Judgment-Sensitive Attitudes. However, as demonstrated in Mad Telepath, this may lead to disaster. Insofar as the Principle of Moral Harmony places a condition of adequacy on any moral theory, Individualistic Consequentialism appears inadequate. We can now present

The Principle of Moral Harmony Argument against Individualistic Consequentialism

1. Individualistic Consequentialism is either Volitional-Focused or Volitional-Rational-Focused.
2. Volitional-Focused Individualistic Consequentialism violates the Principle of Moral Harmony in cases like Asteroid.
3. Volitional-Rational-Focused Individualistic Consequentialism violates the Principle of Moral Harmony in cases like Mad Telepath.
4. Hence, Individualistic Consequentialism violates the Principle of Moral Harmony.
5. If a consequentialist theory violates the Principle of Moral Harmony, it is false.
6. Hence, Individualistic Consequentialism is false.

> *Individualism*: An action possesses deontic properties if and only if, at some point, it is presently available to a single agent.
>
> *Volitional-Focused*: Theories that assign deontic properties to all and only voluntary acts.
>
> *Volitional-Rational-Focused*: Theories that assign deontic properties to voluntary acts and to acts over which agents have rational control.
>
> *Principle of Moral Harmony*: A consequentialist theory must be such that the agents who satisfy it are guaranteed to bring about the best complete state of affairs collectively available to them.

The argument relies on the Principle of Moral Harmony, as it features in Premise 5. But it seems that an adequate consequentialist theory must satisfy this principle. That leaves Premise 2 and Premise 3. Yet, both are supported by appeal to their implications in Asteroid and Mad Telepath. If a defense of Individualism is to be mounted, it will have to undermine one of these claims. In the next section, we suggest that the assertion of Premise 3 is most vulnerable.

7.4 *A Harmonious Form of Individualistic Consequentialism*

Volitional-Rational-Focused Individualistic Consequentialism is more promising than the foregoing suggests. The problem in Asteroid was solved by requiring that agents have certain Judgment-Sensitive Attitudes. This solution introduced a new problem. Because these preferences are determined exclusively by Object-Given Reasons, they may be required even when there is overwhelming State-Given Reason against them. This may lead to disaster. Yet, just as the first problem was solved by appealing to the Judgment-Sensitive Attitudes agents ought to have, perhaps the second problem can be solved in the same way. What's needed is for Volitional-Rational-Focused Individualistic Consequentialism to require agents to have the appropriate preferences in cases like Asteroid but also requires them to lack them in cases like Mad Telepath. We need the preferences agents are required to have to be in some way sensitive to both Object-Given and State-Given Reasons. If such a theory can be defended, then the Principle of Moral Harmony will no longer present a threat to Individualistic Consequentialism. In this section, we pursue this possibility.

In §7.4.1 we offer a challenge to No State Given. The argument highlights an important and overlooked difference between voluntary acts and Judgment-Sensitive Attitudes. Once this difference is noticed, and its implications appreciated, we discover that State-Given Reasons may bear on the Judgment-Sensitive Attitudes agents ought to have. This opens up the possibility of specifying the preferences agents ought to have in such a way that both Object-Given and State-Given Reasons matter.

In §7.4.2 we suggest that, not only is it possible for State-Given Reasons to move agents to withhold forming preferences but this is extremely common. Moreover, in many cases, withholding is what agents ought to do. We then spell out what this implies for the Judgment-Sensitive Attitudes agents ought to have. We arrive at an account that requires agents to have a preference profile that is sensitive to both Object-Given and State-Given Reasons. This is important. Recall why Volitional-Rational-Focused theories violated the Principle of Moral Harmony. The preferences required of agents become a liability when, in cases like Mad Telepath, powerful State-Given Reasons are introduced. Yet, if the preferences required of agents are influenced by State-Given Reasons—if such reasons properly move agents to withhold from forming certain preferences—then we have the makings of a solution to the problem presented by Mad Telepath.

Finally, in §7.4.3 we show how this revised account of the preferences agents ought to have delivers what we need for Volitional-Rational-Focused Individualistic Consequentialism to satisfy the Principle of Moral Harmony.

7.4.1 *The Pragmatic Encroachment Argument against No State Given*

No State Given makes a claim about all Judgment-Sensitive Attitudes, but we'll focus first on belief. This is a sensible starting point, as the case for No State Given appears strongest in this context. Much of the plausibility of No State Given may in fact be the result of generalizing from belief to all Judgment-Sensitive Attitudes. If rational belief formation can be influenced by State-Given Reasons, then it would come as no surprise if preferences were similarly influenced.

We begin with a note of caution. We have to take care when assessing Judgment-Sensitive Attitudes. It is tempting to treat them, for the purposes of deontic assessment, in the same way as we treat voluntary actions. There is, however, an important difference. Most voluntary actions are binary. You can murder or not murder. There's no third option. This has an important implication for deontic assessment. When it comes to most voluntary acts, the property of being permissible and the property of being required are duals.[13] An act is permissible if and only if its negation—refraining from this act—is not required. If murdering is not permissible, then you can conclude that refraining from murdering is required. By contrast, Judgment-Sensitive Attitudes are not binary. There is a third option. Take the proposition It is raining. You might believe that it is true, believe that it is false, or, withhold any belief about it (i.e., suspend judgment). That there are three options matters for deontic assessment. Thus, with attitudes, the inferences we can draw are more limited. If believing that some proposition is true is impermissible, we cannot immediately conclude that believing that it is false is required. If believing that some proposition is true is impermissible, then you ought not to believe it. However, there are two ways to do this. You can believe that it is false, or you can withhold belief. Thus, the property of being permissible and the property of being required are, for Judgment-Sensitive Attitudes, not duals.

Appreciating that Judgment-Sensitive Attitudes are not binary, and so their deontic properties not duals, casts the examples in the previous section—like getting paid a million dollars to believe you're made of glass—in a new light. We might grant that State-Given Reasons can't move you to believe that you're made of glass. They can't get you to form a new belief. But that doesn't deliver No State Given. To demonstrate the truth of that claim, it still needs to be shown that State-Given Reasons can't move you to withhold. And nothing said to this point impugns that possibility.

There is, in fact, a powerful consideration suggesting that State-Given Reasons do play a role in withholding belief. To begin, notice that there is an abundance of cases in which withholding belief concerning some proposition is what an agent ought to do. The exact number of hours Confucius spent writing is something you really ought to suspend judgment about. Yet Object-Given Reasons cannot be what delivers this intuitive verdict. For, in the case of a belief, Object-Given Reasons just are the evidence for or against a proposition's truth. These reasons cannot be reasons to withhold a belief, only to affirm or deny it. Here's Schroeder:

> Why is it that reasons to withhold cannot be evidence? It is because the evidence is exhausted by evidence which supports p and evidence which supports ~p. But the evidence which supports p is [Object-Given Reason] to believe p, and the evidence which supports ~p is [Object-Given Reason] to believe ~p. Consequently the reasons to withhold must come from somewhere else. So they cannot be evidence. (2012: 276)

The Object-Given Reasons for believing that it is raining are all the considerations that increase the likelihood that this proposition is true. The Object-Given

---

13. Our discussion here draws on McNamara (2014) and Schroeder (2018: 676–77).

Reasons for believing it is not raining are all the considerations that increase the likelihood that it's false. That exhausts the evidence, and so exhausts the Object-Given Reasons, concerning this proposition. There are no Object-Given Reasons left to count in favor of withholding. This, on reflection, should be unsurprising. Withholding has no object.

If Object-Given Reasons can't count in favor of withholding, what reasons can? The answer seems to be State-Given Reasons. This suggestion is lent credibility by what is called pragmatic encroachment. Consider this pair of cases:

> Low Stakes: You are driving past the bank on Friday. You had planned to stop and deposit your paycheck, but many people are waiting in line. You have plenty of funds in your account, so you won't need the money anytime soon. You recall the bank being open on Saturdays in the past. You think to yourself, "The bank will be open tomorrow. I'll just come back."

> High Stakes: You are driving past the bank on Friday. You had planned to stop and deposit your paycheck, but many people are waiting in line. Your account is nearly empty. If you don't make the deposit before Monday, you'll be kicked out of your home, your children will have to change schools, and you'll incur huge late fees on your credit card. You'll be in a blackhole of debt, from which you'll never escape. You recall the bank being open on Saturdays in the past. But you think to yourself, "I am not sure if the bank will be open tomorrow. I'll call to see."[14]

Intuitively, the difference in your reaction between the cases is perfectly reasonable. Your inner monologue in both cases is as it should be. In Low Stakes, you ought to believe the bank will be open tomorrow. In High Stakes, that would be a mistake. You ought to suspend judgment. What's interesting about this is that your evidence that the bank will be open is the same in both cases. Your Object-Given Reasons to believe is the same. Yet only in Low Stakes is this sufficient reason for you to believe. What sets the cases apart, and explains why our judgments about them differ, is that the possibility of disaster in High Stakes introduces very strong State-Given Reasons. This is an example of pragmatic encroachment. In High Stakes, if you are mistaken about when the bank is open, there is the possibility of a real disaster. This ramps up the standards for evidence to count as sufficient for belief. More evidence is required before it's permissible to believe in High Stakes that the bank will be open on Saturday.[15]

If this is the correct lesson to draw about High Stakes and Low Stakes, then State-Given Reasons can move you to withhold belief. This positions us to offer

---

14. These cases are modified from Stanley (2005: 3–5).
15. Our discussion of this case follows Schroeder (2012).

The Pragmatic Encroachment Argument against No State Given

1. If No State Given is true, then State-Given Reasons cannot influence the deontic status of having or lacking a Judgment-Sensitive Attitude.
2. State-Given Reasons can influence the deontic status of having or lacking a Judgment-Sensitive Attitude.
3. Hence, No State Given is false.

The argument hinges on Premise 2. That claim is supported by the difference between our intuitive judgments in High Stakes and Low Stakes. At least in the context of belief, State-Given Reasons do seem to influence the permissibility of holding a belief. No State Given is false.

> *No State Given*: The deontic status of having or lacking a Judgment-Sensitive Attitude in no way depends on State-Given Reasons.
>
> *State-Given Reasons*: A reason is state-given if and only if it is a consideration that counts in favor or against holding a certain attitude in virtue of the state of affairs in which that attitude is held.
>
> *Judgment-Sensitive Attitudes*: An attitude is judgment-sensitive if and only if it is one that a rational agent tends to have or lack in response to her taking there to be reasons for or against the attitude.

7.4.2 *The Preference Permissibility Argument against the Object-Given Preference Profile*

We just considered how State-Given Reasons might move you to withhold a belief. Yet, in the cases discussed, this influence is relatively limited. Your State-Given Reasons increased the strength of the Object-Given Reasons needed to permissibly believe that the bank is open on Saturday. However, State-Given Reasons, in the context of preference, have a much more expansive role. This, if correct, has important implications for the preferences agents ought to have. These preferences ought to be sensitive to both the Object-Given and State-Given Reasons in play. And this will provide a valuable resource to Volitional-Rational-Focused theories.

We should stress what may have been obvious from the outset. Judgment-Sensitive Attitudes are not a homogenous bunch. The two we've focused on, beliefs and preferences, are similar in some respects. For both, you exercise rational control in coming to have them by making a judgment about the reasons there are for or against them. There's a cognitive component. But in the case of belief, that judgment is about something cognitive, whereas in the case of a preference, that judgment is about something noncognitive. When you believe, you take things to be a certain way; it's like your mental picture of, say, your home. That's why we say belief-like attitudes are cognitive. They are about something: reality. Your beliefs about your home try to represent your home; and, if accurate, your beliefs are true. By contrast, when you desire, you want things to be a certain way; it's like your mental picture of your dream home. That's why preference-like attitudes are noncognitive. They are not about reality. They don't aim to represent how the world is. That is why your desire for your dream home endures in the face of the obvious fact that you don't live in it. Preferences thus are not the kind of things that can be true or false.[16]

To get a sense of why this difference between belief and preference matters, compare the following two utterances you might make:

> *Belief Judgment without Belief*: "There are decisive Object-Given Reasons to believe that it's raining, but I don't believe that it's raining."
>
> *Preference Judgment without Preference*: "There are decisive Object-Given Reasons to prefer to volunteer at the foodbank on Saturday rather than to sleep in, but I prefer to sleep in."

The first, Belief Judgment without Belief, is extremely odd. Your awareness that you have decisive Object-Given Reason to believe a proposition seems to issue almost automatically in belief. By contrast, the second, Preference Judgment without Preference, is perfectly ordinary. We can effortlessly imagine someone making a judgment about which of two states of affairs is better without thereby coming to have that preference. There is a very small gap between judging that one's Object-Given Reasons support a belief and having that belief. There is a significantly larger gap between judging that one's Object-Given Reasons support a preference and having that preference. The fact that beliefs and preferences differ in this way suggests that, while both are Judgment-Sensitive Attitudes, they may be responsive to reasons in quite different ways. In particular, we might predict that for preferences State-Given Reasons play a more significant role.

To be clear, the proposal under discussion casts State-Given Reasons in a modest role. It claims that such reasons may move you to withhold forming a preference. It does not claim that such reasons can move you to reverse a preference. If you have more Object-Given Reason to prefer sleeping in to being tortured, you cannot, on account of State-Given Reasons, reverse this preference—preferring torture to sleep. But it's one thing to be called to reverse a preference. It's another thing entirely to be called to withhold from forming one. The former asks you to do something you can't. But, as we shall see, withholding for State-Given Reasons is clearly something we are capable of. Indeed, it is so common, and so mundane, as to almost escape notice.[17]

The objects of preferences are states of affairs. For any two states of affairs you can prefer one to the other. And, because states of affairs can be both extremely fine-grained and complicated, the number of possible preferences you could hold

---

16. For more on the nature of beliefs and desires, see §3.5.
17. For how this might occur when an ethical theory is self-effacing, see §1.4.1.

is huge. To appreciate this, note that tomorrow you may shower for some length of time. Maybe it's five minutes. Maybe it's one or two or three seconds longer or shorter. Each variation represents a distinct state of affairs. In almost every case, even when the differences between these states of affairs are extremely slight, there will be Object-Given Reasons to prefer one over the other. And this is just the beginning. When thinking about states of affairs, we need not limit ourselves to those in which you exist. An asteroid could have destroyed Earth at the stroke of midnight in 1909. Or it could have come one or two or three seconds earlier or later. Each of these possibilities yields a different state of affairs. The number of possibilities, and so the number of states of affairs, is hard to fathom. Further, for any two states of affairs, you could prefer one to the other. The number of preferences you could form is astronomical.

Your mental resources, however, are limited. Forming and maintaining a preference comes at some cost. It takes time and mental energy. These costs present State-Given Reasons for you to withhold. Even while these reasons to withhold may be extremely weak—after all it doesn't take too long to form a preference—they are more than adequate to motivate withholding in a huge range of cases. This is because many possible preferences, if you bothered to form them, would make no difference to your life. The vast majority of preferences you could form would impose some small cost and confer no benefit. Notice also, in many of these cases of withholding there is no uncertainty about the relative merits of the states of affairs. You know that the state of affairs where you shower for five minutes tomorrow is better than the state of affairs where an asteroid destroys Earth in 1909. Still, you don't bother to form preferences concerning such states of affairs, not because you don't know which is preferable but because it's simply not worth it. In these cases, it seems that you do enjoy some level of rational control over withholding a preference. You do so by responding to your State-Given Reasons. And, importantly for our purposes, withholding in such circumstances appears to be exactly what you ought to do.

This result—that State-Given Reasons can move you to withhold forming a preference—has important implications. We need to reconsider how to assess preferences so as to account for this possibility. Previously, we assumed that it is permissible to have a certain preference if and only if you have most Object-Given Reason to have or lack that preference. But that assumption must be rejected if the preference profile required of agents is to take account of State-Given Reasons to withhold.

Of course, Object-Given Reasons still play the dominant role. Recall no challenge has been made to the initial result that an agent cannot, and so cannot be required to, engage in preference reversal for State-Given Reasons. If you are going to form a preference, it ought to be determined exclusively by Object-Given Reasons. When it comes to what you prefer, State-Given Reasons lack force. So we can continue to accept

> *Object-Given Impermissibility*: It is impermissible for an agent to prefer state of affairs, S_1, to state of affairs, S_2, if it is not the case that there is more Object-Given Reason to prefer S_1 to S_2.

This principle, in combination with Object-Given Reasons to Prefer, entails that it is impermissible for an agent to prefer S_1 to S_2, if the value of S_1 is equal to or less than that of S_2. Just as you ought not to believe a proposition if its truth is not better supported by the evidence than its falsity, it's impermissible to prefer one state of affairs to another if the former is not better than the latter. Crucially, this does not imply—because the deontic verdicts for preferences are not duals—that you are required to prefer one state of affairs to another if the former is better. You might be required to withhold from preferring.

What's added to the original account is sensitivity to State-Given Reasons to withhold. Here we're concerned, not with whether you should prefer one state of affairs over another but with whether you should be in the business of having a particular preference at all. The main idea is this. As long as the benefits of withholding a preference outweigh the costs of forming it, we can, and we ought to, withhold. From this we can draw two conclusions.

First, the strength of the State-Given Reasons needed to move you to withhold a preference is determined by the value of the state of affairs of withholding it compared to the value of the state of affairs of having it. We are thus led to

> *State-Given Reasons to Withhold*: An agent has more State-Given Reason to withhold from preferring one state of affairs, S_1, to another state of affairs, S_2, if and only if the state of affairs where she withholds from being in the mental state of preferring S_1 to S_2 is better than the state of affairs where she is in the mental state of preferring S_1 to S_2.

For example, Ms. Vertical and Mr. Horizontal, in Mad Telepath, have more State-Given Reason to withhold the Preference for Saving the Children than forming it. The state of affairs where they withhold, and the mad telepath does nothing, is better than the state of affairs where they form it and the mad telepath kills 1,000 adults.

Second, if being in the mental state of having a certain preference brings about a state of affairs that's worse than the state of affairs that would have come about had you withheld, then you ought not to form the preference. We are thus led to

> *State-Given Impermissibility*: It is impermissible for an agent to prefer one state of affairs, S_1, to another state of affairs, S_2, if there is more State-Given Reason to withhold from being in the mental state of preferring S_1 to S_2 than there is to be in this mental state.

Chapter 7: Individualism and Overdetermination

This principle, in combination with State-Given Reasons to Withhold, entails that it is impermissible for an agent to prefer one state of affairs, S_1, to another state of affairs, S_2, if the state of affairs where she is in the mental state of preferring S_1 to S_2 is worse than the state of affairs where she withholds from being in this mental state. For example, in Mad Telepath, it is impermissible for Ms. Vertical and Mr. Horizontal to form the Preference for Saving the Children because the outcome of forming it is worse than the outcome in which they withhold.

If you have a preference that violates neither Object-Given Impermissibility nor State-Given Impermissibility, then that preference is permissible. We can combine these two impermissibility principles to arrive at

> *Preference Permissibility*: It is permissible for an agent to prefer state of affairs, S_1, to state of affairs, S_2, if and only if (i) S_1 is better than S_2, and (ii) the state of affairs where the agent is in the mental state of preferring S_1 to S_2 is at least as good as the state of affairs where the agent withholds from being in this mental state.

If Preference Permissibility is correct, then there are two ways that you, by holding a preference, might act impermissibly. In violation of clause (i), you may prefer the outcome that is not decisively supported by Object-Given Reasons. Or, in violation of clause (ii), you may be in the mental state of holding a preference that you have less than most State-Given Reason to be in. But, if you avoid both violations, then you hold the preference permissibly.

We are now in a position to offer

The Preference Permissibility Argument against the Object-Given Preference Profile

1. Preference Permissibility is true.
2. If Preference Permissibility is true, then having the Object-Given Preference Profile may be impermissible.
3. Hence, having the Object-Given Preference Profile may be impermissible.

Preference Permissibility: It is permissible for an agent to prefer state of affairs, S_1, to state of affairs, S_2, if and only if (i) S_1 is better than S_2, and (ii) the state of affairs where the agent is in the mental state of preferring S_1 to S_2 is at least as good as the state of affairs where the agent withholds from being in this mental state.

Object-Given Preference Profile: The preferences an agent has if she properly responds to all and only her Object-Given Reasons.

The crux of the argument is Premise 1. While this claim is controversial, two observations lend support. First, as we saw above, we often justifiably withhold Judgment-Sensitive Attitudes, but Object-Given Reasons cannot explain why this is so. State-Given Reasons provide the needed explanation. Second, cases of withholding preferences are ubiquitous. We often withhold even when we know that one outcome is better than another. We do this when the benefit of having the preference isn't worth the cost of being in this state of mind. These considerations suggest the truth of Preference Permissibility. Premise 2 is easily seen to be true. Preference Permissibility requires sensitivity to State-Given Reasons, whereas the Object-Given Preference Profile requires insensitivity.

Having made the case for Preference Permissibility, we turn now, in the final subsection, to explain how this enables Volitional-Rational-Focused Individualistic Consequentialism to satisfy the Principle of Moral Harmony.

7.4.3 *The Argument That Volitional-Rational-Focused Individualistic Consequentialism Is Harmonious*

Consider first the verdicts Preference Permissibility delivers in Second-Best Overdetermination cases such as Asteroid. This is straightforward. The Object-Given Reasons for Ms. Vertical and Mr. Horizontal to form the Preference for Saving the Children are overwhelming. Yet, both are Intransigent. Both lack this preference. This, according to Preference Permissibility, is impermissible. If each did what they ought—they formed the Preference for Saving the Children—they'd bring about the best outcome collectively available. In this case, then, there is no violation of the Principle of Moral Harmony.

Now consider what Preference Permissibility implies in Mad Telepath. The mad telepath's threat supplies overwhelming State-Given Reasons for Ms. Vertical and Mr. Horizontal to withhold from forming the Preference for Saving the Children. If they form that preference, although none of the children will die, 1,000 adults will be killed. Clearly, they ought not to form that preference. This seems to be the correct result. But, to show that Individualistic Consequentialism can satisfy the Principle of Moral Harmony, we should answer two more questions. What will happen if both agents act permissibly? And will this be the best outcome collectively available?

What Ms. Vertical and Mr. Horizontal do depends on their preferences and beliefs.[18] Given the threat of the mad telepath, neither agent will have the Preference for Saving the Children. The available outcomes remaining involve the death of either five or twenty children. The Object-Given Reasons decisively favor the former. Both agents believe that this outcome can be brought about by refraining from pressing their respective buttons. Given their permissible preferences and their beliefs, both agents will refrain.

Is this the best outcome collectively available? The answer seems to be Yes. There is no better outcome the agents could bring about. It may be tempting to resist this claim. In particular, you may wonder why it is not possible for Ms. Vertical and Mr. Horizontal to withhold from the Preference for Saving the Children, yet both still push, thereby saving all of the children. A bodily action, as opposed to a mere bodily movement, is the product of a belief-preference pair. In order for

---

18. For more on the account of action this claim presupposes, see §3.5.

a pushing of a button to count as an act—something up for deontic assessment—the agents performing it must do so with a certain preference and a certain belief. Yet, the necessary preference is impermissible. If they had it, the mad telepath would be triggered and 1,000 adults would die.

In this respect, the case would not be importantly different if, in order to save 1,000 adults, Ms. Vertical and Mr. Horizontal had to put on handcuffs that prevented them from pushing their buttons. Given their options, they ought to put on the handcuffs. That's the best they can do. Similarly, in light of the mad telepath's threat, the best they can do is withhold from forming the Preference for Saving the Children. And, given the nature of action, this effectively eliminates the outcome in which both agents press. The mad telepath is the mental equivalent of handcuffs. In withholding from the necessary preference, both are prevented from moving their mind in such a way as to make themselves push the buttons. This is, nonetheless, the best they can do.

We can now offer

The Argument That Volitional-Rational-Focused Individualistic Consequentialism Is Harmonious

1. Preference Permissibility is true.
2. If Preference Permissibility is true, then it's possible for Volitional-Rational-Focused Individualistic Consequentialism to satisfy the Principle of Moral Harmony.
3. Hence, it's possible for Volitional-Rational-Focused Individualistic Consequentialism to satisfy the Principle of Moral Harmony.

Both premises are controversial. We've seen the argument for Premise 1 in the previous subsection. Premise 2 is supported by the implications of Preference Permissibility in Asteroid and Mad Telepath. These cases are designed to test whether a theory can satisfy the Principle of Moral Harmony. Though not dispositive, the fact that Preference Permissibility handles both well is a powerful indicator that a theory incorporating it does not violate the principle.

> *Preference Permissibility*: It is permissible for an agent to prefer state of affairs, S_1, to state of affairs, S_2, if and only if (i) S_1 is better than S_2, and (ii) the state of affairs where the agent is in the mental state of preferring S_1 to S_2 is at least as good as the state of affairs where the agent withholds from being in this mental state.
>
> *Individualism*: An action possesses deontic properties if and only if, at some point, it is presently available to a single agent.
>
> *Volitional-Rational-Focused*: Theories that assign deontic properties to voluntary acts and to acts over which agents have rational control.
>
> *Principle of Moral Harmony*: A consequentialist theory must be such that the agents who satisfy it are guaranteed to bring about the best complete state of affairs collectively available to them.

7.5 Conclusion

In this chapter, we took up a challenge to Individualistic Consequentialism that appeals to the Principle of Moral Harmony. Volitional-Focused Individualistic

Consequentialism violates this principle in Second-Best Overdetermination cases. As we diagnosed it, the problem in such cases is that the agents involved have objectionable preferences. Volitional-Rational-Focused Individualistic Consequentialism remedies this by requiring that agents have certain preferences. But this gave rise to the possibility, demonstrated in Mad Telepath, that the required preferences might themselves lead to an even worse outcome. In response, we investigated the plausibility of Preference Permissibility—a requirement on agents' preferences that is sensitive to State-Given Reasons. Understanding agents' requirements in this way allows for Individualistic Consequentialism to satisfy the Principle of Moral Harmony.

Which move in the argument is the weakest? The problem presented in Mad Telepath is solved by appeal to State-Given Impermissibility. This is a controversial claim. One way to see why this claim is so controversial is to note that the principle might require you to withhold a preference about a pair of outcomes even when one is far better than the other.[19] There's always the possibility that a mad telepath might threaten to destroy Earth unless you withhold from preferring every living person in bliss for a hundred years to every living person in utter agony for twice as long. Yet, when one outcome is so obviously preferable, is it plausible to believe, as State-Given Impermissibility might require, that you ought to withhold?

---

19. The idea that the best counterexamples come from spreading the value of the object of the preference as wide as possible is inspired by Parfit (2011: Appendix A).

References

Conee, E. 2001. "Review of Torbjörn Tännsjö's Hedonistic Utilitarianism." *The Philosophical Review* 110 (3): 428–30.
Feldman, F. 1980. "The Principle of Moral Harmony." *The Journal of Philosophy* 77 (3): 166–79.
*Hieronymi, P. 2006. "Controlling Attitudes." *Pacific Philosophical Quarterly* 87 (1): 45–74.
McHugh, C. 2017. "Attitudinal Control." *Synthese* 194 (8): 2745–62.
McNamara, P. 2014. "Deontic Logic." In *The Stanford Encyclopedia of Philosophy*, edited by E. N. Zalta. Available at https://plato.stanford.edu/archives/fall2018/entries/logic-deontic/.
Parfit, D. 2011. *On What Matters*. Vol. 1. Oxford: Oxford University Press.
*Portmore, D. W. 2018. "Maximalism and Moral Harmony." *Philosophy and Phenomenological Research* 96 (2): 318–41.
Portmore, D. W. 2019. *Opting for the Best: Oughts and Options*. Oxford: Oxford University Press.
*Regan, D. 1980. *Utilitarianism and Co-operation*. Oxford: Clarendon Press.

Scanlon, T. M. 1998. *What We Owe to Each Other*. Cambridge, MA: Harvard University Press.

Schroeder, M. 2012. "Stakes, Withholding, and Pragmatic Encroachment on Knowledge." *Philosophical Studies* 160 (2): 265–85.

Schroeder, M. 2018. "Normative Ethics and Metaethics." In *The Routledge Handbook of Metaethics*, edited by T. McPherson and D. Plunkett, 674–86. New York: Routledge.

Smith, H. M. 1986. "Moral Realism, Moral Conflict, and Compound Acts." *The Journal of Philosophy* 83 (6): 341–45.

Stanley, J. 2005. *Knowledge and Practical Interests*. Oxford: Oxford University Press.

Stratton-Lake, P. 2005. "How to Deal with Evil Demons: Comment on Rabinowicz and Rønnow-Rasmussen." *Ethics* 115 (4): 788–98.

Zimmerman, M. J. 1996. *The Concept of Moral Obligation*. Cambridge: Cambridge University Press.

PART III
Evaluative Principles

8

Hedonism and the Experience Machine

8.1 *Introduction*

Few would deny that pleasure is good-for, and pain is bad-for, those who experience it. If your life were exactly the same except it contained more pleasure, it would be better-for you.[1] And if it contained more pain, it would be worse. Clearly, pain and pleasure matter for one's welfare. But should we go further and say that they are all that matters? Here we've arrived at the question we're concerned with in this chapter:

> Does intrinsic personal value—welfare—consist exclusively in pleasure and pain?

It is tempting to answer Yes. While many different things may be thought to be good-for or bad-for you, all appear reducible to pleasure and pain. Asked why you exercise, you may answer, "Because being unhealthy is bad-for me." Asked why being unhealthy is bad-for you, you may answer, "Because it causes me pain and prevents me from experiencing pleasure." Asked why being pained is bad-for you, or why being pleased is good-for you, you will not know how to answer. Pain and pleasure are where the story ends. They are where the explanation gives out.[2]

This view—that only pain and pleasure ultimately matter for welfare—is known as hedonism. A flatfooted version holds that the extent to which a given pleasure or pain is good-for or bad-for you is proportional to its quantity. This takes us to one of the members of the set of principles examined in this book that together imply Utilitarianism, namely:

> QUANTITATIVE HEDONISM: One's welfare—one's well-being or ill-being—depends solely on one's experiences of pleasure and pain. The extent to which an experience of pleasure or pain is intrinsically good-for or bad-for the subject experiencing it is the product of its intensity times its duration.

---

1. For an overview of welfare, see §1.2.3.
2. This point is due to Hume (1983 [1751]: Appendix I).

This is a simple theory of welfare. Only pleasure is intrinsically good-for you. Only pain is intrinsically bad-for you. And the amount to which these experiences matter is determined entirely by their quantity.

Quantitative Hedonism is attractive in its simplicity. But this simplicity also leaves it vulnerable to a host of objections. For it is insensitive to a range of considerations that, intuitively, do bear on how well one's life goes. In what follows, we articulate and assess what may be the most forceful of these objections.

8.2 *The Experience Machine*

According to Quantitative Hedonism, only experiences of pleasure and pain influence one's welfare. For this reason, it qualifies as a mental state theory. Such theories hold that one's welfare entirely depends on what's in one's head. And it is precisely because of this exclusive focus on what's internal to the subject that mental state theories are thought objectionable. They tell us that lives that are identical in mental respects are necessarily identical in terms of welfare.

To see why this feature of mental state theories is thought problematic, consider first what many would regard as a good life, one whose subject undoubtedly has a high level of welfare:

> Real Life Saver. Having long dreamed of becoming a brain surgeon, Lili has achieved her goal. Her expertise qualifies her to undertake—successfully—operations that few would dare attempt. Lili takes pleasure in her work and in the knowledge that she has saved many lives and improved many more. When away from work, Lili spends time with her loving family. She has also managed, over the years, to cultivate and maintain a number of meaningful friendships.

Lili's life, by any measure, is good-for her. Exceptionally so. By contrast, consider

> Experience Machine. Things are as described in Real Life Saver except that Lili's experiences—while identical—are the product of a machine. She's never performed surgery. She's never saved anyone's life. She has no family and no friends. In reality, she's floating in a tank with electrodes attached to her brain.[3]

Here we're likely to evaluate Lili's welfare quite differently than we did in Real Life Saver. Something's missing. Her life in Experience Machine is a sham. She thinks her work is making the world a better place. She thinks that she has meaningful relationships and that she's accomplished so much. But none of this is true.

---

3. This sort of example was made famous by Nozick (1974: 42–43).

Her interaction with the world is limited to the electrical signals transmitted between her brain and the experience machine. She is profoundly mistaken about the nature of reality.

It's important, when thinking about this pair of cases, that we attend carefully to Lili's welfare and not be distracted by what's irrelevant. For example, it's true that in Real Life Saver lives are saved and meaningful friendships are maintained. In that case, Lili's life is undoubtedly instrumentally good-for others. This is not so in Experience Machine, where neither Lili's expertise nor companionship benefit anyone. Her life is not instrumentally good. So the cases are different. But these differences are not relevant to the central issue. What matters is Lili's welfare. We want to know if her life is as good-for her in Real Life Saver as it is in Experience Machine.

Even when attending only to Lili's welfare, and ignoring any instrumental value her life may have, we're likely to regard the cases quite differently. Lili's life in Experience Machine is worse-for her than in Real Life Saver. This is hard to deny. The intuition that supports this judgment is widely shared and not easily dislodged. But, as stipulated, in both cases her life is identical in mental respects. Evidently, mental states are not all that matter. Something beyond what's in Lili's head influences her welfare.

In the next section, we'll explain in more detail just how this case presents a formidable challenge to Quantitative Hedonism.

8.3 *The Argument from the Experience Machine*

In both Real Life Saver and Experience Machine, Lili's mental states are identical. What it's like for her, mentally, is exactly the same. The excitement of performing a challenging operation brings on the same rush of adrenaline whether the patient is real or the product of an experience machine. The sense of satisfaction she has at the end of the day is equally pleasant whether she's actually accomplished that day's goals or merely experienced accomplishing them. Lili's experiences of pleasure and pain are the same. Thus, if we think there's a difference in welfare in the two cases, we must think there's more to welfare than what's in the head. And, if this is right, then Quantitative Hedonism must be rejected.

We can present this reasoning more precisely. To do so it will be useful to introduce some terminology. As a mental state theory, Quantitative Hedonism holds that one's welfare bears a specific relation to one's mental states. Philosophers have a special term for talking about the kind of connection that's at issue:

> *Supervenience*: A kind of property X supervenes on another kind Y if and only if any two things that share all their Y properties must also share all their

X properties; it's impossible for a thing to change its X properties without changing its Y properties.[4]

For example, take the page of this book. On it, there are a bunch of letters organized in a particular way. Now suppose you compare this page to another one that is microphysically identical—its atomic composition is exactly the same. You would find that this duplicate features the same bunch of letters organized in the same way. This is because typeset properties supervene on microphysical properties. There can be no change in the former without a change in the latter.

With this terminology in place, we can now state a crucial commitment of mental state theories, like Quantitative Hedonism. Such views affirm

> *Mental State Supervenience*: A subject's welfare supervenes on her mind. Changes in a subject's welfare properties must involve changes in her mental properties.

This supervenience claim entails that Lili's level of welfare in Real Life Saver is the same as it is in Experience Machine. Because her mental states are identical, and because, according to Quantitative Hedonism, her welfare supervenes on her mental states, her welfare is identical. If Mental State Supervenience is false, then Quantitative Hedonism, as a mental state theory, is false.

We are now in a position to offer

The Argument from the Experience Machine

1. Lili's life is better-for her in Real Life Saver than in Experience Machine.
2. If Lili's life is better-for her in Real Life Saver than in Experience Machine, then Mental State Supervenience is false.
3. Hence, Mental State Supervenience is false.
4. If Mental State Supervenience is false, then Quantitative Hedonism is false.
5. Hence, Quantitative Hedonism is false.

> *Mental State Supervenience*: A subject's welfare supervenes on her mind. Changes in a subject's welfare properties must involve changes in her mental properties.
>
> *Quantitative Hedonism*: One's welfare—one's well-being or ill-being—depends solely on one's experiences of pleasure and pain. The extent to which an experience of pleasure or pain is intrinsically good-for or bad-for the subject experiencing it is the product of its intensity times its duration.

The only controversial claim is Premise 1. This premise is supported by our intuitive assessments of Lili's life. In Real Life Saver, Lili seems to enjoy greater welfare than she does in Experience Machine. If this premise is true, then we must reject Mental State Supervenience, and with it Quantitative Hedonism. In the next section, we examine the crucial claim of Mental State Supervenience in greater detail.

---

4. This definition is modified from McLaughlin and Bennett (2018).

8.4 *The Argument from Self-Supervenience to Mental State Supervenience*

Those who deny Mental State Supervenience point to the contrast between cases like Experience Machine and Real Life Saver for support. They think it's obvious that Lili's welfare differs between the cases. And they suggest the best explanation for this is that changes beyond one's mental states can be good-for or bad-for a person. On examination, however, it's far from clear that this explanation is correct.

To see why, consider just what one must accept to endorse it. We're interested in Lili's welfare, that is, how good Lili's life is for her. It's easy to see that her mental states bear on this question. It's much harder to see how anything beyond this could be relevant. Skepticism about the possibility of things beyond your mind bearing on your welfare doesn't require sophisticated philosophical argument. The motivating idea is expressed in the popular slogan: What you don't know can't hurt you. By contrast, if we reject Mental State Supervenience we're committed to something rather bold. Things utterly divorced from your mental life can make your life go better or worse-for you. If this is correct, the folk wisdom is wrong. What you don't know can hurt you.

Yet the case for Mental State Supervenience does not rest with folk wisdom. There is a powerful argument in its favor. The argument begins with a relatively uncontroversial observation: changes to a person's welfare must in some way involve changes to that person. After all, if we are to make a claim about someone's well-being or ill-being, we must be making a claim about that person's being. We might call this claim

> *Self-Supervenience*: A subject's welfare supervenes on her being. Changes in a subject's welfare properties must involve changes in her properties.[5]

To say that Lili's life is going well for her is to say that her life has some properties by virtue of which her welfare is high. And if her welfare decreases, this will be because her properties have changed. As Kagan writes:

> Your level of well-being is not a free-floating fact about you; it supervenes on various natural facts. You are well-off by virtue of the fact that the relevant natural facts obtain. But individual well-being is a state of the individual person. So ... differences in individual well-being must supervene on things that constitute differences in the individual person. (1992: 180)

Your welfare, unsurprisingly, supervenes on you. But what features about you, in particular, are relevant? We might begin answering this question by considering an extreme case: death. Are there changes you could undergo that would influence

---

5. This formulation is modified from Moore (2017).

your welfare after your death? There's reason for doubt. To see this, suppose you've written many novels over your life but never enjoyed the critical recognition you hoped for. Near the end of your life, you complete what will be your final book. Right before it hits the press, you die. The book is fantastic. You are posthumously awarded a Pulitzer Prize. It's now true of you, despite your death, that you won this very prestigious award. You have the property of being a winner of the Pulitzer Prize. Yet should we grant that this changes your welfare? If we are to say that it does, then we face something of a puzzle: When did the change occur? It didn't happen when the prize was awarded. At that time, you don't exist anymore. How could it make your life go better-for you? But we can't locate the improvement before your death either. You hadn't yet been awarded the prize. Indeed, the book was yet to be published. How could that which hadn't yet happened improve your life? In this kind of case, we can grant that the fact that you won the award is a fact about you. But we should deny that it is good-for you.[6]

So, changes to you after your death appear unable to change your welfare. A similar line of reasoning suggests that, when you are alive, changes in your nonintrinsic properties are also unable to change your welfare. This is due to the structure of these properties. The nonintrinsic properties you have (e.g., being a certain distance from the moon) are due to the relations you bear to other things. Because part of the relation is external to you, it's difficult to see how a change in this relation could redound to you in a way that could constitute a benefit or harm. To see why, think about an episode of welfare with some duration: a day in your life. Perhaps your day started off poorly, but things got better around noon, and your welfare remained high until you fell asleep. If we let the X-axis represent time, and the Y-axis represent welfare levels, your day might be plotted like Figure 8.1.

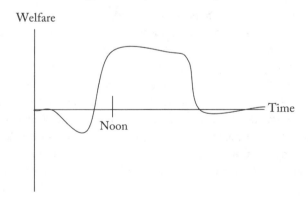

Figure 8.1: *Welfare across a Day*

---

6. The ideas in this paragraph draw on Bradley (2009: ch. 1).

At noon, you were benefited. But, to be made better-off at that specific time, your welfare must be tracking what's going on with you at that time.[7] Indeed, to track the moment-to-moment changes across the day, your welfare must be tracking features that hit close to home. Nonintrinsic properties seem incapable of this.

There is a dilemma facing any account claiming that changes in a subject's welfare properties involve changes in her nonintrinsic properties. Either this account requires a change in one's intrinsic properties at the time one's welfare changes, or it doesn't. Return to your benefiting at noon. If the theory doesn't require a change in your intrinsic properties at noon, then, since nothing internal to you changes, it is mysterious why your welfare changes at precisely noon. To be good-for you it must affect—be a change in—you at that time. If, however, the theory does require a change in your intrinsic properties at noon, then it seems your intrinsic properties are doing the real work. Appealing to nonintrinsic properties is superfluous. So, either it's mysterious how changes in your nonintrinsic properties could result in changes to your welfare at a specific time, or we can make sense of the change in your welfare at a time, but we need not invoke nonintrinsic properties. All of this is to suggest that Self-Supervenience is best understood as holding that a subject's welfare supervenes on her intrinsic properties.

This is not to deny that changes in one's nonintrinsic properties can have important consequences for one's welfare. Suppose through some windfall you become extremely wealthy. The fact that you are wealthy does not itself improve your welfare. It is not intrinsically good-for you. But it may be instrumentally good-for you. Perhaps upon discovering your newfound wealth you smiled and felt pleasure. These changes—having a smile on your face and being pleased—are changes in your intrinsic properties. They depend in no way on the relations you bear to anything else. Changes such as these—changes to your intrinsic properties—do redound to you in the right sort of way to account for the moment-to-moment changes in your welfare.

Now, if we accept Self-Supervenience and accept that your intrinsic properties are the ones that matter, the pressing question is this: What constitutes a change in one's intrinsic properties? One fairly uncontroversial answer is that a subject's intrinsic properties are exhausted by her mental and bodily properties. This claim is modest. It does not assert that a person is her mind and body. It asserts only that a person is not more than these things. Not only is this claim modest, it also provides a nice explanation of why a person's welfare changes over time as it does. Consider again Figure 8.1. The ups and downs in welfare you experience are the result of moment-to-moment changes in your mental and physical properties. When sleeping, your mental and physical properties are not changing much. Accordingly, your welfare line is flat. Then you wake up. You're tired, hungry, and dreading the commute to work. Your welfare line dips. Around noon you get

---

7. This point comes from Broome (2004: 101).

the promotion you've been hoping for. You're happy and feeling satisfied. Your welfare line soars up. In short, we can easily account for changes in welfare over time by looking to changes to your mental and physical properties during that period. For these reasons we might accept that a change in a person's intrinsic properties must be a change in her mind or body.[8]

From here, we're within reach of a significant claim. We noted that changes in nonintrinsic properties, like an increase in one's wealth, might indirectly influence one's welfare. Here we might say something similar about changes in one's bodily properties. Suppose you break a leg. Why might this decrease your welfare? The answer is obvious. If the injury is painful, or if it hampers your ability to make your way in the world, then it is bad-for you. Yet these changes—the pain you feel and the frustration of wearing a cast—are changes in your mental states. These changes, not the change in your leg, are what ultimately explain why your welfare decreases. We can also imagine changes in one's bodily properties that have no effect on one's welfare. Suppose, as before, you break a leg but this time the injury is caused and fully cured all while you were comatose. The fact that you broke your leg never makes its way into your experience. It is hard to see how this change in your bodily properties could have any effect on your welfare. What matters, ultimately, are changes in your mind. Changes in bodily properties matter only insofar as they result in changes to one's mental properties.

Here's where we are. Your welfare supervenes on you. Yet your welfare does not supervene on your nonintrinsic properties. Changes to your nonintrinsic properties matter only instrumentally. So your welfare supervenes on your intrinsic properties. Your intrinsic properties are exhausted by your mental and bodily properties. But your welfare does not supervene on your bodily properties. Changes to your bodily properties matter only instrumentally. Hence, changes in welfare must involve changes in your mental properties.

We now can forward

The Argument from Self-Supervenience to Mental State Supervenience

1. Self-Supervenience is true.

2. If Self-Supervenience is true, then a subject's welfare properties supervene on her intrinsic properties.

3. A subject's intrinsic properties are exhausted by her mental and bodily properties.

4. A subject's welfare properties do not supervene on her bodily properties.

5. Hence, Mental State Supervenience is true.

Self Supervenience: A subject's welfare supervenes on her being. Changes in a subject's welfare properties must involve changes in her properties.

Mental State Supervenience: A subject's welfare supervenes on her mind. Changes in a subject's welfare properties must involve changes in her mental properties.

---

8. This paragraph, and the argument in this section generally, follows Kagan (1992, 1994).

Each premise is substantive, but each is well supported. And, crucially, if the conclusion—the truth of Mental State Supervenience—is accepted, then we need to revise our judgment of Lili's welfare. Despite our initial assessment, it is not the case that Lili's life is better-for her in Real Life Saver than in Experience Machine. For Mental State Supervenience entails that, because her mental states are identical in both cases, so too is her welfare. The powerful intuition motivating the rejection of Quantitative Hedonism is mistaken.

8.5 *The Argument from Invariabilism and Monism to Hedonism*

Perhaps Mental State Supervenience is correct. What was thought to be hedonism's greatest liability is now seen to be a strength. This still leaves us some distance from hedonism. In the remainder, we will show how the gap might be closed.

In the previous section, we introduced Self-Supervenience, which holds that your welfare—what's intrinsically of value-for you—supervenes on you. We then argued that the properties relevant to welfare must be your intrinsic properties, in particular, your mental and bodily properties. Finally, by excluding your bodily properties, we shrunk the supervenience base down to your mental states. We can now, with a pair of additional claims, shrink the supervenience base down still further. If both are accepted, we're left with just one option: hedonism.

The first claim concerns the proper scope of a theory of welfare. Humans vary, but we don't need a different theory for each human. Rather, an explanation of what makes a life go well for the person living it should have application across all of the human species. We should accept

> *Human Invariabilism*: The same theory of welfare is true for every human welfare subject.

According to Human Invariabilism, the correct account of welfare applies to everyone for whom things can go better or worse—from neonatal infants to the elderly. Theories with lesser scope, those that apply only to one age group, for example, must be rejected.[9]

We can clarify Human Invariabilism by considering an instructive but ultimately unsuccessful challenge. A critic might reason as follows. Human Invariabilism purports to be a constraint on theories of welfare. If it is to be a plausible constraint, it should not straightaway exclude many otherwise very attractive theories. Yet it seems to do just this. To see how, consider a good like contemplation, which requires some degree of cognitive sophistication. Many nonobviously false theories say that contemplation increases your welfare. If Human Invariabilism is

---

9. For further defense of invariabilism, including discussion of the objection addressed in the following two paragraphs, see Lin (2018).

to accommodate such theories, then contemplation must be good, not just for you, but for everyone, even for infants. But that seems wrong. Contemplation is inaccessible to infants. If something is inaccessible to infants, then it cannot be good-for them. The only way to avoid this result, while hanging on to Human Invariabilism, is to deny that contemplation is a constituent of welfare. This amounts to excluding many attractive theories. As this critic presents it, Human Invariabilism is a controversial assertion about theories of welfare, not a modest constraint on them.

The critic's reasoning is predicated on a mistake. We should not accept that goods that are inaccessible to subjects are thereby excluded as being good-for them. Suppose in an accident you lost the ability to experience pleasure. Pleasure would then be inaccessible to you, just as contemplation is inaccessible to infants. Still, if we thought that pleasure was good-for you before the accident, we should not let your newly acquired inability change this. If you were to experience pleasure, it would still be good-for you. There is no important difference between your inability and a miserable person who never happens to experience pleasure in her life. For both subjects, pleasure, if it were to be experienced, would be personally good. We should thus not exclude pleasure as a constituent of your welfare simply because you're not capable of experiencing it. We can say similar things about infants and contemplation. That good may be inaccessible to them, but that does not preclude it from being good-for them.

With a clearer idea of what Human Invariabilism claims, we're now in a position to see another reason to accept it. It's parsimonious. Suppose you're in the hospital with a broken leg. You're in a lot of pain. This is bad-for you. Down the hall is an infant, who also has a broken leg. She's in a lot of pain. This is bad-for her. It's reasonable to think that the same explanation for how these injuries decrease welfare applies to you both. You both have broken legs and you both are in pain. Yet, if we reject Human Invariabilism, then, despite the obvious similarities between the two of you, we require two separate theories. We rely on one theory to explain why your welfare is lower and rely on another to explain why the infant's is lowered. This is excessive. We should not multiply theories of welfare beyond necessity.

Though modest, Human Invariabilism, once combined with Mental State Supervenience, delivers an important result. There must be at least one primitive mental state that's good-for people and at least one primitive mental state that's bad-for people. The reasoning is simple. Human welfare subjects have wildly different capacities. A life can go better or worse-for neonates and the elderly, for the severely intellectually disabled and those without disability. Given Human Invariabilism, we need a theory that applies to all such subjects. And, given Mental State Supervenience, this constituent of welfare must be a mental state. All subjects, even the least sophisticated, must be guaranteed to have it to ensure that things can be better or worse-for them. Thus at least some constituents of welfare will be a primitive mental state shared by all subjects.

What mental state, common to all of humanity, could play this role? One overwhelmingly plausible candidate is experiences of pleasure and pain. For the list of mental states common to all human beings is very limited. And once we remove those that don't influence welfare, we seem left with only pleasant and painful experiences. Thus, if Mental State Supervenience and Human Invariabilism are true, then we should include pleasure and pain as constituents of welfare. Hedonism is at least part of the story.

Let us then assume that pleasure is intrinsically good-for you and pain intrinsically bad-for you. This, to be clear, does not exclude anything else as possibly contributing to welfare. It merely shows that one thing will be included: hedonic experiences. To capture the fact that humans at all stages of development are at nonzero welfare levels, we need this much.

We can now turn to our second claim about welfare. This claim concerns whether there is just one kind of thing that is intrinsically good (or bad) for people or if there is more than one. There are many theories of welfare, but all can be classified as either accepting or rejecting

> *Welfare Monism*: There is only one type of thing that is intrinsically good-for welfare subjects and only one type of thing that is intrinsically bad-for welfare subjects.

This claim holds that well-being is limited to one thing, and so too for ill-being. Monistic theories offer a unified approach to people's welfare. Other theories are pluralistic. They claim that there is more than one type of thing that is of intrinsic personal goodness (or badness).

We should start by heading off a potential misunderstanding. A commitment to monism is fully compatible with the apparent diversity of activities that make a life like Lili's good-for its subject. Obviously, Lili undergoes many varied experiences. The pleasure of completing an especially complex operation differs from that of carrying on a long conversation with a close friend. The pain of working long hours is different from the pain of grabbing the wrong end of the scalpel. But all of the things that influence her well-being are of the same kind. They are all pleasant experiences. And all of the things that influence her ill-being are of the same kind. They are all painful experiences. By contrast, some explanations of Lili's welfare are pluralistic. They hold that at least two distinct things are intrinsically good-for her. For example, one may claim that Lili's welfare is high because she experiences pleasure, possesses important knowledge, has many significant achievements, and participates in valuable human relationships. On such a pluralistic view, none of these distinct goods can be reduced to any other. Each good makes its own unique contribution to her welfare.

Why accept Welfare Monism? One initial consideration is simplicity. All else equal, the simpler the theory the better. If we have two equally positioned theories, one monistic the other not, then we have reason to favor the monistic theory. Of course, all else might not be equal. Simplicity only takes us so far. But, by building on Mental State Supervenience, we can mount a defense of Welfare Monism.

Notice, in accepting Mental State Supervenience, a range of pluralistic views are ruled out. For example, among the goods included in the pluralistic view just mentioned were knowledge, achievement, and relationships. These are typical. Pluralism is often thought attractive precisely because it accounts for the purported significance of such goods. But, given that these goods do not supervene on one's mental states, they are ruled out by Mental State Supervenience. Forms of pluralism that posit them are no longer contenders. Also, as noted, once Human Invariabilism is accepted, we know that pleasure and pain must be a constituent of welfare. We've thus narrowed the field of alternatives to Welfare Monism considerably.

The only remaining rivals are forms of pluralism that include pleasure (or pain) as a constituent and posit some additional goods (or bads) compatible with Mental State Supervenience. If one is to reject Welfare Monism, one of these alternatives must be accepted. But marshaling support for such views, as we will show, is especially difficult. What's distinctive about these theories is that they must count pleasure as a constituent of welfare and hold that there are some additional goods (or bads), distinct from pleasure (or pain), but that also supervene on mental states. The trouble facing such theories can be put in the form of a dilemma. Either the goods these theories posit always involve pleasure, or they do not. If a theory claims that they do always involve pleasure, then it is undermotivated. If a theory denies that these additional goods always involve pleasure, then it will have implausible implications.

Consider first a pluralistic theory that posits goods that do not always involve pleasure. If one's welfare really is a product of these various goods, then even if one's life is lacking one of them, if their life includes many others to an extreme degree, one may still enjoy a high level of welfare. In this way a deficiency in one good can be compensated for by a surplus in another. While this may seem plausible in some cases, we should not accept that such compensation is possible. Pleasure appears to be a necessary component of a life good-for its subject. For example, consider a theory that held that pleasure and contemplation are intrinsically good-for you. On this proposal these two things are independently welfare enhancing. This implies that a life could be extremely good, without any pleasure, if extremely high in contemplation. This seems mistaken. As Feldman writes:

> Suppose I dutifully go about [contemplating]. After a tedious and exhausting period of training ... I find the whole thing utterly unsatisfying. The pluralist now tells me that my life is going well for me. I dispute it. I think I might be better-off intellectually ... but my welfare is, if anything, going downhill. (2004: 19)

Pleasure, it seems, is indispensable to being well-off. No other goods, in any amount, can compensate for its absence. Yet pluralistic theories that include at least one good that is not pleasure involving must deny the indispensability of pleasure.[10]

Suppose instead that a theory posits only goods that are always pleasure involving but insists that these goods are plural. For example, consider a theory holding that aesthetic experiences are intrinsically good-for you and that part of what it is to experience beauty is to find something pleasant. To qualify as pluralist, the proponent of such a theory maintains that these are in fact two distinct goods. This position does not have immediately detectable defects. Still, it's not one that enjoys much in the way of support. Any case we might cite as an instance of an aesthetic experience raising your welfare will also be a case of a pleasure experience raising your welfare.

The standard way of testing if something is intrinsically good-for you involves walling off other goods and then seeing if variation in the purported good leads to a variation in welfare. But the theory under consideration holds that pleasure and welfare covary and holds that experiencing beauty always involves pleasure. Obviously enough, then, experiencing beauty and changes in welfare will covary. We cannot wall off pleasure. So we cannot tell whether it's the experience of beauty or just the pleasure that's doing the real work. The standard test thus cannot support this sort of pluralist view.

There is, however, a second way we might seek to support this pluralistic alternative to Welfare Monism. We can look to differences in the magnitude of changes in welfare each theory predicts. The problem is that we are not terribly adept at making such fine-grained judgments. To see this, compare two ways Lili, plugged into the experience machine, might have spent her twenty-fifth birthday. In both versions, Lili's experience contains exactly the same amount of pleasure and pain. In the first version, she spends the afternoon at an art museum featuring some of her favorite works. She experiences much beauty. On the pluralist theory we've been discussing, Lili's life is made intrinsically better in two respects. It contains more pleasure and more experiences of beauty. In the second version, Lili spends the afternoon relaxing in an ugly old warehouse with friends. Despite the drab environment, it was a pleasant outing. According to the theory, her life was made intrinsically better in only one respect. It contains more pleasure. So, if this theory is correct, then we should judge that the life with the virtual trip to the museum is better than the life with the virtual day at the warehouse. After all, both contained the same amount of pleasure, but the trip to the museum furnished additional experiences of beauty.

---

10. For further defense of the thought that pluralism wrongly implies that pleasure is indispensable for a life high in welfare, see Crisp (2006: ch. 4).

While it's clear what the theory predicts about these cases, it's not at all clear that these predictions are accurate. Our intuitions about these cases are simply not sufficiently discriminating to reliably reveal the subtle differences in welfare predicted. It's doubtful you think one of these versions of Lili's birthday is better-for her than the other. And, even if you do, it's doubtful that any such a judgment is reliable. The upshot is that we lack evidence for pluralistic theories that include only goods that are always pleasure involving. The presence of pleasure, and the difficulty of tracking magnitude changes, leaves such theories with minimal support.

We are now in a position to forward

The Argument from Invariabilism and Monism to Hedonism

1. If Mental State Supervenience and Human Invariabilism are true, then pleasure and pain are constituents of welfare.
2. Mental State Supervenience and Human Invariabilism are true.
3. Hence, pleasure and pain are constituents of welfare.
4. If pleasure and pain are constituents of welfare and Welfare Monism is true, then pleasure and pain are the only constituents of welfare.
5. Welfare Monism is true.
6. Hence, pleasure and pain are the only constituents of welfare.

> *Mental State Supervenience*: A subject's welfare supervenes on her mind. Changes in a subject's welfare properties must involve changes in her mental properties.
>
> *Human Invariabilism*: The same theory of welfare is true for every human welfare subject.
>
> *Welfare Monism*: There is only one type of thing that is intrinsically good-for welfare subjects and only one type of thing that is intrinsically bad-for welfare subjects.

Human Invariabilism is supported by the thought that we should not multiply theories beyond necessity. If the preceding arguments are sound, the only rivals to Welfare Monism are views that posit additional goods (or bads) beside pleasure (or pain) that can satisfy Mental State Supervenience. But such theories face a dilemma. If the additional goods and bads posited don't involve pleasure, then the theory delivers implausible results. If the goods and bads do involve pleasure, then the theory makes predictions that are difficult to reliably test. Either way, these alternatives to Welfare Monism appear to lack adequate support.

8.6 *Conclusion*

In this chapter, we've tried to show how the Argument from the Experience Machine might be resisted. Along the way, we've made a number of arguments on behalf of Quantitative Hedonism. Which is the weakest?

There's a case to be made that it's the argument for Mental State Supervenience. This argument relies on the claim that changes in your welfare must involve changes in your intrinsic properties. While there is some reason to believe this claim, there's also a powerful consideration against it. If a person's welfare supervenes on her intrinsic properties, then much of our ordinary thinking about welfare is deeply mistaken. To see why, notice what this supervenience relation implies. As Nagel writes:

> It means that even if a man is betrayed by his friends, ridiculed behind his back, and despised by people who treat him politely to his face, none of it can be counted as a misfortune for him so long as he does not suffer as a result. It means that a man is not injured if his wishes are ignored by the executor of his will, or if, after his death, the belief becomes current that all the literary works on which his fame rests were really written by his brother, who died in Mexico at the age of twenty-eight. (1970: 76)

We regularly cite examples of people's lives being made worse off by things that influence only nonintrinsic properties. What these examples make clear is that the restriction to intrinsic properties is highly revisionary. If we're unwilling to accept that undiscovered libel, deception, posthumous mistreatment, and the like make no difference to your life, then we must accept that nonintrinsic properties do influence your welfare.

The question now, of course, is whether an account that embraces nonintrinsic properties can be maintained. To be viable, it would require a principled way to distinguish between those nonintrinsic properties that matter and those that don't. It is, however, no easy task to extend welfare beyond what's in your head without overreaching.

References

*Bradley, B. 2009. *Well-Being and Death*. Oxford: Oxford University Press.
Broome, J. 2004. *Weighing Lives*. Oxford: Oxford University Press.
*Crisp, R. 2006. *Reasons and the Good*. Oxford: Oxford University Press.
Feldman, F. 2004. *Pleasure and the Good Life*. Oxford: Oxford University Press.
Hume, D. 1983 [1751]. *An Enquiry Concerning the Principles of Morals*. Indianapolis: Hackett.
*Kagan, S. 1992. "The Limits of Well-Being." *Social Philosophy and Policy* 9 (2): 169–89.
Kagan, S. 1994. "Me and My Life." *Proceedings of the Aristotelian Society* 94: 309–24.
Lin, E. 2018. "Welfare Invariabilism." *Ethics* 128 (2): 320–45.

McLaughlin, B, and K. Bennett. 2018. "Supervenience." In *The Stanford Encyclopedia of Philosophy*, edited by E. N. Zalta. Available at https://plato.stanford.edu/archives/win2018/entries/supervenience/.

Moore, A. 2017. "Objectivism about Animal and Alien Well-Being." *Analysis* 77 (2): 328–36.

Nagel, T. 1970. "Death." *Noûs* 4 (1): 73–80.

Nozick, R. 1974. *Anarchy, State, and Utopia*. New York: Basic Books.

9

Welfarism and Sadistic Pleasure

9.1 *Introduction*

There are two importantly different senses of intrinsic value.[1] We might say, for example, that pleasure is intrinsically good-for the person who is pleased. Here we are making a claim about personal value; pleasure makes a life better-for the person living it. But we might also say that pleasure is just plain intrinsically good. Here we're making a claim about impersonal value; pleasure makes the world a better place. A pleasant experience is good-simpliciter. Yet to what extent are these two notions connected? Do things that have the property of being good-for you also have the property of being good-simpliciter? We've arrived at the question we're concerned with in this chapter:

> Do only states of affairs with the property of being personally valuable have the property of being impersonally valuable?

Reason to answer in the affirmative is supplied by the remarkable coincidence between welfare and basic value. When something is good-for someone (e.g., pleasure), it usually is also basically good. When something is bad-for someone (e.g., pain), it usually is also basically bad. Moreover, when we imagine a complete state of affairs devoid of all creatures for whom things can go better or worse, it seems we are imagining a world in which nothing is good-simpliciter or bad-simpliciter. Ugly rock formations or beautiful sunsets, when no one is around, are of no evaluative significance. Desolate states of affairs are ones in which nothing matters.[2] Generalizing these observations, we arrive at one of the members of the set of principles examined in this book that together imply Utilitarianism, namely:

> WELFARISM: All and only episodes of welfare are of basic value. All and only episodes of well-being are basically good. All and only episodes of ill-being are basically bad.

Welfarism tells us impersonal value runs in lockstep with personal value. Something is a basic good if and only if it is intrinsically good-for someone. And

---

1. For more on these two senses of value, see §1.2.3.
2. This point is suggested by Sidgwick (1907: I.IX.4).

something is a basic bad if and only if it is intrinsically bad-for someone. This connection offers an attractive way of understanding the relationship between the notions of good-for and good-simpliciter.

Despite its apparent merits, Welfarism faces a powerful objection. If one accepts Welfarism, one must accept that well-being is always basically good, no matter the context. But, for many, context matters. In what follows, we present and evaluate the most powerful version of this objection.

9.2 *Sadistic Pleasure*

Most agree that pleasure is well-being enhancing. If you are pleased by success at work, that's good-for you. Many will also agree that your being pleased by success at work is good-simpliciter. But not all episodes of pleasure are in this way innocent. Consider

> Sadistic Pleasure. Every day after work, Sid sits down to watch videos of people suffering. The pain of others brings Sid tremendous pleasure. The more painful the experiences, the more intense Sid's pleasure.[3]

Set aside concerns about the subjects of these videos. Their suffering is certainly bad. Instead, focus only on Sid. Even with this narrow focus, something is unsettling. Unlike being pleased by a job well done, Sid's pleasure is brought on by the suffering of others. Intuitively, this pleasure is not an unadulterated good. It's in some way deficient. This intuition is widely shared and persistent. It thus makes it very hard to accept that Sadistic Pleasure is

> *All Good*: Sid's sadistic pleasure is good-for Sid, it is good-simpliciter, and is in no way bad-simpliciter.

All Good is particularly unintuitive. Even if we haven't identified precisely what is troubling about the case, we may still be confident that there is a problem.

Our reluctance to accept All Good runs deep. It is not just the shallow thought that Sid is a jerk, and All Good fails to capture that. The worry, rather, is that an evaluative theory that yields this result verges on schizophrenic. The feelings and attitudes that Sid has toward what is bad-simpliciter seem, by the lights of this very theory, mistaken, inappropriate, and incongruous. Rather than being pained by what is bad and being pleased by what is good, Sid is pleased by what is bad and pained by what is good. To accept that Sadistic Pleasure is All Good, one must endorse an evaluative theory that violates what we'll call the

---

3. This example is modified from Chisholm (1968).

> *Principle of Evaluative Congruity*: An evaluative theory must not be such that it's entirely intrinsically good-simpliciter when what's good-for someone is directly produced by what's intrinsically bad-simpliciter.

Theories that satisfy the Principle of Evaluative Congruity are free from a certain defect. Such theories deny that it is entirely intrinsically good-simpliciter when someone's well-being is directly produced by what's bad-simpliciter. This principle underwrites the intuition that All Good is a mistake.[4]

We should take care to clarify exactly what the Principle of Evaluative Congruity asserts and to distinguish it from other less attractive claims. To this end, we highlight two ways in which the principle is qualified. First, to say that something is *entirely* intrinsically good-simpliciter is to both assert that it is good-simpliciter and to deny that it also gives rise to some other bad-simpliciter. If, for example, Sid's pleasure is entirely good-simpliciter, then it is not also bad-simpliciter that it is pleasure taken in the pain of others. That's what the "entirely" does in this formulation. Second, it matters crucially that the thing that is good-for someone is the *direct* result—and not a random byproduct—of what's bad-simpliciter. To see what this amounts to, contrast Sid's pleasure with an unproblematic case. It is quite common that when one's well-being is enhanced another's is diminished. If you beat a friend at a board game, the pleasure you take in winning might be good-for you, and her losing, because it pains her, bad-for her. But in this case your well-being is not directly produced by what is bad-simpliciter—your friend's ill-being. What pleases you is your victory. Her loss is a necessary condition for that, and some pain will likely accompany her defeat, but you relish the win, not her disappointment. Her pain is involved in what contributes to your well-being, but only indirectly. Cases such as this are perfectly ordinary and give rise to no special concern. By contrast, Sid's case is concerning. What's good-for Sid is directly what's bad-for others. Sid is pleased, not merely by the depiction of pain and suffering but by actual pain and suffering. Sid does not enjoy what's portrayed in horror movies. He enjoys what's bad-for others. If Sid discovered that those featured in his videos suffered in no way but instead were very happy actors, he would be pained.

As a matter of intuitive judgment, Sadistic Pleasure is not All Good. The Principle of Evaluative Congruity offers an account of why this is so. All Good, however, follows from a pair of the principles considered in this book. Utilitarianism violates the Principle of Evaluative Congruity. In the next section, we'll explain how.

9.3 *The Argument from Sadistic Pleasure*

Two of the principles explored in this book imply the truth of All Good. We can start with

---

4. The ideas in this paragraph draw on Olson (2004: §3.2).

> QUANTITATIVE HEDONISM: One's welfare—one's well-being or ill-being—depends solely on one's experiences of pleasure and pain. The extent to which an experience of pleasure or pain is intrinsically good-for or bad-for the subject experiencing it is the product of its intensity times its duration.

Quantitative Hedonism tells us that Sid's welfare can be enhanced if and only if he experiences pleasure. Sid's sadistic pleasures are accordingly good-for him. How good they are for him is determined by how intense they are and how long they last. Since it is very intense, the pleasure he takes in the suffering of others is very good-for him.

The next step on our way to All Good comes from the principle that is the focus of this chapter, namely, Welfarism. We can usefully decompose Welfarism into two claims. First, it asserts a sufficient condition for something to qualify as good-simpliciter or bad-simpliciter, namely, that it is good-for someone or bad-for someone. Second, it asserts a necessary condition for something to qualify as good-simpliciter or bad-simpliciter, namely, that it is good-for someone or bad-for someone. This has two corresponding implications for our assessment of Sadistic Pleasure. First, given the sufficient condition, insofar as Sid's pleasure is good-for Sid, it's also good-simpliciter. What's good-simpliciter is simply a matter of what's good-for people. So, Sid's pleasure is good-simpliciter. Second, given the necessary condition, there are no other sources of intrinsic goodness or badness apart from well-being and ill-being. There is thus no intrinsic bad introduced by Sid's unsettling psychology.

Quantitative Hedonism entails that Sid's pleasant experiences are good-for him. Welfarism entails that they are also good-simpliciter and precludes the possibility that any intrinsic bad has been introduced. Thus, if one accepts these two principles, one must accept All Good. And, as we have seen, if a theory implies All Good, then it violates the Principle of Evaluative Congruity.

We are now in a position to articulate

The Argument from Sadistic Pleasure

1. If Quantitative Hedonism and Welfarism are both true, then the Principle of Evaluative Congruity is false.
2. The Principle of Evaluative Congruity is true.
3. Hence, either Quantitative Hedonism or Welfarism is false.

> *Quantitative Hedonism*: One's welfare—one's well-being or ill-being—depends solely on one's experiences of pleasure and pain. The extent to which an experience of pleasure or pain is intrinsically good-for or bad-for the subject experiencing it is the product of its intensity times its duration.
>
> *Welfarism*: All and only episodes of welfare are of basic value. All and only episodes of well-being are basically good. All and only episodes of ill-being are basically bad.
>
> *Principle of Evaluative Congruity*: An evaluative theory must not be such that it's entirely intrinsically good-simpliciter when what's good-for someone is directly produced by what's intrinsically bad-simpliciter.

The truth of Premise 1 is seen by reflection on what Quantitative Hedonism and Welfarism imply in Sadistic Pleasure. Premise 2 is supported by our intuitive judgment that something is amiss in Sadistic Pleasure and that the best explanation of what's amiss is captured by the Principle of Evaluative Congruity. We are thus under pressure to abandon one or both of these principles. In the next section, we'll suggest that Sadistic Pleasure is best understood as targeting Welfarism.

9.4 *The Well-Being in Ill-Being Argument against Welfarism*

We've seen that Quantitative Hedonism and Welfarism entail that Sadistic Pleasure is All Good. But what's troubling about the case isn't the account of welfare that's been assumed. We need not accept Quantitative Hedonism to deliver similar violations of the Principle of Evaluative Congruity. Instead we need only to accept a theory of welfare that countenances the possibility of

> *Well-Being in Ill-Being*: What's good-for someone is directly produced by what's bad-for someone.

Although accounts of welfare differ, most will admit the possibility of Well-Being in Ill-Being.

To see this, notice that, while Sadistic Pleasure centers on Sid's pleasure in other's pain, we could easily modify the case to accommodate alternatives to Quantitative Hedonism. For example, one prominent welfare theory holds that well-being consists in the satisfaction of one's desires, while ill-being consists in one's desires going unsatisfied. To show that such a theory permits Well-Being in Ill-Being we need only suppose that Sid desires that the desires of others go unsatisfied. On this view, when others' desires go unsatisfied this satisfies Sid's desires. Their ill-being is his well-being. What's troubling about Sadistic Pleasure, and permits Well-Being in Ill-Being, is its structure. The details can be adjusted as needed. We could, for example, revise the case so that Sid desires, loves, hopes for others getting what they are averse to, hate, and hope against. Or we could say that Sid is pleased, delighted, satisfied by the thought of others being pained, depressed, and dissatisfied. Given the case's flexibility, nearly all subjective accounts of welfare—where what's good- or bad-for someone depends on her psychology—can be shown to accept the possibility of Well-Being in Ill-Being. Even objective theories of welfare are vulnerable. Consider another prominent account, the objective list theory. This view holds that well-being consists in the possession of various objective goods (e.g., friendship, knowledge, beauty, and achievement), while ill-being consists in lacking these goods or the possession of various objective bads (e.g., betrayal, ignorance, ugliness, and failure). Yet nearly all objective lists include some of the psychological items just mentioned (e.g., pleasure and pain). And this inclusion is all that's needed to arrive at Well-Being in Ill-Being.

Many theories of welfare, not just Quantitative Hedonism, permit Well-Being in Ill-Being. If any of these theories is combined with a commitment to Welfarism, then, under certain conditions, it will violate the Principle of Evaluative Congruity. This is because, in accepting Welfarism, one accepts that all and only what is good-for someone is good-simpliciter, and all and only what's bad-for someone is bad-simpliciter. And hence, any instance of Well-Being in Ill-Being will be an instance in which something that's entirely good-simpliciter is directly produced by what's bad-simpliciter.

The Argument from Sadistic Pleasure can now be understood as targeting Welfarism. We can forward

The Well-Being in Ill-Being Argument against Welfarism

1. If Well-Being in Ill-Being and Welfarism are both true, then the Principle of Evaluative Congruity is false.
2. The Principle of Evaluative Congruity is true.
3. Hence, either Well-Being in Ill-Being or Welfarism is false.
4. Well-Being in Ill-Being is true.
5. Hence, Welfarism is false.

Well-Being in Ill-Being: What's good-for someone is directly produced by what's bad-for someone.

Welfarism: All and only episodes of welfare are of basic value. All and only episodes of well-being are basically good. All and only episodes of ill-being are basically bad.

Principle of Evaluative Congruity: An evaluative theory must not be such that it's entirely intrinsically good-simpliciter when what's good-for someone is directly produced by what's intrinsically bad-simpliciter.

We can grant the truth of Premise 1 and Premise 4. Thus, if we are to resist the conclusion, we must deny Premise 2. We must hold that the Principle of Evaluative Congruity, despite appearances, is false. How might this be accomplished?

We can start by noting that if Well-Being in Ill-Being is true, there are only two ways to satisfy the Principle of Evaluative Congruity in cases like Sadistic Pleasure. We could either show

Not Good: Sid's sadistic pleasure is in no way good-simpliciter.

Or, we could show

Some Bad: Sid's sadistic pleasure is in some way bad-simpliciter.

In the next two sections, we will examine both possibilities. At least one must be defensible if the Principle of Evaluative Congruity is to remain credible.

Before moving on, we should note that we'll be sticking with the case of Sadistic Pleasure. So we'll continue using pleasure as an example of something that is good-for someone. This will help retain the focus on the version of Utilitarianism explored in this book. We should stress, however, that the arguments to come could be modified to accommodate different accounts of welfare.

9.5 *The Intrinsic Goodness Argument against Not Good*

One way to vindicate the Principle of Evaluative Congruity, and to reveal the falsity of All Good, is to show that Sadistic Pleasure is Not Good. If this view is shown to be correct, then, although Sid's pleasure is good-for him, it fails to qualify as good-simpliciter. But it is important to note that Not Good can take two forms. On the first, more extreme version, one denies that pleasure, or any other constituent of well-being, is ever intrinsically good-simpliciter. This is a bold claim. To accept it one must believe that any pleasure, even the most innocent sort, lacks intrinsic goodness. This strains credulity. As Nagel writes, "That pleasure is impersonally good and pain impersonally bad are propositions that one really needs reasons to doubt rather than reasons to believe" (1986: 162). In the absence of reasons to doubt the goodness of pleasure, we should reject the extreme version of Not Good. On the second, less extreme version of Not Good one holds that what is good-for people is often, but not always, good-simpliciter. In some cases what is good-for someone is precluded from qualifying as good-simpliciter. And Sid's pleasure is a case in point. We shall focus on this more plausible version of Not Good.

On this less extreme alternative, we arrive at Not Good via the

> *Conditional View*: Something can be basically good (or bad) in certain circumstances but not basically good (or bad) in other circumstances.[5]

By adopting the Conditional View, we are able to secure the intuitively correct verdict in Sadistic Pleasure. Sid's pleasure is good-for him but it is not good-simpliciter. Because his pleasure is the direct product of what's bad-simpliciter, it fails to meet the necessary conditions to qualify as good-simpliciter. This view is also able to say the right thing about ordinary cases of innocent pleasure. When you take pleasure in a job well done, this is good-for you. It is also good-simpliciter. Your pleasure, but not Sid's, qualifies as basically good. The Conditional View allows us to satisfy the Principle of Evaluative Congruity by embracing the less extreme version of Not Good.

To accept this less extreme version of Not Good is to deny Welfarism. According to Welfarism, all episodes of well-being are basic goods. According to Not Good, only certain episodes of well-being are basic goods. That is, the Conditional

---

5. For defense of the Conditional View, see Hurka (1998). For criticism, see Bradley (2002).

View allows the defender of Not Good to deny Welfarism's sufficient condition, namely, if something is an episode of well-being, then it is good-simpliciter. While this denial enables one to say the seemingly correct things about Sadistic Pleasure, problems loom.

The Conditional View makes an assertion about intrinsic goods that, on inspection, appears to be in conflict with their very nature. If the Conditional View is true, then something, such as pleasure, can be intrinsically good under some circumstances but not under others. The innocent pleasure you take in a job well done qualifies, but Sid's sadistic pleasure, given its source, does not. It is, however, not clear how the goodness of an intrinsic good could be conditional in this way. Reflection on the very notion of intrinsic goodness seems to preclude such a possibility.

For something to be intrinsically good is for it to be good in itself, independent of its relations to other things. This idea is captured by Moore, who characterizes intrinsic goodness as follows: "To say that a kind of value is 'intrinsic' means merely that the question whether a thing possesses it, and in what degree it possesses it, depends solely on the intrinsic nature of the thing in question" (1951: 260). On this suggestion, a thing's being intrinsically valuable is a matter of its having a certain intrinsic nature. We can think of a thing's intrinsic nature as its intrinsic properties. Some things, like agony, do not depend for their badness on anything else. Such things are intrinsically bad. Even if something good came from it, the agony itself would still be intrinsically bad. The badness of the agony supervenes on its intrinsic properties.[6]

This understanding of intrinsic value supplies us with a test. Contemplate a purportedly valuable state of affairs, *as such*. As Chisholm explains, "as such" stresses that this is to be the "contemplation of just that state of affairs as distinguished, for example, from the contemplation of some wider state of affairs which one may think that the given state of affairs brings along with it" (1981: 100). This isolates the purported good.[7] We can then ask: Under these conditions, does the thing retain its value? If Yes, it is intrinsically valuable. If No, it's not. Now consider a five-dollar bill. By contemplating it in isolation we see that it lacks any property worth calling good. It's just a rectangular piece of paper with some numbers, letters, and a face on it. By contrast, by contemplating an episode of pleasure in isolation—setting aside what it causes or what it's caused by—we see that it would still be good.

These remarks about the nature of intrinsic goodness bear directly on the plausibility of the Conditional View. They reveal that intrinsic goodness cannot be conditional in the way suggested. Here again is Moore:

---

6. For more on supervenience, see §8.3.
7. Lemos (1994: 10–11) calls this "intentional isolationism."

> It is impossible for what is strictly one and the same thing to possess that kind of value at one time, or in one set of circumstances, and not to possess it at another; and equally impossible for it to possess it in one degree at one time, or in one set of circumstances, and to possess it in a different degree at another, or in a different set. (1951: 260–61)

What has intrinsic value in any circumstance has intrinsic value in every circumstance. And this delivers the

> *Unconditional View*: If something is basically good (or bad) in any circumstance, then that thing is basically good (or bad) in all circumstances.

Pleasure is clearly intrinsically good. It is good in isolation. We are thus licensed to infer from the fact that any pleasure is good that all pleasure is good.

The Unconditional View rules out the interpretation of Sadistic Pleasure offered by the less extreme version of Not Good. Sid derives pleasure from others' pain. And, of course, this pain is intrinsically bad-simpliciter. But the cause of Sid's pleasure is not among its intrinsic properties. So if we admit that the innocent pleasure you take in a job well done is itself good—it's good in isolation—then we must also admit that Sid's pleasure is itself good. Both pleasures must be good-simpliciter, since, as a matter of its intrinsic properties, the pleasure itself is exactly alike in both cases. In short, if the Unconditional View is true, then, to accept Not Good, we must implausibly accept that no pleasure is good.[8]

We are now in a position to offer

The Intrinsic Goodness Argument against Not Good

1. If the Unconditional View is true, then the Conditional View is false.
2. The Unconditional View is true.
3. Hence, the Conditional View is false.
4. If the Conditional View is false, then Not Good is false.
5. Hence, Not Good is false.

> *Unconditional View*: If something is basically good (or bad) in any circumstance, then that thing is basically good (or bad) in all circumstances.
>
> *Conditional View*: Something can be basically good (or bad) in certain circumstances but not basically good (or bad) in other circumstances.
>
> *Not Good*: Sid's sadistic pleasure is in no way good-simpliciter.

This argument hinges on Premise 2 and Premise 4. And the case for both is strong. Premise 2 is supported by reflection on the nature of intrinsic goodness. Since the intrinsic properties of pleasure qualify it as good-simpliciter—pleasure is good in isolation—pleasure under any conditions is good-simpliciter. Premise 4 is also well supported. What made Not Good plausible was

---

8. The presentation of this argument draws on Rachels (2004) and Cullity (2019).

the possibility that pleasure is good-simpliciter most of the time, but not always. And sadistic pleasure is a case when it is not good. On examination, however, this appears untenable. If the pleasure of some innocent pleasure is intrinsically good, then the pleasure of Sid's sadistic pleasure is too.

If the above argument is sound, we must reject Not Good. We should grant that Sid's pleasure is itself good-simpliciter. Thus, if the Principle of Evaluative Congruity is true, only one possibility remains. Sadistic Pleasure must give rise to Some Bad. We turn now to assess this view.

9.6 *The Argument from Innocuous Sadism*

Another way to vindicate the Principle of Evaluative Congruity is to show that Sadistic Pleasure introduces Some Bad. On this proposal one need not deny that Sid's pleasure is good-for Sid or that it's good-simpliciter. Rather one points to Sid's sadism as the troubling feature of the case. The suggestion here is that it is bad-simpliciter when what's good-for someone (e.g., Sid's pleasure) is directly produced by what's intrinsically bad-simpliciter (e.g., the pain of others). This suggestion seems to properly diagnose that Sid is, for lack of a better term, messed up. He's vicious. He's pleased by what's bad-simpliciter: the pain of others. And it is bad-simpliciter to be vicious in this way. The attractive idea motivating Some Bad is captured by Brentano, who writes, "Pleasure in the bad is, as pleasure, something that is good, but at the same time, as an incorrect emotion, it is something that is bad" (1969: 90). It is bad to hold a positive evaluative attitude toward what's bad.[9] Such unfitting attitudes are themselves intrinsically bad-simpliciter.[10]

As with Not Good, to accept Some Bad amounts to a denial of Welfarism. According to Welfarism, only episodes of ill-being are basic goods. According to Some Bad, something other than ill-being—Sid's sadism—is a basic bad. That is, Some Bad, by holding that unfitting attitudes are bad-simpliciter, denies one of Welfarism's necessary conditions, namely, that only if something is an episode of ill-being is it bad-simpliciter. In adopting this view, one is able to reject All Good and so satisfy the Principle of Evaluative Congruity. But, as before, problems loom.

Return to the Unconditional View. If something is bad-simpliciter in any circumstance, then it is bad-simpliciter in every circumstance. This claim is supported by reflection on the nature of intrinsic badness. If this is correct, and if Sid's sadism is bad-simpliciter in Sadistic Pleasures, then sadism must be bad-simpliciter in every circumstance. But is sadism always bad?

In answering this question, it will help to consider

---

9. For an extended defense of this position, see Hurka (2001).
10. For more on unfitting attitudes, see §1.4.1 and §7.4.

> Innocuous Sadism. Ying is a renowned Army doctor who has saved countless lives by performing lifesaving surgeries on combatants injured in battle. Due to the severity of the injuries she treats, Ying often must begin operating before anesthetics have kicked in. Her initial incisions thus cause her patients unavoidable pain. Early in her career Ying was distressed by this pain. But one day, inexplicably, she ceased to be upset by it. Rather, it caused her mild pleasure. Ying also has a highly compartmentalized psychology. She only feels pleasure witnessing pain in these very specific circumstances. This change in Ying has thus had no repercussions for her life or the lives of those around her.

Ying, under these special conditions, takes pleasure in others' pain. We can grant that this feature of her psychology is unfitting. It's fitting to be pained by what's bad and pleased by what's good. This much let us simply assume. For both Welfarism and Some Bad imply that she has unfitting attitudes toward pain. Both hold that pain is bad-simpliciter. But Some Bad goes on to make a further claim about Ying's response. It insists that it is intrinsically bad-simpliciter that Ying has these unfitting responses. But should we accept this further claim?

There are two salient features of Innocuous Sadism that seem relevant to determining whether having these unfitting attitudes is itself bad. First, the pain that pleases Ying is unavoidable. She inevitably encounters it in the course of her work. She does not seek it out. Second, Ying's sadism has no negative consequences. It hasn't changed her behavior at all. She continues to excel at her job and continues to be distressed by pain in any other context. Given these two features—that the pain is unavoidable and that her emotional response has had no negative consequences—it's not at all clear that Ying's sadism is bad-simpliciter.

Think for a moment about why it might be bad to have an unfitting response to what's bad-simpliciter. The natural answer is that the proper response to bad things is to prevent or extinguish them, while the proper response to good things is to promote or preserve them. That is, our psychological makeup should be such that we welcome goods and avoid bads. Someone who's psychologically reversed—welcoming bads and avoiding goods—is vicious. And it is bad to be vicious in this way because, obviously enough, such viciousness—assuming the person is not entirely inept at making the world fit her mind—leads to more bads and less goods. The good of having fitting or appropriate attitudes is thus intimately linked to our role as beings capable of bring about goods and bads. If one is disposed to promote and preserve what's bad and to prevent and extinguish what's good, then one is likely to bring about bad states of affairs. But if this is the full answer as to why viciousness is bad (or such virtue is good), then an agent's unfitting attitudes (or fitting attitudes) are merely instrumentally bad (or good). They are not themselves of intrinsic impersonal value. Their value depends on their role in agents' motivational sets, and the value of these sets in turn depends on the fact that agents can make the world better or worse overall.[11]

To see if this is indeed the full answer, imagine a world where the usual link between psychological responses and the promotion or prevention of intrinsic impersonal value is severed. Suppose, for example, that our world is just as it is except that a handful of evaluative spectators are watching our activities. These spectators are capable of forming fitting and unfitting attitudes in response to the states of affairs they observe. Yet they have no agential involvement. If they are pained by pain of those they watch, nothing else happens. If they are pleased by the pain of those they watch, nothing else happens. What should we say about the value of these spectators' attitudes? Are their unfitting attitudes themselves bad? The answer seems to be No. Insofar as the spectators make no difference to the world they watch, the fittingness of their attitudes appears to be evaluatively neutral. This suggests that our answer above as to why it might be bad to have an unfitting response was the full answer. It's bad because of what agents with unfitting attitudes bring about. The bad of having unfitting attitudes is merely instrumental.

We have suggested that neither Ying's sadism nor the sadism of evaluative spectators is intrinsically bad. Rather their unfitting attitudes are merely instrumentally bad. If this is correct, then, by appeal to the Unconditional View, we may conclude that sadism, in all instances, is not bad-simpliciter. And so we may reject Some Bad. We should, however, pause here to acknowledge that some may still be reluctant to accept this conclusion. The feeling that there's something bad about taking pleasure in others' pain can be hard to shake. And what is to prevent someone from invoking the Unconditional View to instead argue from Sid's troubling emotional response in Sadistic Pleasure to the conclusion that all instances of sadism are intrinsically bad? Sadistic Pleasure and Innocuous Sadism elicit conflicting intuitive judgments. Why should we regard Innocuous Sadism as the more credible?

In reply, we should recognize that our intuitive judgments about Sadistic Pleasure are liable to lead us astray. In drawing conclusions about such cases, we're vulnerable to a specific kind of error, namely:

Instrumental-Intrinsic Confusion: Mistakenly treating what is merely of instrumental value as intrinsically valuable.

In imagining Sid's circumstance, we are likely to conclude that what is instrumentally bad must also be intrinsically bad. This kind of mistake is not uncommon. The difference between the two kinds of value can easily be blurred. This is especially likely when three conditions are met: when an intrinsic good is also regularly instrumentally bad, when the interval between the goods and bads obtaining is brief, and when the amount of good is dwarfed by the amount of bad.

---

11. For more on an agent's motivational set, see §1.4.2.

Sadistic Pleasure meets the three conditions that invite Instrumental-Intrinsic Confusion. When people like Sid take pleasure in others' pain, they frequently then inflict pain on others. There is little time between the pain that's caused and the pleasure that results. And, in many cases, the pain may be tremendous and lasting—truly horrific—while the sadist enjoys only a fleeting rush of pleasure. When we are told that Sid watches videos of people in pain we immediately wonder if he isn't also regularly producing pain himself. We're motivated to keep our distance. But these worries, notice, are tracking the wrong thing. We're latching on to the instrumental badness of Sid's sadism and imbuing it with intrinsic significance. We're suffering from Instrumental-Intrinsic Confusion.

For these reasons we should not regard our intuitions about the two cases, Sadistic Pleasure and Innocuous Sadism, as equally reliable. There are good reasons to doubt our assessment of Sid and, more generally, to question what we think about sadism. As Smart (1973: 25–26) writes:

> Our repugnance to the sadist arises, naturally enough, because in our universe sadists invariably do harm. If we lived in a universe in which by some extraordinary laws of psychology a sadist was always confounded by his own knavish tricks and invariably did a great deal of good, then we should feel better disposed towards the sadistic mentality.

Given the nature of sadism, and the world as it is, it is unsurprising that we feel that something is amiss with Sid. But this does not reveal the intrinsic value of unfitting attitudes. Rather, it merely reflects the fact that sadism is so often instrumentally bad.

We are now in a position to articulate

The Argument from Innocuous Sadism

1. If the Unconditional View and Some Bad are both true, then sadism is always intrinsically bad-simpliciter.
2. Sadism is not always intrinsically bad-simpliciter.
3. Hence, either the Unconditional View or Some Bad is false.
4. The Unconditional View is true.
5. Hence, Some Bad is false.

Unconditional View: If something is basically good (or bad) in any circumstance, then that thing is basically good (or bad) in all circumstances.

Some Bad: Sid's sadistic pleasure is in some way bad-simpliciter.

Premise 4 was defended in the previous section. The central claims of this argument are thus made in Premise 1 and Premise 2. And both are well supported. Premise 1 follows from the Unconditional View and the core of Some Bad. Premise 2 is supported by appeal to our intuitions in Innocuous Sadism and reinforced by the thought that having fitting attitudes itself is merely instrumentally good.

Taken together, the arguments of the last two sections amount to a serious challenge to the Principle of Evaluative Congruity. We considered the two ways that the principle might be vindicated and found both wanting.

9.7 Conclusion

This chapter began by showing how Sadistic Pleasure, once combined with the Principle of Evaluative Congruity, can be used to reject Welfarism. We examined how one might respond to this challenge. But some moves may be questioned. Which claim is most vulnerable?

There's a case to be made that it's the Unconditional View. It might be argued that this view is predicated on a conception of intrinsic value that is overly restrictive. To see how this charge might be motivated, consider the following example. On December 31, 1862 there were a number of identical pens in a drawer in the White House. In this circumstance, no pen, considered in itself, seems intrinsically good. On January 1, 1863 Abraham Lincoln reached in the drawer, picked up one of the pens, and signed the Emancipation Proclamation. This particular pen seems now to have taken on a special evaluative status.[12] We might think that it should be preserved, not because we expect it to ever be useful but, because having played a role in history, it is valuable for its own sake. Yet, whether or not something has played a role in history is not a matter of its intrinsic properties. Thus, if we accept that the pen is valuable for its own sake on account of its role, we must reject as excessively restrictive the conception of intrinsic value that underwrites the Unconditional View. Some things (e.g., Lincoln's pen) appear to be intrinsically good in one circumstance but not in another.[13]

If this is a counterexample to the Unconditional View, the goods in question must indeed be intrinsically good. But we may doubt that historically important pens really have intrinsic value. Perhaps we regard such objects in this way because they inspire, rallying us behind good causes, or because they have come to represent part of our national identity. If so, then this challenge to the Unconditional View is just a further instance of Instrumental-Intrinsic Confusion.

---

12. This example is modified from Kagan (1998).

13. Drawing on examples like these, Korsgaard (1983) argues that intrinsic value is not of central moral importance.

References

Bradley, B. 2002. "Is Intrinsic Value Conditional?" *Philosophical Studies* 107 (1): 23–44.

Brentano, F. 1969. *The Origin of Our Knowledge of Right and Wrong*. London: Routledge and Kegan Paul.

Chisholm, R. M. 1968. "The Defeat of Good and Evil." *Proceedings and Addresses of the American Philosophical Association* 42: 21–38.
Chisholm, R. M. 1981. "Defining Intrinsic Value." *Analysis* 41: 99–100.
*Cullity, G. 2019. "Exceptions in Nonderivative Value." *Philosophy and Phenomenological Research* 98 (1) 26–49.
Hurka, T. 1998. "Two Kinds of Organic Unity." *The Journal of Ethics* 2 (4): 299–320.
*Hurka, T. 2001. *Virtue, Vice, and Value*. Oxford: Oxford University Press.
Kagan, S. 1998. "Rethinking Intrinsic Value." *The Journal of Ethics* 2 (4): 277–97.
*Korsgaard, C. M. 1983. "Two Distinctions in Goodness." *Philosophical Review* 92 (2): 169–95.
Lemos, N. M. 1994. *Intrinsic Value: Concept and Warrant*. Cambridge: Cambridge University Press.
Moore, G. E. 1951. *Philosophical Studies*. New York: The Humanities Press.
Nagel, T. 1986. *The View from Nowhere*. Oxford: Oxford University Press.
Olson, J. 2004. "Intrinsicalism and Conditionalism about Final Value." *Ethical Theory and Moral Practice* 7 (1): 31–52.
*Rachels, S. 2004. "Six Theses about Pleasure." *Philosophical Perspectives* 18 (1): 247–67.
Sidgwick, H. 1907. *The Methods of Ethics*. 7th ed. London: Macmillan.
Smart, J. J. C. 1973. "An Outline of a System of Utilitarian Ethics." In *Utilitarianism: For and Against*, 3–67. Cambridge: Cambridge University Press.

10

Proportionalism and Worthiness

10.1 *Introduction*

You need a root canal. The procedure will take place Saturday morning in Operating Room 1. You dread what you know will be a painful experience. This pain is bad-for you. It's also bad-simpliciter. It's basically bad that someone will be in pain. The same thing—the pain from the operation—thus appears to be doubly bad. It's personally and impersonally bad. To this we can add: The extent to which this pain is bad corresponds to its magnitude. The worse the operation is for you personally, the worse it is impersonally. This, at least, is how things appear. Is this appearance deceptive? Here we've arrived at the question we're concerned with in this chapter:

> Does the amount of personal value track the amount of basic value?

The answer seems to be Yes. The degree to which a pain is intrinsically bad-for you is the same as the degree to which it will be basically bad. The two are proportional. If we claim this relationship holds across the board, then we are led to one of the members of the set of principles examined in this book that together imply Utilitarianism, namely:

> PROPORTIONALISM: The basic value of an episode of welfare is strictly proportional to its value-for the subject. The extent to which an episode of well-being is basically good is strictly proportional to how good it is for the subject. The extent to which an episode of ill-being is basically bad is strictly proportional to how bad it is for the subject.

Proportionalism offers what seems to be the most straightforward affirmative answer to this chapter's central question.[1]

This proposal is attractive in part because it's difficult to identify any factors that would justify a departure from it. Why would the pain that's bad-for you be more or less bad-simpliciter? Suppose your operation is rescheduled and relocated. The procedure will be just as painful, but it will now take place on Sunday and in Operating Room 2. Should this spatiotemporal difference matter? Is

---

1. For an overview of evaluative properties, see §1.2.3.

there any reason to believe the ordeal will be any more or less bad-simpliciter? Presumably not. Now suppose there's been a mix-up. You don't need a root canal after all. A different patient does. The procedure will be just as painful for her as it would have been for you. Should this alter how bad-simpliciter it is that someone will be in pain? Again, presumably not. The badness of the root canal appears insensitive to where and when it occurs and unaffected by who experiences it.

Proportionalism serves as a kind of default. We need reasons to move away from the view. In what follows, we present and evaluate what is perhaps the most formidable challenge to Proportionalism.

10.2 *Saint or Sinner*

In ordinary cases, we're happy to grant that something good-for a person is also, and to the same extent, good-simpliciter. And, like the pain of a root canal, what's bad-for someone is also, and to the same extent, bad-simpliciter. As just noted, it seems that the goodness or badness is indifferent to where and when it occurs and who it's experienced by. Yet, the last of these possibilities may demand a second look. Is it possible that facts about the identity of the welfare recipient justify a departure from Proportionalism?

To get an affirmative answer to this question, we need to identify some feature a person might possess that would result in her well-being or ill-being being disproportionately good-simpliciter or bad-simpliciter. In theory, any feature could be claimed to have this significance. Take, for example, the proposal that the welfare of left-handed people has only half the basic value of non-left-handed people. Although unserious, it's worth noting how this proposal's structure departs from Proportionalism. It identifies a feature—a dominant hand—that diminishes the basic goodness (or badness) of a person's well-being (or ill-being). And so the possessor of the welfare matters. And it matters a lot. If you are left-handed, you convert well-being (or ill-being) to basic goodness (or badness) at only half the rate of your non-left-handed counterparts. Something that's very bad-for you might be only a little bad-simpliciter.

No sane person thinks one's dominant hand has such evaluative significance. But other features are more plausible candidates. Consider

> Saint or Sinner. On Monday, the newspaper headline reads, "Saint Endures Horrific Surgery." Teresa, widely known for her strict adherence to morality's demands and virtuous character, underwent a 24-hour emergency operation. Unfortunately, due to a rare condition, the anesthetics were totally ineffective and Teresa was in excruciating pain the entire time. On Tuesday, however, the newspaper headline reads, "Correction: Saint Actually Sinner." Interest in the

story led to further investigation, which revealed that Teresa is in fact a serial wrongdoer with a truly vicious character.[2]

Many are likely to react to this case in the following way. Monday's news is tragic. The pain of the surgery is very bad-simpliciter. But this badness is exacerbated by the fact that the person who suffered was so saintly. Tuesday's news is something of a relief. Of course, the pain Teresa endured in surgery was bad-for her. Her loss in personal value doesn't change. Yet, when we learn that, rather than a saint, Teresa's a sinner, our evaluation of the surgery, in terms of its impersonal value, changes. The pain of the surgery—no longer a cosmic injustice—appears less bad-simpliciter.

In the next section, we'll explain how our intuitive reaction to this case can be marshaled against Proportionalism.

10.3 *The Basic Value Depends on Worthiness Argument against Proportionalism*

In Saint or Sinner, our evaluation of the badness of Teresa's suffering is modulated by our beliefs about her saintliness. Even if the extent of Teresa's suffering is in no way diminished, it is now judged to be less bad-simpliciter that it happened. The intuition motivating this judgment is articulated by Kant, who writes, "What now is the highest good? It is the unification of the greatest happiness with the greatest degree of capacity to be worthy of this happiness. If there is to be a highest good, then happiness and the worthiness thereof must be combined" (Metaphysik L1, 28: 337).[3] Kant's suggestion is an attractive one. Unlike being left-handed, the fact that someone is worthy of happiness seems a plausible basis on which to adjust the rate at which they convert welfare to basic goodness or badness. This Kantian thought may lead us to accept

> *Basic Value Depends on Worthiness*: The basic value of an episode of well-being or ill-being is, at least in part, determined by worthiness.

This idea offers a neat explanation of our intuitive reaction to Saint or Sinner. Initially we thought the painful surgery was performed on a saint. Given Basic Value Depends on Worthiness, this was very bad indeed. When we learn on Tuesday that she was instead a sinner, we revise our assessment. We're inclined to react to Tuesday's news positively.

We are now in a position to articulate

---

2. This example is inspired by Ross (1930: 35).
3. Quoted from Guyer (2000: 93).

The Basic Value Depends on Worthiness Argument against Proportionalism

1. If Basic Value Depends on Worthiness is true, then Proportionalism is false.
2. Basic Value Depends on Worthiness is true.
3. Hence, Proportionalism is false.

> *Basic Value Depends on Worthiness*: The basic value of an episode of well-being or ill-being is, at least in part, determined by worthiness.
>
> *Proportionalism*: The basic value of an episode of welfare is strictly proportional to its value for the subject. The extent to which an episode of well-being is basically good is strictly proportional to how good it is for the subject. The extent to which an episode of ill-being is basically bad is strictly proportional to how bad it is for the subject.

The first premise is uncontroversial. The crucial claim is made in Premise 2, and it enjoys much support. Basic Value Depends on Worthiness captures an idea that's widely shared. It makes sense of our intuitive judgment in Saint or Sinner. If Basic Value Depends on Worthiness can be given adequate defense, then Proportionalism must be rejected.

10.4 *Graphing Proportionalism*

In the coming sections, we'll sketch and assess the two most promising attempts to defend Basic Value Depends on Worthiness.[4] To understand how these alternatives work, we'll need to first introduce a helpful tool: graphs.[5] What's at issue in this chapter is the relationship between levels of welfare and levels of basic value. The accounts we'll be evaluating relate these two values differently. To better understand the proposals on offer, it will be instructive to graphically represent the differences between them.

We'll start with Proportionalism. Its simplicity makes it easy to graph. Examine Figure 10.1. The X-axis represents lifetime welfare.[6] Episodes of well-being move us eastward; episodes of ill-being move us westward. The Y-axis represents levels of basic value. Basic goodness increases as we move northward; basic badness increases as we move southward. According to Proportionalism, the relationship between these values is strictly proportional. An episode of well-being is exactly as good-for its subject as it is basically good. Any movement eastward is accompanied by a movement of equal distance northward. Similarly, an episode

---

4. In distinguishing between two versions of Basic Value Depends on Worthiness, we follow Persson (1997).

5. In representing the competing approaches graphically, we follow standard practice in the desert literature. See, for example, Hurka (2001), Feldman (1995, 1997), and Kagan (2012). The graphs below follow Kagan.

6. Focusing on whole lives is a simplifying assumption. It is for the most part innocuous and allows us to avoid complications concerning the relationship between worth and time. For discussion, see Kagan (2012: 11–12).

Figure 10.1: *Proportionalism*

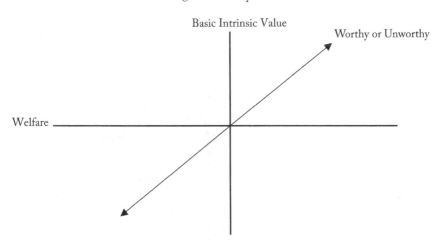

of ill-being is exactly as good-for its subject as it is basically bad. Any movement westward is accompanied by a movement of equal distance southward. This proportional relationship, which holds whether the person in question is worthy or not, is represented by the straight line cutting at a 45-degree angle through the origin.

Before we can graph Saint or Sinner, we should make a simplifying assumption. Let's suppose that, given the ups and downs of her existence, Teresa's lifetime welfare score, excluding the surgery, would be zero. With this assumption, we can here, and for future graphs, assume that Teresa starts her surgery at the origin. For Proportionalism, given it's a prolonged episode of ill-being, we will see a movement west along the X-axis accompanied by a movement of equal length south along the Y-axis. The length of this movement indicates the amount of basic badness of the episode of suffering. To see how this works, examine Figure 10.2.

Because the relationship between good-for and good-simpliciter is always the same—regardless of worthiness—the single line is sufficient to depict every agent. Views that accommodate Basic Value Depends on Worthiness, by contrast, look quite different. Such accounts must allow that an episode of well-being corresponds to more or less basic goodness depending on the subject's worthiness. Those who are worthy and those who are unworthy will thus be represented with different lines. This marks one significant difference between Proportionalism and its alternatives. There is another difference as well, but it depends on how the details of the alternatives are filled in. There are countless ways this could be done. We won't attempt to canvas every possibility. But we will develop two representative accounts. Both accommodate Basic Value Depends on Worthiness. Neither, we shall see, is free from problems.

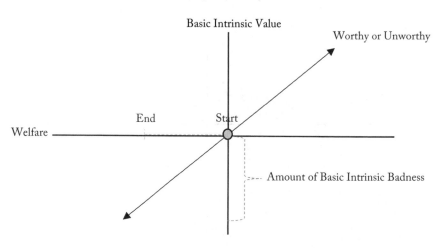

Figure 10.2: *Proportionalism for Saint or Sinner*

10.5 *The Fit Idea Argument against the Merit View*

One natural way to elaborate Basic Value Depends on Worthiness appeals to *merit*. This is the familiar idea that people, things, performances, and the like ought to be recognized for their quality. Recall the intuitive judgment elicited in Sinner or Saint. Initially, when Teresa was reported to be a virtuous person who had devoted her life to doing good deeds, we judge that it ought to be that she's benefited, not made to suffer. When it was later reported that she was actually a vicious person who had perpetrated many bad deeds, we drop this judgment. On this explanation, Tuesday's news is a positive development because it revealed that Teresa was not a meritorious saint worthy of the best, but an unworthy sinner. Since this first alternative to Proportionalism appeals to the idea of merit, let's call it the

> *Merit View*: Basic intrinsic goodness (or badness) of the same amount of well-being (or ill-being) is greater if it befalls the worthier person.

On this view, we determine how good (or bad) a given amount of well-being (or ill-being) is by multiplying it by the subject's worthiness. The greater the merit— the worthier one is—the greater the difference between the two values. This reflects the conviction that the welfare of the worthy is worth more.[7]

The Merit View is appealing. In addition to explaining our intuitions about Saint or Sinner, it accounts for thoughts we're likely to have about distributive

---

7. Our discussion of the Merit View draws on Kagan (2012: §2.4) and Feldman (1995).

justice. If you had to choose someone to undergo an episode of ill-being, would it be Teresa-the-Saint or Teresa-the-Sinner? The latter option seems the more just of the two. The reason is this: justice demands we prioritize the more meritorious. When shares of welfare are to be doled out, it is appropriate that the distribution reflect the relevant merits. A distribution in which the worthy have more welfare than the less worthy is more just.

There are many ways to spell out the details of the Merit View. We're not aiming to be comprehensive, so we won't attempt to canvass them all here. Instead, we are trying to devise the least controversial account that can accommodate Basic Value Depends on Worthiness. To this end, we'll make the following assumption: The base rate at which well-being is converted into intrinsic goodness is 1. This is the rate for the most unworthy. Every episode of well-being, regardless of the subject, has at least an equal level of intrinsic goodness. But, because the worthy are meritorious, their welfare has a higher multiplier. The higher a person's lifetime worthiness, the higher the multiplier. Yet no one's multiplier is less than 1.

The rationale for this assumption is twofold. First, by stipulating the base rate to be 1, we insulate the Merit View from certain objections. For example, if instead we were to allow that some people convert welfare to basic goodness with a multiplier of zero, then it would be possible that some subjects function, in effect, as welfare black holes. For these people, no matter how intense an episode of well-being, its basic goodness would always be zero. Similarly, their episodes of ill-being would be in no way intrinsically bad. An account that is indifferent to whether someone endures extreme suffering or enjoys unlimited ecstasy warrants suspicion. Or, to take another example, if we were to allow that some people have a negative conversion rate then we'd face an even more unwelcome result. For these unfortunate subjects an episode of well-being would be basically bad, and an episode of ill-being would be basically good. The implication that endless suffering is increasingly wonderful should be avoided. That said, an account may permit either of these possibilities. We haven't offered anything like an airtight case against them. But their defenders face an uphill battle. There's a second, pragmatic reason to stipulate that the base rate is 1. By doing so, we are able to show more clearly how the Merit View and Proportionalism differ. Given this assumption, we can understand the Merit View as differing from Proportionalism in only one respect. The Merit View holds that certain people, because worthier, convert well-being (or ill-being) into basic goodness (or badness) more efficiently. The Merit View, as described, is depicted in Figure 10.3.

When a unworthy sinner and a worthy saint suffer the same episode of ill-being, this will correspond to different amounts of basic badness. Return to Saint or Sinner. We assumed that, absent the surgery, Teresa's lifetime welfare is zero. Beginning at the origin, the surgery will take us the same distance west

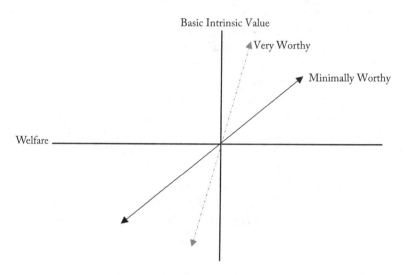

Figure 10.3: *The Merit View*

on the X-axis, regardless of whether we are talking about Teresa-the-Saint or Teresa-the-Sinner. The distance this move will take us down the Y-axis, however, will differ greatly. Teresa-the-Saint's surgery will take us much farther south than Teresa-the-Sinner. In effect, when our judgment changes from Monday to Tuesday, this corresponds in the graph to the difference between the line of the worthier and that of the minimally worthy. We get the result we were looking for: the basic badness of Teresa-the-Saint's suffering is greater.

The Merit View is a legitimate alternative to Proportionalism and accommodates the intuition elicited in Saint or Sinner. Nonetheless, the view, on examination, has a serious defect. It fails to capture something crucial about Basic Value Depends on Worthiness. When we reflect on what it means to be worthy of something, we are likely to agree with the Merit View that it's good when the worthy get prioritized. But we're also inclined to a further thought, namely, that there is something in particular that the worthy deserve. If someone is worthy of an award then it is important that they receive it. Once they have, we're not compelled to give them another. If someone is worthy of a prison term, once they've served it, we're not compelled to give them another. If a saint is worthy of a certain amount of well-being, it's important that she receive it, but once she has, we're not compelled to give her more. The general idea is expressed by Kagan:

> For each person there is an absolute level [of welfare] that the person deserves to be at. This is what the person deserves absolutely. If people have what they deserve, this is good.... If people have less than they deserve, then this is less good, or perhaps even bad.... [If] someone has more than they deserve, this is less good, or perhaps even bad. (1999: 300)

If Kagan is correct, accounts accepting Basic Value Depends on Worthiness need to accommodate the

> *Fit Idea*: When there is a perfect fit between one's welfare level and one's level of worthiness, any change in welfare decreases the amount of basic goodness.[8]

This idea tells us that welfare contributes to intrinsic goodness up to a point. This point is set by one's level of worthiness. If one has a perfect fit between worthiness and welfare, any change in welfare is a change for the worse.

The Merit View, however, is incompatible with the Fit Idea. Notice, the lines on the graph in Figure 10.3 extend northeast and southwest forever. This indicates that whether you are worthy or unworthy, you always convert welfare to basic value at the same rate. This conversion is independent of how much or little you've already received. The Merit View cannot make sense of the idea that someone is worthy of anything in particular. There are not two things: your welfare and the level of welfare you deserve. There is only one thing: your merit. On this picture, we can say that well-being is better-simpliciter when enjoyed by the worthy than the unworthy. But we cannot say that someone, given her merits, is closer or farther from getting what she deserves. We cannot accommodate the Fit Idea.

We can now put forward

The Fit Idea Argument against the Merit View

1. To properly capture Basic Value Depends on Worthiness, an account must accommodate the Fit Idea.
2. The Merit View cannot accommodate the Fit Idea.
3. Hence, the Merit View cannot properly capture Basic Value Depends on Worthiness.

> *Basic Value Depends on Worthiness*: The basic value of an episode of well-being or ill-being is, at least in part, determined by worthiness.
>
> *Fit Idea*: When there is a perfect fit between one's welfare level and one's level of worthiness, any change in welfare decreases the amount of basic goodness
>
> *Merit View*: Basic intrinsic goodness (or badness) of the same amount of well-being (or ill-being) is greater if it befalls the worthier person.

Only Premise 1 is controversial, and it is supported by our run-of-the-mill thoughts about worthiness. On reflection it seems that people are not simply worthy; they are worthy of something in particular. And they can be closer or farther from getting it. This—the Fit Idea—is essential to Basic Value Depends on Worthiness. Since the Merit View can't accept this, we ought not to accept the Merit View. Yet perhaps another alternative to Proportionalism can.

---

8. For further elaboration, see Arrhenius (2017).

10.6 *The Polarity Preservation Argument against the Desert View*

Our second alternative to Proportionalism aims to improve on the Merit View by incorporating the apparent connection between worthiness and desert. It accommodates the Fit Idea. On this view, everyone, by virtue of their level of lifetime worthiness, deserves some specific level of welfare. The basic goodness of someone's lifetime welfare is highest when this level matches exactly what she deserves. When people get more or less welfare than they deserve, the basic goodness of their lifetime welfare is lower. This account, in short, adjusts welfare for desert. As a result, the graph for this view will depict angled lines that look like mountains, not straight lines as with the Merit View and Proportionalism. The peaks of these mountains mark where a subject's lifetime desert level and her lifetime welfare level perfectly match.

The Merit View, recall, had the benefit of explaining why we're inclined to prioritize the worthy. This benefit can be retained, consistent with the Fit Idea, but we'll need to make two additional claims. First, if there is some amount of welfare that people deserve, what should we think when they get more than this? What should we think of *overserving*? We should think that, for all subjects, welfare beyond what is deserved reduces the basic value of their lifetime welfare, but this reduction is more severe when the unworthy are overserved than when the worthy are. The basic badness of overserving the worthy is less than basic badness of overserving the unworthy by the same amount. Second, what happens when people get less than they deserve? What should we think of *underserving*? We should think that, for all subjects, welfare below what is deserved reduces the basic value of their lifetime welfare, but this reduction is more severe when the worthy are underserved than when the unworthy are. The basic badness of underserving the worthy is greater than the basic badness of underserving the unworthy by the same amount.

These two points, about overserving and underserving welfare, must be reflected in the graph. To do this, the western slopes of the mountains representing the less worthy will incline more gradually than the western slopes of the more worthy. And the eastern slopes of the less worthy will decline more quickly—they will be steeper—than those of the more worthy. In this way we can combine the Fit Idea with the thought that we should prioritize the welfare of the worthy.

We can now articulate the main idea of this second alternative to Proportionalism. Let's call it the

> *Desert View*: When there is a perfect fit between one's welfare level and one's level of worthiness, any change in welfare decreases the amount of basic goodness. Getting more welfare than one is worthy of is less basically bad the higher one's worthiness level. Getting less welfare than one is worthy of is less basically bad the lower one's worthiness level.[9]

---

9. Our articulation of the Desert View follows Kagan (2012).

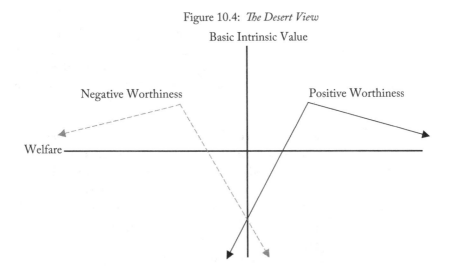

Figure 10.4: *The Desert View*

This view, depicted in Figure 10.4, takes a very different shape than Proportionalism or the Merit View. As noted, the Fit Idea leads us to mountains. The peak of each mountain represents the place at which what one deserves perfectly matches what one receives. To reflect the importance of prioritizing the worthy, we made two additional claims. Overserving the worthier is better. Underserving the worthier is worse. As a result, the mountains rotate clockwise around their peaks as worthiness decreases.

The Desert View offers a very attractive way of elaborating Basic Value Depends on Worthiness. Return to Saint or Sinner, again assuming that Teresa's lifetime welfare level, excluding the surgery, is zero. The episode of ill-being she suffered was very bad-for her. But whether it was also bad-simpliciter or good-simpliciter depends on whether she is a saint or a sinner. If she is a saint, with positive worthiness, then her welfare level of zero is far below what she deserves. Accordingly, the basic badness of an episode of ill-being would be extremely high. By contrast, if she is a sinner, with negative worthiness, we get a very different result. Teresa, with a lifetime welfare score of zero, is already getting far more than she deserves. She deserves to suffer. And suffering, thanks to the surgery, is what she gets. It takes her closer to what she deserves. What's bad-for her is good-simpliciter. So here too we get the result we were looking for: the basic badness of Teresa-the-Saint's suffering is greater.

While the Desert View succeeds in certain respects, it seems to violate a plausible claim about the relationship between welfare and basic value. Let's call this

> *Polarity Preservation*: Episodes of well-being are always basically good. Episodes of ill-being are always basically bad.

Assuming hedonism for the moment, Polarity Preservation allows us to claim that all pleasure is itself good, and good-for the person experiencing it. Pleasure is always doubly good. The basic value of well-being is always, at least to some extent, positive. Similarly, all pain is itself bad, and bad-for the person experiencing it. Pain is always doubly bad. The basic value of ill-being is always, at least to some extent, negative.

Polarity Preservation is consistent with Proportionalism and the Merit View, but not the Desert View. This is because Polarity Preservation is incompatible with the Fit Idea. To accept the latter, one must hold that sometimes an episode of well-being can be basically bad, and an episode of ill-being can be basically good. And this is simply to deny Polarity Preservation. Both the Fit Idea and Polarity Preservation have much to be said in their favor. But one must be rejected. Which should it be? To get clear about this, we should focus on the kinds of cases in which polarity is not preserved. This occurs whenever a person's welfare is greater than that which she deserves. Whenever one is getting more than one's due, an episode of ill-being is good-simpliciter. It moves them closer to getting what they deserve. And, for the same reason, an episode of well-being is bad-simpliciter. So deciding between the Fit Idea and Polarity Preservation comes down to this. Should we believe that, once past one's peak, polarity flips?

In answering this question, notice first that to accept the Fit Idea we must accept that it can be good-simpliciter when even the saintliest suffer. Someone who is exceptionally worthy, admirable in every way, may have welfare beyond her desert level. This may be true even if this saint is extremely worthy. In such cases an episode of ill-being would in fact be intrinsically good. What's bad-for a saint may be good-simpliciter. This is an unattractive implication. Should we believe that it is ever bad when a saint enjoys well-being?

Many people will concede that the Fit Idea has these counterintuitive implications. But they are swift to point out that what Polarity Preservation implies about sinners is equally unattractive. In Saint or Sinner, one is likely to think that the episode of ill-being would be worse-simpliciter if inflicted on Teresa-the-Saint than Teresa-the-Sinner. But further, one is also likely to think that this episode of ill-being, when inflicted on Teresa-the-Sinner, is in fact good-simpliciter. Those with negative worthiness are deserving of ill-being. It's good-simpliciter when they get it. Shouldn't we believe that it's sometimes good when a sinner gets the ill-being she deserves?

Both views, concerning polarity flipping past a peak, have a strike against them. The Fit Idea tells us that suffering—even for exceptional saints—can be good. Polarity Preservation tells us that it is never good-for anyone—even the most wicked sinner—to suffer. Both of these implications are unintuitive. Yet, in terms of the reliability of our intuitions, Polarity Preservation has an advantage—for the counterintuitive implications of Polarity Preservation are especially vulnerable to a certain kind of error, namely,

> *Instrumental-Intrinsic Confusion*: Mistakenly treating what is merely of instrumental value as intrinsically valuable.

This error is easily made. Intrinsic goods often come with a bright halo. It's easy to think that instrumental goods that fall within their circumference give off light of their own. For example, that incentives and disincentives are effective in altering people's behavior is well known. In many domains we're used to threatening punishment for misbehavior and promising reward for compliance. Such policies are surely instrumentally valuable. Moreover, the good that's brought about is often immediate. Whether it's a child sent to timeout, a citizen fined for speeding, or a criminal sentenced for theft, very soon after the punishment is imposed the perpetrator, and those who witness it, are motivated to comply. This makes it very easy to mistakenly regard the instrumental good of punishment as something that's intrinsically good. The thought that people deserve ill-being helps us get along given the world we live in and the kind of creatures we are. It directs our behavior, supplying incentives and disincentives, when natural inclination isn't up for the task. As a result, when it comes to worthiness, we are prone to fetishizing, treating what is of merely instrumental significance as if it has intrinsic significance.

We can say more. It may be conceded that people take satisfaction in knowing that the unjust are punished. Most of us have powerful retributivist tendencies. This is part of what makes punishment instrumentally valuable. Not only does it serve to disincentivize misbehavior, the administration of punishment also satisfies the very strong desires of the compliant. No one wants to feel like a dupe. And when those who deviate from the rules are made to pay a price, the value of compliance is reaffirmed. But, having made this concession, one need not take the further step of claiming that this retributivist tendency tracks anything of intrinsic value. Our thoughts that it is good when the unworthy suffer, rather than reflecting some important truth about desert, may be relics of our evolutionary past. As Parfit writes:

> These attitudes are like some simpler emotions that are had by the animals that are most like us. If evolution can explain why many people have these reactive attitudes, that might give some support to the view that these attitudes, and the widely held belief that such attitudes are justified, are not responses to reasons. (2011: 429)

That the judgments that cut against Polarity Preservation are vulnerable to Instrumental-Intrinsic Confusion means that we should not put much stock in them. The same is not true of the counterintuitive implications of the Fit Idea. Nothing about the abundance of well-being for the saintly courts this confusion. The belief that it can never be bad to increase the welfare of the saintliest appears reliable.

We are now in a position to offer

The Polarity Preservation Argument against the Desert View

1. If Polarity Preservation is true, then the Fit Idea is false.
2. Polarity Preservation is true.
3. Hence, the Fit Idea is false.
4. If the Fit Idea is false, then the Desert View is false.
5. Hence, the Desert View is False.

Premise 1 and Premise 4 are uncontested. The argument thus hinges on Premise 2. This idea is independently attractive. It gains an edge over the Fit Idea when we recognize that, where these views diverge, the counterintuitive implications of Polarity Preservation are especially prone to Instrumental-Intrinsic Confusion while the counterintuitive implications of Polarity Preservation are not.

> *Polarity Preservation*: Episodes of well-being are always basically good. Episodes of ill-being are always basically bad.
>
> *Fit Idea*: When there is a perfect fit between one's welfare level and one's level of worthiness, additional welfare decreases the amount of basic goodness.
>
> *Desert View*: When there is a perfect fit between one's welfare level and one's level of worthiness, any change in welfare decreases the amount of basic goodness. Getting more welfare than one is worthy of is less basically bad the higher one's worthiness level. Getting less welfare than one is worthy of is less basically bad the lower one's worthiness level.

10.7 *The Circularity Argument against Worthiness*

The two previous sections have articulated problems for the most promising ways of fleshing out Basic Value Depends on Worthiness. We turn now to a further challenge, one that points to a deeper problem. With two plausible assumptions—that worthiness depends on living up to what morality demands, and that what morality demands depends on worthiness—any moral theory that incorporates Basic Value Depends on Worthiness will be viciously circular. This section fleshes out this worry.[10]

We've yet to discuss what makes someone more or less worthy. Worthiness may depend on a number of factors: character traits, motives, attitudes, and the like. But, to take the first step toward circularity, we need only accept the fairly uncontroversial claim that

> *Worthiness Depends on Acting Morally*: Lifetime worthiness is, at least in part, determined by the degree to which one conforms to morality's demands.

---

10. The whole section draws heavily on Kagan (2017).

This claim is part of the explanation for our judgments in Saints or Sinners. Teresa-the-Saint is worthy, in part, because she strictly conforms to morality's demands. Teresa-the-Sinner is less worthy, in part, because she is grossly immoral.

The next step needed for circularity is also fairly uncontroversial. This is the claim that

> *Acting Morally Depends on Basic Value*: What morality requires is, at least in part, determined by basic value.

This claim is, of course, accepted by Utilitarians. But one need not accept Utilitarianism to accept it. One need only think that basic goods and bads play some role in fixing moral obligations. Notice, even nonconsequentialist theories that posit constraints on maximizing the good usually incorporate thresholds—points at which, when enough good is at stake, the constraint is overridden. And this is sufficient to commit oneself to Acting Morally Depends on Basic Value. So understood, this claim is, in fact, very modest. To deny it one must hold that basic goods are utterly irrelevant to determining moral requirements. That's a hard position to defend.

This pair of claims, together with Basic Value Depends on Worthiness, make for a serious problem. They form a circle. And it's not the innocuous sort. We'll show the problem from both theoretical and practical perspectives, starting with the former.

Moral theories not only enumerate the deontic properties our acts possess but also explain why acts have the deontic properties they do.[11] But can a theory that is circular in the way described explain why we ought to do what we ought to do? It seems not. To see this, suppose we are believers in a theory that aims to accommodate Basic Value Depends on Worthiness. Now suppose someone presses a series of questions. The first is this: "What facts explain whether or not I act morally?" Our answer, if we accept Acting Morally Depends on Basic Value, will include facts about basic goodness. The questioner continues: "So, what facts explain basic goodness?" Our answer, if we accept Basic Value Depends on Worthiness, will include facts about worthiness. The questioner then follows up: "So, what facts explain worthiness?" Our answer, if we accept Worthiness Depends on Acting Morally, will include facts about acting morally. The questioner, now justifiably dissatisfied, recounts the circular journey we've taken: "To explain whether I act morally, I must look to facts about basic value. To explain basic value, I must look to facts about worthiness. To explain worthiness, I must look to facts about whether I act morally. Now we're back where we started. We've gone in an explanatory circle (depicted in Figure 10.5) so tight it explains nothing." This series of questions makes vivid that theories that accept Basic Value Depends on Worthiness are explanatorily impotent.

---

11. For more on the enumerative and explanatory tasks of an ethical theory, see §1.2.

Figure 10.5: *Worthiness Circularity*

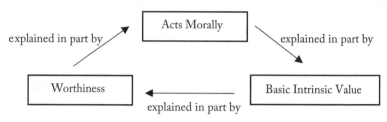

We can also bring out the vicious circularity of such a theory from the practical point of view. Consider

> Painkillers for the Worthy. You and a stranger lie in pain near death at the hospital. Both of you have lived lives which, except for these final moments, are exactly the same in terms of welfare and levels of worthiness. You have one dose of a painkiller. You can take it yourself or medicate the stranger. You medicate the stranger.

In medicating the stranger, did you act permissibly or not?

Suppose medicating her was permissible. In that case, you acted in conformity with morality. This increases your lifetime worthiness. You also spared the stranger some pain, and you suffered some yourself. Yet, if this is correct, then perhaps our initial verdict is mistaken. For, by medicating the stranger, the less worthy received relief while the worthier suffered. So perhaps we should suppose that, instead, medicating the stranger was impermissible. In that case, you failed to satisfy morality's demands and thus decreased your lifetime worthiness. As before, you also spared the stranger some pain, and you suffered some yourself. But this suggests that our second verdict must also be mistaken. For, by medicating the stranger, the worthier received relief while the less worthy suffered. The viciousness of the circle is again apparent. Did you act permissibly? If we initially answer Yes, we seem forced to revise our answer to No. If we initially answer No, we seem forced to revise our answer to Yes. Neither deontic verdict is stable.

Against Basic Value Depends on Worthiness, we can now offer

The Circularity Argument against Worthiness

1. Basic Value Depends on Worthiness, Worthiness Depends on Acting Morally, and Acting Morally Depends on Basic Value together form a vicious circle.

2. If Basic Value Depends on Worthiness, Worthiness Depends on Acting Morally, and Acting Morally Depends on Basic Value together form a vicious circle, then one of these claims is false.

3. Worthiness Depends on Acting Morally is true.

4. Acting Morally Depends on Basic Value is true.
5. Hence, Basic Value Depends on Worthiness is false.

> *Basic Value Depends on Worthiness*: The basic value of an episode of well-being or ill-being is, at least in part, determined by worthiness.
>
> *Worthiness Depends on Acting Morally*: Lifetime worthiness is, at least in part, determined by the degree to which one conforms to morality's demands.
>
> *Acting Morally Depends on Basic Value*: What morality requires is, at least in part, determined by basic value.

Premise 1 is undisputed and Premise 2 is difficult to deny. We've shown, from both theoretical and practical perspectives, that the three claims together form a vicious circle. Few would regard such an account as acceptable. The argument thus hinges on the very modest claim of Premise 3 and the well-supported claim of Premise 4. If sound, this argument undermines the central challenge to Proportionalism. The basic value of welfare does not depend on worthiness.

10.8 *Conclusion*

The aim of this chapter has been to articulate the challenge made vivid in Saint or Sinner. Along the way we've made a number of arguments on behalf of Proportionalism. The most powerful of these is the Circularity Argument against Worthiness. Can this argument be resisted?

The most vulnerable principle used to generate the circularity is Worthiness Depends on Acting Morally. One might deny this principle and so break out of the circle. Here's a plausible alternative. Instead of acting morally, worthiness may depend on being properly motivated. That is, we could hold that those with the right motives, independent of the moral status of their acts, are worthy. Those with the wrong motives are unworthy. In locating worthiness in one's motives, we may still retain the intuition that it's not as bad-simpliciter that Teresa-the-Sinner suffered as it would have been if Teresa-the-Saint was the patient. After all, we're inclined to believe not only that saints act morally but also that they are properly motivated.[12]

Yet to accept this alternative, in a way that avoids the circularity, requires a total separation of worthiness from morality. But notice, when we claim that saints are properly motivated, we likely mean that saints are motivated as morality requires. If what makes one's motives proper is that they are in conformity with what morality demands, we've not actually denied Worthiness Depends on Acting Morally. We've simply expanded the circle. The question that's now pressing is this: Is there a way to make sense of worthiness that's completely independent from acting morally?

---

12. Kagan (2017) offers this as his preferred way of avoiding the circularity.

References

Arrhenius, G. 2017. "Desert as Fit: An Axiomatic Analysis." In *The Good, the Right, Life and Death*, edited by K. McDaniel, J. R. Raibley, F. Feldman, and M. J. Zimmerman, 3–17. London: Routledge.

*Feldman, F. 1995. "Adjusting Utility for Justice: A Consequentialist Reply to the Objection from Justice." *Philosophy and Phenomenological Research* 55 (3): 567–85.

Feldman, F. 1997. *Utilitarianism, Hedonism, and Desert: Essays in Moral Philosophy*. Cambridge: Cambridge University Press.

Guyer, P. 2000. *Kant on Freedom, Law, and Happiness*. Cambridge: Cambridge University Press.

Hurka, T. 2001. "The Common Structure of Virtue and Desert." *Ethics* 112 (1): 6–31.

Kagan, S. 1999. "Equality and Desert." In *What Do We Deserve*, edited by L. P. Pojman and O. McLeod, 298–314. Oxford: Oxford University Press.

Kagan, S. 2012. *The Geometry of Desert*. Oxford: Oxford University Press.

*Kagan, S. 2017. "Indeterminate Desert." In *The Good, the Right, Life and Death*, edited by K. McDaniel, J. R. Raibley, F. Feldman, and M. J. Zimmerman, 45–70. London: Routledge.

Parfit, D. 2011. *On What Matters*. Vol. 2. Oxford: Oxford University Press.

*Persson, I. 1997. "Ambiguities in Feldman's Desert-Adjusted Values." *Utilitas* 9 (3): 319–27.

Ross, W. D. 1930. *The Right and the Good*. Oxford: Clarendon Press.

11

Additive Aggregation and The Repugnant Conclusion

11.1 *Introduction*

A complete state of affairs—a whole way the world could be—has many parts. Some are basically good: your being pleased to a certain extent today at noon. Others are basically bad: your being pained to a certain extent tomorrow at midnight. We might agree which of these states of affairs are basically good and which are basically bad. We might also agree about the amount of their basic goodness and the amount of their basic badness. But this leaves open another question:

> What's the relationship between the basic values contained within a complete state of affairs and the overall value of that complete state of affairs?

An answer to this question will come in the form of a combinatorial principle.[1] This principle will take the basic values contained within a complete state of affairs as inputs and give us its overall value as the output.[2]

To get a sense of what such a principle does, consider an analogy: the evaluation of your favorite album. Suppose you have evaluated each individual song. The first is good, the second is great, the third is a bit of a miss, and so on. This is not yet an evaluation of the album as a whole. To arrive at this judgment requires something further. You need a combinatorial principle. You need a way to move from the basic value (the value of each song) to the overall value (the value of the album). To be clear, such a principle does nothing to alter the basic values at play. Those remain fixed.[3] The greatness of the second track of your favorite album wouldn't change were it released as a single. Rather the principle tells us how to move from the evaluation of parts to the evaluation of the whole.

The most straightforward combinatorial principle is simple summing. What's the overall value of your favorite album? To get the answer, we sum all the goodness

---

1. For discussion of simple summing, see §1.3.3.
2. For an overview of the distinction between basic value and overall value, see §1.2.3.
3. This point is due to Moore (1993 [1903]: 81) and Feldman (2000: 333–34).

of the good tracks, sum all the badness of all the bad tracks, and then subtract the latter from the former. And the same idea applies to the evaluation of states of affairs. What's the overall value of the complete state of affairs? It is exactly as valuable as the sum of the value of its parts. This takes us to one of the members of the set of principles examined in this book that together imply Utilitarianism, namely:

> ADDITIVE AGGREGATION: The overall value of a complete state of affairs is determined by simple summing on a single numerical scale, adding the amount of each basic good and subtracting the amount of each basic bad. The higher the sum total, the better overall is the complete state of affairs.

This idea—that we can evaluate a complete state of affairs by summing the basic goods and bads—is an attractive one. Indeed, given that the basic values contained within a complete state of affairs are neither enhanced or diminished when determining their overall value, it seems that alternatives to Additive Aggregation have a lot of explaining to do. What evaluative alchemy could yield a compound whose value differs from the sum of its value atoms?

Despite its appeal, Additive Aggregation is thought defective. It implies that many minor goods or bads, if sufficiently numerous, can outweigh the contribution of fewer major ones. And this can deliver results that many regard as repugnant. In this chapter, we present and evaluate a forceful version of this challenge.

11.2 *The Repugnant Conclusion*

The suggestion that basic goods and bads combine additively introduces no evaluative mysteries. If a complete state of affairs contains exactly ten units of basic goodness, the overall goodness is ten. Because it's such a straightforward suggestion, it's not hard to see how Additive Aggregation could be true. Yet this principle can lead to an unsettling conclusion. Consider

> Modeling Worlds. You've always been curious about the way the world could have been. Recently, you've developed a computer program that allows you to model different possibilities. This early prototype is primitive. You can only adjust two things: the number of people and their lifetime welfare. Still, it's a lot of information. Your computer can only handle twenty-six worlds. To view these worlds, you adjust a slider starting with World-A on the far left and ending with World-Z on the far right. For each movement of the slider, the population doubles but the lifetime welfare of each of the inhabitants decreases by 1. World-A is inhabited by 1,000 people, each with a welfare

level of 1,000. World-B is inhabited by 2,000 totally different people, each with a welfare level of 999. Each time the slider moves to the right the same function is applied. The world's population is doubled, with a new set of people, and the welfare each person there enjoys is ever so slightly reduced.

Today you've set out to place your slider on the best of these possible worlds. Since everyone's life has the same total welfare at a given world, we can use a simple bar chart. We let the height of each bar represent the quality of life at a world and the width represent the number of people (see Figure 11.1).

World-A is obviously a very good place. But, when compared with World-B, it's hard to deny that there's been an improvement. The inhabitants of World-A are better-off, but only by a tiny bit. The miniscule decrease in the lifetime welfare for each person is more than compensated for by the sheer increase in the number of good lives lived. The total welfare of this world is 1,998,000, nearly twice that of World-A. The complete state of affairs is, on the whole, better. It seems you should move your slider a notch to the right. The next step also seems innocent. As nice as World-B is, the same reasoning that moved you to deem World-B better than World-A also moves you to deem World-C better than World-B. The inhabitants of World-C are slightly less well-off than those of World-A and World-B. But, as before, this slight difference appears trivial when compared to the dramatic increase in the number of lives well worth living. The total welfare of this world is 3,988,000, nearly twice that of World-B. It seems you should move your slider another notch to the right.

So far, each world in the series appears better than the previous one. While the well-being enjoyed by the inhabitants of each world decreases slightly as the sequence progresses, the dramatic increase in population more than compensates. But the reasoning that leads you to conclude that World-B is better than World-A, and World-C better than World-B, leads you to conclude that World-Z is the best of all. Because its inhabitants are so numerous, even if each has only a minimally good life, its total well-being is greater than any other in the sequence. Yet a moment's reflection reveals this to be an unwelcome destination. Every member of the population of World-Z has a life barely worth living. If we accept that each move of the slider to the right marks an improvement, we are led to what Parfit has coined the

> *Repugnant Conclusion*: Compared with the existence of many people whose quality of life would be very high, there is some much larger number of people whose existence would be better, even though these people's lives would be barely worth living. (2016: 110)

This conclusion, aptly named, strikes many as counterintuitive. It's hard to believe that a world filled only with lives barely worth living is better than one populated

Figure 11.1: *Modeling Worlds*

by fewer but much better-off people.[4] If you started with the slider on World-Z, you almost surely would move it left.

Many have thought that a theory that implies the Repugnant Conclusion must be abandoned. If this is correct, then we must abandon Utilitarianism. For, as we will explain in the next section, three of the core principles explored in this book together imply this conclusion.

11.3 *The Argument from the Repugnant Conclusion*

In Modeling Worlds, your program adjusted two things: the number of people and the level of lifetime welfare. This makes an evaluative difference for anyone who accepts

> WELFARISM: All and only episodes of welfare are of basic value. All and only episodes of well-being are basically good. All and only episodes of ill-being are basically bad.

Welfarism holds that well-being and ill-being matter in their own right and that they are the only things that matter in this way. This implies that the difference in total welfare levels on World-A through World-Z amounts to differences in things that matter intrinsically.

We could accept Welfarism, however, without arriving at the Repugnant Conclusion. We could do so by denying that equal amounts of well-being are equally basically good.[5] But this move is not open to those who accept

> PROPORTIONALISM: The basic value of an episode of welfare is strictly proportional to its value-for the subject. The extent to which an episode of well-being is basically good is strictly proportional to how good it is for the subject. The extent to which an episode of ill-being is basically bad is strictly proportional to how bad it is for the subject.

Proportionalism holds that the basic goodness of a given amount of well-being matches the amount of good it provides for its subject. In accepting this principle, one accepts that the goodness of an instance of well-being is indifferent to whose it is, where it is, and when it is. Nor does it matter how it is distributed. So each

---

4. The Repugnant Conclusion was made famous by Parfit (1984: ch. 17). An early discussion of it can be found in Sidgwick (1907: IV.1).

5. By appealing to desert, Feldman (1997: ch. 10) takes this approach to blocking the Repugnant Conclusion. For arguments against adjusting for desert, see §10.6–10.7.

unit of well-being on a world will be equal to one unit of basic goodness. There are, for example, one million units of basic goodness on World-A.

Welfarism and Proportionalism tell us what has basic value and how much. But this leaves open the question of how each separate factor combines. And this takes us to the principle that's the focus of this chapter, namely, Additive Aggregation. This principle tells us how to take the basic goods and bads and arrive at the evaluation of the complete state of affairs overall: add them up. So, if there are one million units of basic goodness on World-A, we can say that the value overall of that world is one million.

Combining Welfarism, Proportionalism, and Additive Aggregation yields the view that the goodness of a complete state of affairs, its overall evaluation, is strictly proportional to the total amount of welfare. Since all the people in World-A to World-Z enjoy positive lives, we can simply multiply the number of people times their well-being. Welfarism, Proportionalism, and Additive Aggregation together imply that World-Z is far and away the best in the sequence. Its total welfare, and hence its overall value, is 3.3 trillion. From these three principles we arrive at the Repugnant Conclusion.

We are now in a position to articulate

The Argument from the Repugnant Conclusion

1. If Welfarism, Proportionalism, and Additive Aggregation are true, then the Repugnant Conclusion is true.
2. The Repugnant Conclusion is false.
3. Hence, either Welfarism, Proportionalism, or Additive Aggregation is false.

Premise 2 is supported by the intuitive judgment that a world inhabited by many people with lives barely worth living is not better than one inhabited by fewer people with very good lives. Welfarism, Proportionalism, and Additive Aggregation have led to what appears to be an unacceptable result. But which of these principles, exactly, is the culprit? In the next section, we'll explain why the problem seems traceable to Additive Aggregation.

Welfarism: All and only episodes of welfare are of basic value. All and only episodes of well-being are basically good. All and only episodes of ill-being are basically bad.

Proportionalism: The basic value of an episode of welfare is strictly proportional to its value for the subject. The extent to which an episode of well-being is basically good is strictly proportional to how good it is for the subject. The extent to which an episode of ill-being is basically bad is strictly proportional to how bad it is for the subject.

Additive Aggregation: The overall value of a complete state of affairs is determined by simple summing on a single numerical scale, adding the amount of each basic good and subtracting the amount of each basic bad. The higher the sum total, the better overall is the complete state of affairs.

Repugnant Conclusion: Compared with the existence of many people whose quality of life would be very high, there is some much larger number of people whose existence would be better, even though these people's lives would be barely worth living.

11.4 *The Argument against Additive Aggregation*

We've seen that Welfarism, Proportionalism, and Additive Aggregation together entail the Repugnant Conclusion. However, one need not accept anything as strong as the combination of Welfarism and Proportionalism to get there. Combining Additive Aggregation with a much weaker, and less controversial, claim will suffice. One must hold only that lives with positive lifetime welfare are, to some extent, basically good. Stated more precisely, this modest commitment claims that

> *Positive Lives Are Good*: If one's lifetime welfare is positive—the amount of well-being exceeds the amount of ill-being—then one's existence is, to some extent, intrinsically good-simpliciter.[6]

Together, Additive Aggregation and Positive Lives Are Good deliver the Repugnant Conclusion. Why? Because, each of the worlds in the sequence we considered was importantly similar. Indeed, it seems we can stipulate away any other morally relevant factors such that, except for the difference in welfare and population, all else is equal between the worlds in the sequence. If that's correct, then a commitment to Positive Lives Are Good and Additive Aggregation is sufficient to arrive at the Repugnant Conclusion.

Positive Lives Are Good is very plausible. This is due to its modesty. Unlike Welfarism, it does not rule out the possibility that there are intrinsic goods beyond well-being. And, unlike Proportionalism, it makes no claim about how much goodness such a life has. It asserts only that the existence of a life with positive lifetime welfare is, to some extent, itself good-simpliciter. Beyond its modesty, Positive Lives Are Good is attractive on its own merits. A life worth living, even if only barely, appears to be good. To deny this claim, one would be forced to claim that either lives that are good-for the subjects living them are evaluatively neutral or bad. Since both of these claims seem far less plausible, we can assume that Positive Lives Are Good is true.

The Repugnant Conclusion follows from Additive Aggregation and Positive Lives Are Good. Positive Lives Are Good takes the critical heat off Welfarism and Proportionalism. We've also suggested that the more modest commitment of Positive Lives Are Good is very plausible. We can thus conclude that the principle challenged by the Argument from the Repugnant Conclusion is Additive Aggregation. This principle is essential to delivering the Repugnant Conclusion, and, unlike Positive Lives Are Good, it's far from uncontroversial.

---

6. Positive Lives are Good is modified from Parfit (2016: 110). Unlike what he calls the "Simple View," however, it makes a claim only about intrinsic goodness.

The Argument from the Repugnant Conclusion can now be understood as targeting Additive Aggregation. This takes us to

The Argument against Additive Aggregation

1. If Positive Lives Are Good and Additive Aggregation are both true, then the Repugnant Conclusion is true.
2. The Repugnant Conclusion is false.
3. Hence, either Positive Lives Are Good or Additive Aggregation is false.
4. Positive Lives Are Good is true.
5. Hence, Additive Aggregation is false.

> *Positive Lives Are Good*: If one's lifetime welfare is positive—the amount of well-being exceeds the amount of ill-being—then one's existence is, to some extent, intrinsically good-simpliciter.
>
> *Additive Aggregation*: The overall value of a complete state of affairs is determined by simple summing on a single numerical scale, adding the amount of each basic good and subtracting the amount of each basic bad. The higher the sum total, the better overall is the complete state of affairs.
>
> *Repugnant Conclusion*: Compared with the existence of many people whose quality of life would be very high, there is some much larger number of people whose existence would be better, even though these people's lives would be barely worth living.

If we want to resist the conclusion then we must deny Premise 2. We must hold that the Repugnant Conclusion, despite appearances, is true. To this end, we might pursue a pair of strategies. First, we might forward a positive argument that we should accept the Repugnant Conclusion. If successful, this would show the Argument against Additive Aggregation to be unsound. Second, we might challenge the credibility of the intuition motivating the rejection of the Repugnant Conclusion. This would, if successful, undermine our confidence in Premise 2, and thereby strip the argument of its force. We'll discuss each of these strategies in turn.

11.5 *The Argument to Accept Repugnance*

If the argument of the previous section is sound, then those who deny the Repugnant Conclusion must also deny Additive Aggregation. But if one is motivated to deny Additive Aggregation out of a desire to avoid its counterintuitive implications, then, in so doing, one had better not endorse a principle that itself delivers results that are just as counterintuitive, or more so. Yet the alternatives to Additive Aggregation face serious objections. These objections teach important lessons. And these lessons can be converted into a powerful argument for the truth of the Repugnant Conclusion.

One seemingly attractive proposal presents itself as a quick fix. In our sequence above, Additive Aggregation focuses only on the sum total of well-being in a complete state of affairs without regard to how any individual fares. Perhaps all that is required is a shift of focus. Perhaps we should adopt the

> *Average View*: The overall value of a complete state of affairs is determined by summing each person's lifetime welfare levels and dividing it by the total number of lives. The higher the average, the better overall is the complete state of affairs.[7]

The Average View avoids the Repugnant Conclusion. World-A has a higher average welfare level than World-Z. Indeed, its average is greater than any other world in the sequence.

While the shift from total to average welfare solves one problem, it introduces many others. An initial observation is that, in accepting the Average View, one must deny the intuitive judgment that kicked off the sequence, namely, that World-B is better than World-A. We might be willing to revise our pretheoretical judgment about this move if doing so were necessary to avoid the Repugnant Conclusion. This implication may be tolerable. But the Average View has another, less tolerable defect.

What enables the Average View to avoid the Repugnant Conclusion is its insensitivity to total levels of welfare. This insensitivity delivers counterintuitive results. The following case makes this vivid:

> Happy Additions. To the extremely well-off people of World-A, one million other equally well-off people are added. Call this world Populous-World-A.

The Average View, because it focuses only on average levels of welfare, will evaluate all states of affairs with the same average level of welfare as being equally good overall, regardless of population size. Populous-World-A, on this view, thus marks no improvement on World-A. That is hard to believe. The initial inhabitants of Populous-World-A are just as well-off as before. The only apparent difference is that one million additional people exist, each of whom lives an extremely good life. To hold, with the Average View, that this change has no influence on the value of the world strains credulity.

What explains why Populous-World-A is an improvement over World-A? The answer seems to be this: when positive lives are added to a world, and no other bads are introduced, this makes the world better overall. This thought is very hard to resist once one has accepted Positive Lives Are Good. To accept Positive Lives Are Good but agree with the Average View's verdict in Happy Additions, one would need to deny that

---

7. For critical discussion of this view, see Parfit (1984: §143).

> *More Intrinsic Goods Are Better*: Adding something intrinsically good-simpliciter to a complete state of affairs, while adding nothing intrinsically bad-simpliciter, makes the complete state of affairs better overall.

Accepting this claim, in combination with Positive Lives Are Good, delivers the intuitively correct verdict in Happy Additions. And, like Positive Lives Are Good, it is very modest. It makes no claim about the extent to which the complete state of affairs is rendered better, and no claim is made when other bads have been introduced. So the only cases to which More Intrinsic Goods Are Better applies are cases that involve the mere addition of positive lives (i.e., the addition of people who have lives worth living, who affect no one else, and whose existence does not create inequality, injustice, or anything else of the sort).[8]

Beyond underwriting the intuitively correct verdict in Happy Additions, More Intrinsic Goods Are Better is independently plausible. To claim that something is intrinsically good is to claim that this thing is good in itself. Its goodness depends on its intrinsic properties, independent of any relations it bears to other things. Such a thing would be good regardless of the circumstances in which it obtains.[9] Thus, if something intrinsically good is added to a state of affairs, it seems that it must make at least some positive contribution. And, if that positive contribution is not counterbalanced by some other bad, then the complete state of affairs will be better overall. In cases like Happy Additions, since the addition of a life worth living is not accompanied by a bad, the Average View is forced to deny More Intrinsic Goods Are Better.

The combination of Positive Lives Are Good and More Intrinsic Goods Are Better implies that, absent the introduction of some bad, the addition of positive lives makes the complete state of affairs, at least to some extent, better overall. The second alternative to Additive Aggregation is promising because it accommodates this plausible idea while avoiding the Repugnant Conclusion. This is the

> *Lexical View*: This view is like Additive Aggregation, except that the overall value of some complete states of affairs cannot be determined on a single numerical scale. A complete state of affairs containing an extremely good life is better than any complete state of affairs containing any number of moderately good lives, and a complete state of affairs containing an extremely bad life is worse than any complete state of affairs containing any number of moderately bad lives.[10]

---

8. For discussion of mere addition, see Parfit (1984: §142) and Huemer (2008).
9. For a defense of these claims about intrinsic value, see §9.5.
10. For discussion of the Lexical View, see Portmore (1999) and Broome (2004: 24–25).

According to this view, each additional life worth living makes a positive contribution to the evaluation of the state of affairs. So the view accepts Positive Lives Are Good and More Intrinsic Goods Are Better. Yet the Lexical View avoids the Repugnant Conclusion. It manages this by adopting a very different approach to the comparative value of different lives.

To understand the idea driving the Lexical View, it may be helpful to first consider some more mundane comparisons. Compare licking a lollipop to falling in love. Both are good. But their goodness is so different you'd have trouble measuring them on the same scale. Or consider an advertising jingle and your favorite song. Even here, when you're comparing two things of the same kind—two pieces of music—the vast difference between them makes meaningful comparison a challenge. Indeed, we might claim that this is more than just a problem of figuring out how to compare them. Our inability to compare is evidence of something deeper. There simply is no answer to how they compare. A lollipop is good. And falling in love is good. But no amount of the former equals the latter. The incomparability is due to the very nature of the values. The values are such that no number of lollipops could ever equal falling in love and no number of advertising jingles could add up to your favorite song. The Lexical View makes a similar claim about the differences between extremely different lives. Just as no number of jingles is as good as even one of your favorite songs, no number of lives barely worth living ever contributes as much to a state of affairs as an exceptionally good life.[11]

This view is a bit unnatural. We are accustomed to thinking of amounts of value as positions on a numerical scale. When you learned how to count, someone probably told you to focus on the relationship between size and order. By focusing on this relationship, you could figure out how much of something there is by matching the names of the numbers with the things you are counting. So long as you count in the correct order, the last number you say tells you the size of the set. Because this is how you learned to think about magnitudes, it is tempting to think that it is the only way to think about them. But, if the Lexical View is true, we must think differently. The value of each life cannot be put onto a single scale or be assigned some positive or negative number. When it comes to the evaluation of a complete state of affairs, some lives are simply on a different scale.

We can now make explicit the core idea that allows the Lexical View to block the slide to the Repugnant Conclusion. The view rejects

> *Positive Life Continuity*: For any two positive lifetime welfare levels, call them *Higher* and *Lower*, enough Lower lives render the evaluation of a complete state of affairs better overall than a single Higher life.[12]

---

11. The examples in this paragraph are modified from Griffin (1986: 83–89).
12. For defense of the negative version of this view, see Norcross (1997: 138–39) and Arrhenius (2005).

In rejecting Positive Life Continuity, the contribution of each life to the evaluation of a complete state of affairs may not be comparable. The existence of one of these lives is better than the existence of any amount of less good lives. When this occurs, the overall value of a complete state of affairs cannot be determined on a single numerical scale. There is a discontinuity—addition simply does not apply—when comparing these different lives.

But how plausible is this discontinuity? Return to Modeling Worlds. Each subsequent world is populated by inhabitants whose lives only differ in minor respects. The changes from World-A to World-Z are gradual. And we could modify the case to make them even more so. Yet, in denying Positive Life Continuity, the Lexical View holds that at some point in the sequence there is a very significant shift. One complete state of affairs is inhabited by lives sufficiently good to qualify as Higher. The adjacent state of affairs is inhabited by lives that are Lower. Suppose this change happens between World-J and World-K. The Lexical View implies some very surprising things about these worlds. The view, of course, holds that World-J is better than World-K. But it also holds that World-J would remain better than World-K even if its population dwindled to one. Call this world, inhabited by only a single person with a Higher life, Lonely-World-J. On the Lexical View, Lonely-World-J is better than World-K. The inhabitants of World-K, though their lives are similar in many respects as those of Lonely-J, live Lower lives. This is hard to believe. And the problems don't end here. On the Lexical View, Lonely-World-J will always receive a higher evaluation than World-K, regardless of the number of lives it contains. Even if we added millions or billions of additional equally good lives to World-K, the result would never be better than Lonely-World-J. These results should give us pause.

Of course, if there were some significant break in the kinds of welfare between the people on K and J, then the defender of the Lexical View could point to this difference to address the worries just raised. The problem is that it seems that we can put the things that contribute to our welfare benefits on a continuum that makes it very difficult to justify discontinuity. Perhaps when we compare radically different things, like falling in love and licking a lollipop, it may be hard to see how any number of the one could ever be as good as the other. But when we consider things that are not so different, for example, mere acquaintances, friends, and lovers, it becomes much harder to identify the break needed to justify lexical dominance. As Parfit writes:

> The good things in life do not come in quite different categories. . . . Though Haydn is not as good as Mozart, he is very good. And there is other music which is not far below Haydn's, other music not far below this, and so on. Similar claims apply to the other best experiences, activities, and personal

relationships, and to the other things which give most to the value of life. Most of these things are on fairly smooth continua, ranging from the best to the least good. Since this is so, it may be hard to defend the view that what is best has more value than any amount of what is nearly as good. (1986: 164)

If what causes welfare benefits can indeed be placed on this continuum, then it seems we should accept Positive Life Continuity and so reject the Lexical View.

Drawing on the problems faced by these alternatives, the defender of Additive Aggregation can forward

The Argument to Accept Repugnance

1. Positive Lives Are Good, the More Intrinsic Goods the Better, and Positive Life Continuity are all true.
2. If Positive Lives Are Good, More Intrinsic Goods Are Better, and Positive Life Continuity are all true, then the Repugnant Conclusion is true.
3. Hence, the Repugnant Conclusion is true.

As we've seen, each of the principles mentioned has much to be said in its favor. They are intuitively plausible, and their denial leads to some rather unpalatable conclusions.[13] The chief advantage of Additive Aggregation, then, is that it is compatible with these principles. The downside, of course, is that it leads to the Repugnant Conclusion.

The question we now face is this: Which do we have more reason to believe? Should we accept the Repugnant Conclusion? Or should we reject Positive Lives Are Good, More Intrinsic Goods Are Better, or Positive Life Continuity? In the next section, we take up this matter.

> *Positive Lives Are Good*: If one's lifetime welfare is positive—the amount of well-being exceeds the amount of ill-being—then one's existence is, to some extent, intrinsically good-simpliciter.
>
> *More Intrinsic Goods Are Better*: Adding something basically good to a complete state of affairs, while adding nothing basically bad, makes the complete state of affairs better overall.
>
> *Positive Life Continuity*: For any two positive lifetime welfare levels, call them *Higher* and *Lower*, enough *Lower* lives render the evaluation of a complete state of affairs better overall than a single *Higher* life.
>
> *Repugnant Conclusion*: Compared with the existence of many people whose quality of life would be very high, there is some much larger number of people whose existence would be better, even though these people's lives would be barely worth living.

---

13. Premise 2, for example, may be denied by rejecting the transitivity of "better than"; see Temkin (2012: chs. 5–7). For skepticism concerning the denial of transitivity, see Broome (2004: 50–52) and Huemer (2013: 332–36).

11.6 *The Argument for the Unreliability of Repugnance*

Many people are confident that the Repugnant Conclusion must be false. To be sure, the conclusion is an unwelcome one. The idea that a complete state of affairs filled with lives barely worth living could ever be better than a complete state of affairs with a smaller but much better-off population is certainly counterintuitive. But is our resistance on this matter a reliable guide to the truth?

Return to Modeling Worlds. We began by imagining a complete state of affairs populated by a few people living very good lives. Each world in the sequence was in two ways different from that which came before. First, the difference in well-being for each individual was very small. Inhabitants of World-A and World-B were both very well-off. Inhabitants of the latter lived only slightly less spectacular lives. Second, the difference in population on each world got increasingly large. Doubling the number of inhabitants as we moved from world to world resulted in exponential population growth. Either of these two variables alone might render our assessments less than reliable. Below, we raise a worry concerning each.

We can start with our ability to track quality. The worry is that, when we reflect on the lives of those in World-Z, we fail to accurately apprehend the goodness of their lives. The people of World-A have lives well worth living. The people of World-Z have lives barely worth living. One might naturally assume not only that this difference indicates a significant difference in levels of well-being but that the inhabitants of World-Z are positively miserable. The fact that their lives are in fact worth living, that they do enjoy some well-being, may easily be overlooked. We may be tempted to conclude that these lives simply do not contribute to the goodness of the complete state of affairs when we should conclude that they contribute, but only a little. The significance of very small amounts may be indiscernible when juxtaposed with very large amounts.

Here is a different way of bringing out the concern. Reflect for a moment on our own welfare levels. While some people do indeed live wonderful lives, none enjoys the unadulterated bliss that is present on World-A—not even close. Even in the best circumstances moments of ecstasy are few and far between. Our lives are filled with inconvenience, annoyance, and frustration. Our experiences, by and large, are neutral or worse. Moments of real joy only punctuate what is on the whole an unspectacular existence. These observations might lead us to conclude that, in point of fact, our world is not terribly far from World-Z. If that's correct, our evaluation of the lives led in World-Z is distorted. We proceed from the mistaken belief that our own lives are very good, vastly better than those of the inhabitants of World-Z. Yet, once our assumptions about what constitutes a life worth living are appropriately calibrated, once we see that our own lives are much like those on World-Z, then our attitudes change. Since we do not recoil from our own lives and the lives of those around us, we should not recoil from the lives of those on World-Z.[14]

We can next turn to our ability to track quantity. The worry is that we cannot properly assess cases involving very large numbers. Our number sense can usefully handle a wide range of cases. But when we turn to extreme cases—like the Repugnant Conclusion—we cannot rely on the way things seem. As Broome writes:

> We have no reason to trust anyone's intuitions about very large numbers, however excellent their philosophy. Even the best philosophers cannot get an intuitive grasp of, say, tens of billions of people. That is no criticism; these numbers are beyond intuition. . . . For very large numbers, we have to rely on theory, not intuition. When people first built bridges, they managed without much theory. They could judge a log by eye, relying on their intuition. Their intuitions were reliable, being built on long experience with handling wood and stone. But when people started spanning broad rivers with steel and concrete, their intuition failed them, and they had to resort to engineering theory and careful calculations. The cables that support suspension bridges are unintuitively slender. (2004: 56–57)

We can accurately evaluate a few people living very good lives, but when we try to evaluate of few billion, or trillion, intuition fails. We can only understand how welfare influences the evaluation of a state of affairs concerning small groups—our family and friends. But we have no reason to think that we have a similar understanding of 3.3 trillion people. If we simply port over how we make such judgments for these small number cases, there's no reason to think our judgments will be accurate. Even the slightest hiccup in moral mathematics will compound, leading to unimaginable distortions.

The foregoing considerations are offered, not as evidence that the Repugnant Conclusion is true but to cast doubt on the intuition to the contrary. We should be cautious about accepting our judgments as reliable. With this in mind, return to the Positive Lives Are Good Argument against Aggregation. For any argument to succeed, we must have more confidence in each premise than in the negation of the conclusion.

We are now in a position to offer

---

14. The ideas in this paragraph draw on Tännsjö (2002).

The Argument for the Unreliability of Repugnance

1. To have reliable evaluative intuitions about the Repugnant Conclusion, we must be able to properly imagine the quality and quantity of the lives on states of affairs like World-Z.
2. We are unable to properly imagine the quality or quantity of the lives on states of affairs like World-Z.
3. Hence, we do not have reliable evaluative intuitions about the Repugnant Conclusion.

> *Repugnant Conclusion*: Compared with the existence of many people whose quality of life would be very high, there is some much larger number of people whose existence would be better, even though these people's lives would be barely worth living.

If this argument is sound, then our confidence that the Repugnant Conclusion is false is unwarranted. Without this confidence, the Positive Lives Are Good Argument against Additive Aggregation is weak.

We can combine the lessons of this section and the last. Forced to choose between accepting the Repugnant Conclusion or rejecting either Positive Lives Are Good, More Intrinsic Goods Are Better, or Positive Life Continuity, the former may be the choice to make. Accepting the Repugnant Conclusion may not be as wrongheaded as it initially seemed.

11.7 *Conclusion*

The aim of this chapter has been to examine how Additive Aggregation fares in the face of the challenge posed by the Repugnant Conclusion. Along the way we've made a number of arguments on behalf of Additive Aggregation. Which of these is the weakest?

In defending Positive Life Continuity, we appealed to the thought that lives could be placed on a smooth continuum. At one end would be the worst lives, at the other would be the best, and in between would be lives that differ only in the smallest details. If we accept Welfare Monism—the idea that there is only one type of thing that is intrinsically good-for you and only one type of thing that is intrinsically bad-for you—the thought that there's no discontinuity between these lives seems irresistible.[15] But if we deny Welfare Monism, it seems that continuity can be resisted. For example, we might claim that experiencing pleasure, being moral, and friendship are each, in their own right, things that make your life go well. And once this plurality is posited, we're well positioned to reject Positive Life Continuity. We can maintain that, say, the value of experiencing pleasure, the value of being moral, and the value of having friends cannot be compared. How many pleasant experiences would it take to equal the value of a friendship? How

---

15. For more on Welfare Monism, see §8.5.

many friendships would it take to equal the value of being moral? If we cannot answer these questions, then we can reject the suggestion that lives can be placed on a smooth continuum. Even if we try to limit the continuum to one value (e.g., hedonic value), adjusting this value along the continuum will have an impact on the other values. Here's Dorsey:

> The mistake [in the smooth continuum argument] is easy to spot. [It] ... does not consider the instrumental effects of these various states on other indices of value.... If [we accept value monism], it is difficult to claim that there is a reasonable stopping point on the sequence, a point at which one inserts a lexical priority. But assume now ... that a broken ankle carries with it a certain degree of pain, while the next point in the sequence carries with it slightly more pain, but that a broken ankle and not the very next point in the sequence is compatible with the achievement of some other index of value.... Though on a hedonist or other monist dimension, the two points look as though they could clearly be traded off against each other, when we import a further dimension of value to which these various hedonic achievements may be instrumental, this becomes far less plausible. (2009: 49)

As the passage suggests, the rejection of Positive Life Continuity depends on the plausibility of a nonmonistic theory of welfare with incomparable goods. But is such a position defensible?

References

Arrhenius, G. 2005. "Superiority in Value." *Philosophical Studies* 123 (1–2): 97–114.
Broome, J. 2004. *Weighing Lives*. Oxford: Oxford University Press.
Dorsey, D. 2009. "Headaches, Lives and Value." *Utilitas* 21 (1): 36–58.
Feldman, F. 1997. *Utilitarianism, Hedonism, and Desert: Essays in Moral Philosophy*. Cambridge: Cambridge University Press.
Feldman, F. 2000. "Basic Intrinsic Value." *Philosophical Studies* 99 (3): 319–46.
Griffin, J. 1986. *Well-Being: Its Meaning, Measurement, and Moral Importance*. Oxford: Oxford University Press.
*Huemer, M. 2008. "In Defence of Repugnance." *Mind* 117 (468): 899–933.
Huemer, M. 2013. "Transitivity, Comparative Value, and the Methods of Ethics." *Ethics* 123 (2): 318–45.
Moore, G. E. 1993 [1903]. *Principia Ethica*. Rev. ed. Cambridge: Cambridge University Press.
Norcross, A. 1997. "Comparing Harms: Headaches and Human Lives." *Philosophy & Public Affairs* 26 (2): 135–67.
Parfit, D. 1984. *Reasons and Persons*. Oxford: Clarendon Press.
*Parfit, D. 1986. "Overpopulation and the Quality of Life." In *Applied Ethics*, edited by P. Singer, 145–64. Oxford: Oxford University Press.

Parfit, D. 2016. "Can We Avoid the Repugnant Conclusion?" *Theoria* 82 (2): 110–27.
*Portmore, D. W. 1999. "Does the Total Principle Have Any Repugnant Implications?" *Ratio* 12 (1): 80–98.
Sidgwick, H. 1907. *The Methods of Ethics*. 7th ed. London: Macmillan.
Tännsjö, T. 2002. "Why We Ought to Accept the Repugnant Conclusion." *Utilitas* 14 (3): 339–59.
Temkin, L. S. 2012. *Rethining the Good: Moral Ideals and the Nature of Practical Reasoning*. Oxford: Oxford University Press.

Appendix A
Principles to Utilitarianism

This book examines a set of principles that together imply Utilitarianism. For ease of reference, each is listed below. The first five state the normative principles. The next four state the evaluative principles. These principles, treated as premises, constitute a valid argument to the conclusion: an agent's presently available alternative has the property of being permissible if and only if (and because) the performance of any of her other presently available alternatives would not have brought about an outcome with a higher sum total of pleasure minus pain.[1] If these nine principles are true, then the argument is sound.

Normative Principles

> MAXIMIZING IS SUFFICIENT: An agent's presently available alternative has the property of being permissible if the performance of any of her other presently available alternatives would not have brought about a complete state of affairs that's better overall.

> MAXIMIZING IS NECESSARY: An agent's presently available alternative has the property of being permissible only if the performance of any of her other presently available alternatives would not have brought about a complete state of affairs that's better overall.

> OBJECTIVISM: The deontic properties of an agent's presently available alternatives depend solely on the complete states of affairs they would bring about if performed, not her perspective on these states of affairs.

> ACTUALISM: The deontic properties of a presently available alternative depend solely on the complete state of affairs that would be brought about were the agent to perform it compared to the complete states of affairs that would be brought about if the agent were to perform any of her other presently available alternatives.

> INDIVIDUALISM: An alternative possesses deontic properties if and only if, at some point, it is presently available to a single agent.

---

[1]. For consistency, we will use "alternatives" rather than "actions" for all the normative principles below. For the formulation of Utilitarianism that assigns deontic properties to every member of every set of presently available actions for every agent, see §6.8.

Evaluative Principles

> QUANTITATIVE HEDONISM: One's welfare—one's well-being or ill-being—depends solely on one's experiences of pleasure and pain. The extent to which an experience of pleasure or pain is intrinsically good-for or bad-for the subject experiencing it is the product of its intensity times its duration.
>
> WELFARISM: All and only episodes of welfare are of basic value. All and only episodes of well-being are basically good. All and only episodes of ill-being are basically bad.
>
> PROPORTIONALISM: The basic value of an episode of welfare is strictly proportional to its value for the subject. The extent to which an episode of well-being is basically good is strictly proportional to how good it is for the subject. The extent to which an episode of ill-being is basically bad is strictly proportional to how bad it is for the subject.
>
> ADDITIVE AGGREGATION: The overall value of a complete state of affairs is determined by simple summing on a single numerical scale, adding the amount of each basic good and subtracting the amount of each basic bad. The higher the sum total, the better overall is the complete state of affairs.

Appendix B
Alternative Principles

In this book, considerable space is devoted to the arguments for and against a set of principles that lead to Utilitarianism. In this appendix, we identify the chief alternatives to these principles. Under the name of each principle, we give a brief description of rival views, along with references where more in-depth discussion can be found.

Maximizing Is Sufficient

Deontological Views: Such views incorporate at least one requirement to refrain from performing a certain familiar act-type (e.g., murder) even though performing such an act would minimize the total number of act-tokens of this act-type and have no other morally relevant implications. Deontological Views can be divided into two categories. Views in the first category focus on the person performing the action, and so are called agent centered. See, for example, Foot (1967). Views in the second category focus on the victim, and so are called patient centered. See, for example, Kamm (1996).

Maximizing Is Necessary

Satisficing Views: It is not the case that permissible acts are only those that bring about the best complete state of affairs. The line for what qualifies as a permissible action is drawn below what's optimal. An agent acts permissibly as long as the performance of the act, of the agent's presently available alternatives, brings about a complete state of affairs that's good enough. See, for example, Slote (1984).

Agent-Centered Option Views: Such views hold that there are situations in which it is permissible for you to perform a certain act that brings about the best complete state of affairs but that it is also permissible for you to refrain from performing this act thereby bringing about a worse complete state of affairs. Agent-Centered Option Views can be divided into two categories. Views in the first category allow situations in which it is permissible for the agent to bring about a complete state of affairs that's worse overall but better for herself. These views endorse what are called agent-favoring options. See, for example, Scheffler (1982). Views in the second category allow situations in which it is permissible for the agent to bring about a complete state of affairs that is worse overall and worse for herself. These views endorse what are called agent-sacrificing options. See, for example, Lazar (2018).

Objectivism

Perspectivism: The deontic properties of an agent's presently available alternatives depend on the agent's perspective on the complete states of affairs that they would bring about if performed. In consequentialist form, it holds that an agent's presently available alternative has the property of being permissible if and only if the performance of any of the agent's other presently available alternatives would not have brought about a complete state of affairs that's perspectively better. There are a number of forms of perspectivism, which differ based on how perspective value is defined. That is, they differ insofar as they take different parts of the agent's perspective to be relevant for deontic assessment. For example, views may focus on what the agent believes, knows, expects, or reasonably expects. On the most prominent form of perspectivism, which is modeled on decision theory, the agent's present evidence is used to assign an expected value—which is a function of the value and the likelihood of getting it—to the outcomes of the alternatives. See, for example, Jackson (1991) and Zimmerman (2008).

Actualism

Possibilism: The deontic properties of a presently available alternative depend solely on the complete state of affairs that could be brought about were the agent to perform it compared to the complete states of affairs that could be brought about if the agent were to perform any of her other presently available alternatives. In consequentialist form, it holds that an agent is required to perform a certain action if and only if her performing this action is part of the act-set from present until the time of her last action that brings about a complete state of affairs better than any alternative act-set. See, for example, Feldman (1986) and Zimmerman (1996). For discussion of how the debate concerning Actualism and Possibilism is linked to the debate concerning Objectivism and Perspectivism, see Jackson (2014) and Zimmerman (2017).

Individualism

Collectivism: An action possesses deontic properties if and only if, at some point, it is presently available to an individual or collection of agents. On this view, deontic assessment applies not only to what individuals do but also to what groups do. For example, this view might hold that an individual agent acts permissibly if and only if she brings about the best outcome individually available and that we act permissibly if and only if we bring about the best outcome collectively available. See, for example, Jackson (1987) and Parfit (unpublished manuscript).

Quantitative Hedonism

Qualitative Hedonism: One's welfare depends solely on one's experiences of pleasure and pain. The extent to which a pleasure or pain is intrinsically good-for or bad-for the subject experiencing it is the product of its intensity times its duration times some quality rating (e.g., whether the pleasure is higher or lower). See, for example, Mill (2003 [1861/1859]: U 2.5) and Crisp (2006).

Desire-Satisfactionism: One's welfare depends solely on having your desires satisfied. The extent to which a desire's being satisfied or not satisfied is intrinsically good-for or bad-for the subject is proportional to its strength. See, for example, Hare (1981) and Heathwood (2016).

Objective List Theory: One's welfare depends solely on one's life containing certain objective goods and lacking certain objective bads. See, for example, Fletcher (2013).

Welfarism

Value Pluralism: There is more than one thing of basic value. Different forms of Value Pluralism posit different goods. Things that are commonly claimed to be of basic value include pleasure and pain, respect and disrespect, virtue and vice, equality and inequality, achievement and failure, love and hate, beauty and ugliness, knowledge and ignorance. See, for example, Moore (1993 [1903]) and Ross (1930).

Recursive Views: Having certain attitudes toward certain basic values is itself of basic value. On the most prominent version of this view, pleasure, knowledge, and achievement are basically good, and loving (desiring, pursuing, or taking pleasure in) these goods for themselves is also basically good. See, for example, Brentano (1969) and Hurka (2001).

Proportionalism

Desert Adjusted Views: Things go best when people get what they deserve. When there is a perfect fit between one's welfare level and one's desert level, any change in welfare is a change for the worse. See, for example, Feldman (1997) and Kagan (2012).

Prioritarianism: The basic value of an episode of welfare depends on the recipient's initial level of welfare. Well-being is of greater basic goodness and ill-being is of greater basic badness, the lower the recipient's lifetime welfare level. See, for example, Parfit (1997, 2012).

ADDITIVE AGGREGATION

Organic Unities: The overall value of a complete state of affairs is not necessarily the sum of all the basic goodness minus the sum of all the basic badness. Holding the basic values fixed, the overall value of the complete state of affairs can be more (or less) than the sum of its basic goods and bads. See, for example, Moore (1993 [1903]) and Chisholm (1986). For an important defense of this view, see Regan (2003: 667–70).

References

Brentano, F. 1969. *The Origin of Our Knowledge of Right and Wrong*. London: Routledge and Kegan Paul.

Chisholm, R. M. 1986. *Brentano and Intrinsic Value*. Cambridge: Cambridge University Press.

Crisp, R. 2006. "Hedonism Reconsidered." *Philosophy and Phenomenological Research* 73 (3): 619–45.

Feldman, F. 1986. *Doing the Best We Can: An Essay in Informal Deontic Logic*. Dordrecht: D. Reidel.

Feldman, F. 1997. *Utilitarianism, Hedonism, and Desert: Essays in Moral Philosophy*. Cambridge: Cambridge University Press.

Fletcher, G. 2013. "A Fresh Start for the Objective-List Theory of Well-Being." *Utilitas* 25 (2): 206–20.

Foot, P. 1967. "The Problem of Abortion and the Doctrine of Double Effect." *Oxford Review* 5: 5–15.

Hare, R. M. 1981. *Moral Thinking*. Oxford: Clarendon Press.

Heathwood, C. 2016. "Desire-Fulfillment Theory." In *The Routledge Handbook of Philosphy of Well-Being*, edited by G. Fletcher, 135–47. New York: Routledge.

Hurka, T. 2001. *Virtue, Vice, and Value*. Oxford: Oxford University Press.

Jackson, F. 1987. "Group Morality." In *Metaphysics and Morality: Essays in Honour of J. J. C. Smart*, edited by P. Pettit, R. Sylvan, and J. Norman, 91–110. Oxford: Basil Blackwell.

Jackson, F. 1991. "Decision-Theoretic Consequentialism and the Nearest and Dearest Objection." *Ethics* 101 (3): 461–82.

Jackson, F. 2014. "Procrastinate Revisited." *Pacific Philosophical Quarterly* 95 (4): 634–47.

Kagan, S. 2012. *The Geometry of Desert*. Oxford: Oxford University Press.

Kamm, F. M. 1996. *Morality, Mortality: Rights, Duties, and Status*. Vol. II. Oxford: Oxford University Press.

Lazar, S. 2018. "Moral Status and Agent-Centred Options." *Utilitas* 31 (1): 83–105.

Mill, J. S. 2003 [1861/1859]. Utilitarianism *and* On Liberty: *Including Mill's "Essay on Bentham" and Selections from the Writings of Jeremy Bentham and John Austin*. 2nd ed. Oxford: Blackwell.

Moore, G. E. 1993 [1903]. *Principia Ethica*. Rev. ed. Cambridge: Cambridge University Press.

Parfit, D. 1997. "Equality and Priority." *Ratio* 10 (3): 202–21.

Parfit, D. 2012. "Another Defence of the Priority View." *Utilitas* 24 (3): 399–440.
Parfit, D. "What We Together Do." Unpublished manuscript.
Regan, D. H. 2003. "How to Be a Moorean." *Ethics* 113 (3): 651–77.
Ross, W. D. 1930. *The Right and the Good*. Oxford: Clarendon Press.
Scheffler, S. 1982. *The Rejection of Consequentialism: A Philosophical Investigation of the Considerations Underlying Rival Moral Conceptions*. Oxford: Oxford University Press.
Slote, M. 1984. "Satisficing Consequentialism." *Proceedings of the Aristotelian Society* 58: 139–63.
Zimmerman, M. J. 1996. *The Concept of Moral Obligation*. Cambridge: Cambridge University Press.
Zimmerman, M. J. 2008. *Living with Uncertainty: The Moral Significance of Ignorance*. Cambridge: Cambridge University Press.
Zimmerman, M. J. 2017. "Prospective Possibilism." *The Journal of Ethics* 21 (2): 117–50.

Appendix C
Theory Assessment

In ethics, we often do not have an airtight case for one theory. When deciding which theory to accept, we are thus forced to compare. On what basis might we judge one theory superior to another?

In answering this question, we are trying to identify some general features that, if possessed, make a theory more likely to be true. The task is a challenge because in ethics there are few uncontroversial indicators of moral progress. If we had clear signs of success, then we could appeal to the features that successful theories have in common. Lacking such signs, we need to take a different tack. Fortunately, there are many areas of inquiry in which we develop theories, and in many cases, we have reason to believe we've made progress. Consider how developments in engineering, technology, and medicine in the last century have profoundly changed our lives. Here we have a domain with clear signs of progress: science. We might thus draw on the virtues and vices that we learn from scientific theorizing and port them over to ethics. Of course, we should not expect ethics to proceed in just the same way as science. But there are substantial similarities.[1]

Let's start with what's common. Both science and ethics are in the business of explaining phenomena. A scientific theory seeks to explain observations about the world around us. For example, when we look at the night sky the stars appear to change location from night to night. What explains this? We begin with some speculation or a hunch. Having perceived the phenomena to be explained, we propose a principle or set of principles—purported laws of motion—that would explain these observations. Then, drawing on these principles, we make testable predictions about the behavior of objects. When these predictions are accurate, that lends some credence to the proposed principles. What was once speculation is now more credible. When these principles are found to reliably explain and predict the relevant data, we provisionally accept them as a theory. If instead the principles fail to predict and explain, they are rejected or revised.

As with science, ethical theory also seeks to explain phenomena. But we're not concerned with empirical data. There is no such thing as a deontic telescope or evaluative magnifying glass. We cannot measure rightness or goodness the way we can measure the rate at which an object falls. This is an important difference. Yet it shouldn't be exaggerated. We lack empirical data, but we do have something else: the way things seem to us morally. We have our considered moral judgments.

---

1. We are not the first to appeal to science in this way, see Thomson (1986: 257–58) and Kagan (2001).

Consider the following list of pretheoretical ethical beliefs, many of which you probably have.

Normative Judgments	Evaluative Judgments
Saving lives at little cost is required.	Pleasure is good-for you.
Preventing pain is a reason to act in a certain way.	Pain is bad-for you.
Favoring your children is permissible.	Health is good-for you.
Torturing is impermissible.	Friendships are good.
Keeping promises is required.	Not getting one's due is bad.

An ethical theory seeks to explain and unify these judgments under a single principle or set of principles. And, as with scientific theories, moral principles make predictions about what we ought to do, who we ought to be, and what is of value in circumstances that we've yet to consider. Whereas scientists perform actual experiments and take actual measurements, when thinking about ethics we often rely only on experiments we run in our minds. We use thought experiments to see if principles yield results in line with our own judgments. If our judgments match those predicted by the principle, that lends some credence to the theory. When the two differ, that gives us reason to reconsider. When these principles reliably align with our considered judgments in a wide range of cases, we provisionally accept them. If instead the principles fail to predict and explain, we might revise or reject them.

So far, we've drawn attention to a pair of important similarities between science and ethics. In both domains, we devise principles that attempt to explain a data set; and, in both, these principles can be tested with reference to the accuracy of their predictions. This suggestion, to be sure, does not imply that the data relevant to both domains are the same—they're not. Nor does it presuppose that the inferences we're licensed to draw from predictive failures are the same—they're not. Nonetheless, the approach we take to assessing scientific theories can be of help in assessing ethical theories. For some of the very same considerations that suggest scientific theories are more or less likely to be true seem to apply equally to ethical theories. In what follows we identify four such considerations.

We'll begin with two criteria that are noncomparative; they can be used to assess a theory in isolation. The first criterion comes from the idea that an adequate theory will explain all instances of the relevant phenomenon, and not just an arbitrary subset. An adequate theory will explain all of the data that need explaining. For example, we expect our laws of motion to cover, obviously enough, all things in motion. If such a theory were unable to account for very small objects or those at very high velocities, it would fail. Newtonian mechanics fails in this way. It breaks down when applied to things traveling near the speed of light and subatomic particles. We'll say that a theory that explains only part of what needs explaining fails on account of being

> *Incomplete*: A theory is incomplete just when it accounts for only part of the phenomenon it sets out to explain.

An ethical theory may fail in the same way. We expect an ethical theory to deliver deontic verdicts for all acts. So if, for example, a theory was silent on acts that influence nonhuman animals or future generations, it would be Incomplete.

The second criterion follows immediately from the idea that we want our theory to be true. A theory that makes incompatible predictions or imposes contradictory requirements cannot be true. Theories that are in this way contradictory must be rejected. For example, if a theory says that an object will, at the same time, be in motion and be motionless, it contradicts itself. It fails on account of being

> *Inconsistent*: A theory is inconsistent just when it implies a contradiction.

An ethical theory may fail in the same way. Suppose that a theory both claimed that you are required to keep all your promises no matter what and required you to be a teetotaler no matter what. But now suppose you are playing a game with your friend, and you promise to drink whatever is in his cup if you lose. You lose. His cup happens to be full of alcohol. According to this theory, you are required to keep your promise, and so required to drink alcohol. But you are also required to abstain from drinking alcohol. So, on this occasion, you are both required to drink and required to refrain from drinking alcohol. Such a theory is inconsistent. This theory must be rejected.[2]

The next two criteria are essentially comparative. To assess a theory along these dimensions requires that you see how it fares when compared with rival theories. Both of these criteria are justified on the grounds that they pick out something constitutive of good explanations. Consider what a theory is supposed to do. It explains some phenomenon. When comparing two theories—in any domain—we are justified in favoring the one that offers the better explanation.

The third criterion stems from the idea that we want to avoid conflicts between what a theory claims is true and what we observe. Between two otherwise comparable theories, the one that's harder to square with our observations and background assumptions is worse. We should opt for the alternative. We might call this comparative feature

> *Doxastic Coherence*: One theory is more doxastically coherent than another when it fits with our assumptions and observations better than the other.[3]

Unfortunately, it is not easy to determine how to respond when a theory fails to cohere with our assumptions and observations. For in some cases a theory will

---

2. The last two paragraphs draw on Griffin (1986).
3. What we have in mind here is roughly Reflective Equilibrium, see Rawls (2001: §10).

not match our predictions, but not because the theory is false. Sometimes the background assumptions from which we proceed are wrong, and sometimes the prediction we posit is mistaken. For example, Newton's theory of universal gravitation was thought to incorrectly predict the orbit of Uranus. But this prediction was predicated on the false assumption that there are only seven planets. Rather than rejecting the theory, scientists questioned the background assumptions. This turned out to be the right move, as it led to the discovery of Neptune. The apparent failed prediction wasn't actually a reason to abandon Newton's theory, but a reason to reconsider our understanding of the solar system. When a theory is confronted by disconfirming evidence, something must give. Whether that's the theory or the background assumptions—or the observation itself—is not always clear.[4]

Adjudicating such disputes is even more challenging in the domain of morality. A theory in ethics may make what seem like erroneous predictions—it may imperfectly fit our considered judgments—yet not warrant rejection. To see why this is all but inevitable, consider the list of judgments an ethical theory might be invoked to explain. Virtually no theory can account for them all. Many of the intuitive judgments we make about morality, on examination, are revealed to conflict with each other. You may believe that, if you can prevent a terrible outcome, such as the death of a child, at little cost to yourself, then you are required to do so. You may also believe that you're permitted to spend considerable sums to provide for your family. Yet it's not at all clear that both of these claims can be correct, and it's hard to have any level of confidence about their relative credence. What conclusion should we draw when a theory accounts for one but not the other of these judgments? In cases of conflict, we face a difficult choice. We must give up on something: the theory, the judgment, or the other assumptions operating in the background.

The final criterion is simplicity. All else being equal, a simpler explanation is better than a more complex one. Why should we prefer simpler explanations? Because the justificatory burden of positing fewer types of entities is lower. Each time we elaborate a theory with additional constructs we incur a cost. The theory gets more complex. When this complexity adds nothing by way of explanatory power, it is unjustified. The appeal of simplicity can be seen in another way. Notice, if we start with a true theory and supplement it with false claims about extraneous entities that do not actually exist, the resulting theory may still be able to account for the phenomena that need explaining. By contrast, if we start with a true theory and eliminate some of the true claims that comprise it, the resulting theory will not be able to account for phenomena that need explaining. This asymmetry provides additional reason to favor a simpler over a more complex theory. Thus, if we have two theories that are both complete and coherent and explain our

---

4. This paragraph draws on Duhem (1954 [1914]: 185–87).

observations equally well, we're justified in favoring the one that's simpler. This takes us to

> *Qualitative Parsimony*: A theory is more qualitatively parsimonious than another when it posits fewer types of entity to explain what needs to be explained.

The appeal to Qualitative Parsimony is common in science. For example, both Lorentz and Einstein proposed theories that explained why, as they approached the speed of light, rulers contract and clocks slow down. But Lorentz's theory needed to posit electromagnetic ether, while Einstein's did not. For this reason Einstein's theory was thought superior. But Qualitative Parsimony is equally applicable when assessing theories in ethics.[5]

To see why simplicity matters, consider the following ethical theory. Begin with the complete list of all your moral judgments. Then, create a big conjunctive principle—filled with numerous exceptions and qualifying clauses—which captures, insofar as possible, all of these judgments. This gerrymandered principle may actually be most doxastically coherent. That is, it will deliver verdicts that align most closely with your considered judgments. And perhaps, if you took care, you could work this principle up into something that's complete and consistent. But you would properly regard this contrived monstrosity as deeply flawed. And you would do so on grounds of Qualitative Parsimony. This very long conjunctive principle, to account for all of the relevant judgments, would have to posit a huge number of different types of entity.[6]

To see this, return to our moral judgments listed above. Consider just three claims: health is good-for you, pleasure is good-for you, and pain is bad-for you. The very long conjunctive principle we've created would explain all of these judgments, but each one would require that we posit an additional entity. This seems unnecessary. Once we've accepted that pleasure is good-for you and pain is bad-for you, it's hard to see why we'd also need to hold that health is in its own right good-for you. What makes it true that health is good-for you seems to be fully accounted for by the personal goodness of pleasure and the personal badness of pain. This suggests that a simpler theory, one that's equally adequate as an explanation, may be readily available. And we should prefer such a theory on account of Qualitative Parsimony. The question, of course, is how far this kind of simplifying project can go while still being consistent, complete, and doxastically coherent.

Here we've arrived at a final complication. The ethical theory we should believe must not be Inconsistent nor Incomplete. But these two noncomparative criteria will leave many contenders. And among those we cannot assume that one theory will dominate the others when assessed by the comparative criteria.

---

5. This paragraph draws on Lewis (1986: 87–88).
6. This paragraph draws on Kagan (1989: 11–15).

Rather we will likely get mixed results. One theory will fare better than another in terms of Doxastic Coherence but worse in terms of Qualitative Parsimony. We thus need to know how to trade off. What is a better indicator of a theory's truth, greater Doxastic Coherence or greater Qualitative Parsimony?

Any proposal for weighing these criteria against each other will be extremely controversial. But it is worth remembering what it is that an ethical theory is fitting: us. How much weight you ought to assign to Doxastic Coherence as compared to Qualitative Parsimony will depend on your confidence in the considered judgments of human beings. How much credence should we place in commonsense moral judgments? Here, we may have arrived at a place where drawing on science distorts rather than illuminates.

References

Duhem, P. 1954 [1914]. *The Aim and Structure of Physical Theory*. Translated by P. W. Wiener. Princeton, NJ: Princeton University Press.

*Griffin, J. 1986. *Well-Being: Its Meaning, Measurement, and Moral Importance*. Oxford: Oxford University Press.

Kagan, S. 1989. *The Limits of Morality*. Oxford: Oxford University Press.

*Kagan, S. 2001. "Thinking about Cases." *Social Philosophy and Policy* 18 (2): 44–63.

Lewis, D. 1986. *Counterfactuals*. Rev. ed. Oxford: Basil Blackwell.

*Rawls, J. 2001. *Justice as Fairness: A Restatement*. Cambridge, MA: Harvard University Press.

Thomson, J. J. 1986. *Rights, Restitution, and Risk: Essays in Moral Theory*. Cambridge, MA: Harvard University Press.

Glossary

Act-Type/Token: The distinction between a general category of act and particular instances of it. For example, murder is an act-type of which serial killers perform many tokens.

Ad hoc: Contrived for a specific purpose.

Agency: To have the capacity to recognize and respond to reasons.

Agent: One who performs an action.

Agent-Favoring Option: A situation in which it is morally permissible for you to perform a certain act that brings about the best complete state of affairs, but it is also morally permissible for you to refrain from the performance of this act, thereby bringing about a complete state of affairs that is worse overall but better-for you.

Agent-Neutral Reasons: Reasons that do not make essential reference to the agent to whom they apply; reasons for everyone.

Agent-Relative Consequentialism: An agent's presently available alternative has the property of being permissible if and only if the performance of any of the agent's other presently available alternatives would not have brought about a complete state of affairs that is intrinsically better-relative-to-her.

Agent-Relative Reason: Reasons that make essential reference to the agent; reasons for a particular person.

Agent-Relative Value: A state of affairs, S_1, is better agent-relative-to-you than a state of affairs, S_2, if and only if you have more (agent-relative and agent-neutral) reason to prefer S_1 to S_2.

Agent-Sacrificing Option: A situation in which it is morally permissible for you to perform a certain act that brings about the best complete state of affairs, but it is also morally permissible for you to refrain from the performance of this act, thereby bringing about a complete state of affairs that is worse overall and worse-for you.

Alternative Actions: One act is an alternative to another just when their joint performance is impossible.

Approximation Strategy of a Utilitarian: The strategy that a Utilitarian agent believes would, if followed, bring about the greatest sum total of pleasure minus pain in the long run, given what she believes about her own psychology and circumstances.

Argument: A series of statements, one of which (the conclusion) is claimed to be supported by the others (the premises).

Basic Value: The intrinsic value-simpliciter of a state of affairs consisting purely of a single intrinsic value.

Glossary

Belief: To believe that p is to be disposed to act in ways that would tend to satisfy one's desires, whatever they are, in a world in which p (together with one's other beliefs) were true. Beliefs have mind-to-world direction of fit.

Commonsense Morality: A collection of general rules commonly regarded by ordinary people as capturing the moral truth. For example, commonsense morality holds that murder is impermissible and favoring the near and dear is permissible.

Complete State of Affairs: A complete state of affairs is such that, for every other state of affairs, it is either included or precluded. A state of affairs includes another if it is not possible for it to obtain and for the other not to obtain. A state of affairs precludes another if it is not possible that it obtains and that the other also obtains.

Concepts: Contents of thoughts; ways of conceiving of things as being.

Conceptual Truth: A proposition the truth of which is guaranteed by the concepts involved. For example, it's conceptually true that vixens are female foxes.

Conditional: A sentence of the form "If p then q." Here p is called the *antecedent*, while q is called the *consequent*.

Conjunction: The conjunction of p and q is true if and only if p is true and q is true.

Consequentializing: Take whatever consideration might lead to a break with consequentialism's deontic verdicts, and reinterpret it as part of what makes a complete state of affairs better or worse.

Consistency: A set of propositions is consistent if and only if there is at least one logically possible world in which all of the propositions in the set are true.

Constraint: A requirement to refrain from performing a certain familiar act-type—e.g., murder—even though performing such an act would minimize the total number of act-tokens of this act-type and have no other morally relevant implications.

Contingent Truth: A proposition that is true in the actual world but is false in at least one possible world.

Counterexample: An example that shows the falsity of some proposition.

Counterfactual: A conditional of the form "If p were the case, then q would be the case."

Decision Procedure: A set of rules that the agent can use, given her beliefs at the time of action, to identify whether an action is to be performed.

Decision-Deontic Confusion: Mistakenly treating what is part of a decision procedure as if it were part of a deontic theory.

Decisive Reason: Reasons to act in a certain way that overpower any other reason (or combination of reasons) not to act in this way.

Deontic Force: An act's deontic force is strictly proportional to the total strength of the set of reasons that bear on the performance of the act.

Deontic Properties: A property that can be ascribed with a deontic predicate, e.g., is permissible, is impermissible, is optional, is required.

Deontic Theory: A theory that assigns deontic properties to acts.

Descriptive Properties: A property that can be ascribed with a descriptive predicate, e.g., is red, is flat, is round, is heavy.

Desire: To desire that p is to be disposed to act in ways that would tend to bring it about that p in a world in which one's beliefs, whatever they are, are true. Desires have world to mind direction of fit.

Desire-Satisfactionism: One's welfare depends solely on having one's desires satisfied. The extent to which a desire's being satisfied or not satisfied is intrinsically good-for or bad-for the subject is proportional to its strength.

Doxastic: Having to do with belief.

Entailed Action: An action is entailed if and only if it is among an agent's presently available actions and its performance is entailed by the performance of some of her other presently available actions.

Equivocation: When an ambiguous term appears in an argument such that the meaning of the term changes across the argument.

Evaluative Properties: A property that can be ascribed with an evaluative predicate, e.g., is good-for, is bad-for, is good, is bad, is valuable, is desirable.

Existence Internalism about Reasons: If there is a reason for an agent to act in a certain way, then her acting in this way promotes the object of one of her desires.

Fact: A true proposition.

Fitting Attitude: An attitude is fitting if and only if it accurately represents its object.

Grounding: A metaphysically necessary explanation. If p grounds q, then we are saying what it is in virtue of which something is q—in this case p. For example, being water is grounded in being H_2O.

If and Only If: A sentence that states both a necessary and a sufficient condition; a biconditional. The "if" captures the sufficient condition. The "only if" captures the necessary condition.

Ill-Being: What makes a life intrinsically worse-for the subject living it. Personally bad-for makers.

Impermissibility-Blame Confusion: Mistakenly assuming that an agent who freely and knowingly fails to satisfy an other-regarding moral requirement is thereby to be blamed.

Impermissible: An action is impermissible if and only if refraining from the action is required.

Glossary 251

Inference to the Best Explanation: Tells us to infer the truth of a given hypothesis from the fact that this hypothesis would explain the available evidence better than any other available hypotheses.

Instrumental Reason: A fact has the property of being an instrumental reason if and only if it is not the case that this fact itself counts in favor of acting in a certain way; its normative force depends on some other fact.

Instrumental Value: A fact has the property of being instrumentally valuable if and only if it is not the case that this fact is itself good or bad; its goodness or badness depends on how it relates to something else.

Instrumental-Intrinsic Confusion: Mistakenly treating what is merely of instrumental value as intrinsically valuable.

Intrinsic Reason: A fact has the property of being an intrinsic reason if and only if this fact itself counts in favor of acting in a certain way; its normative force does not depend on any other fact.

Intrinsic Value: A fact has the property of being intrinsically valuable if and only if this fact is itself good or bad; its goodness or badness does not depend on how it relates to anything else.

Irreversible Action: An action is irreversible if and only if once begun it cannot physically be stopped short of completion.

Judgment-Sensitive Attitudes: An attitude is judgment-sensitive if and only if it is one that a rational agent tends to have or lack in response to her taking there to be reasons for or against the attitude. For example, beliefs, desires, and fears.

Lexical Dominance: X lexically dominates Y if and only if any amount of X is better than any amount of Y.

Moral Rationalism: Necessarily, if an agent is morally required to perform some act, then she has decisive reason, all things considered, to perform this act.

Motivational Set: A set of motives including such things as attitudes, emotions, loyalties, and projects.

Necessary Condition: A condition p is a necessary condition for some q when the falsity of p guarantees the falsity of q. That is, q cannot be true unless p is true. For example, one is a mother only if one is female. That is, being female is a necessary condition for being a mother.

Non-Entailed Action: An action is nonentailed if and only if it is among an agent's presently available actions and its performance is not entailed by the performance of any of her other presently available actions.

Normative Properties: A property that can be ascribed with a normative predicate, e.g., is permissible, is impermissible, is optional, is required, is a reason for, is a reason against.

Normative Reason: A consideration that counts in favor of, or justifies, acting in a certain way.

Object-Given Reasons: A reason is object-given if and only if it is a consideration that counts in favor or against holding an attitude in virtue of the object or the content of that attitude.

Objective List Theory: One's welfare depends solely on one's life containing certain objective goods and lacking certain objective bads.

Optimific: An action is optimific if and only if, of the agent's presently available actions, its performance brings about the best complete state of affairs, in other words, no other action would produce a better outcome.

Optional: An action is optional if and only if it is permissible to either perform or refrain from the action.

Ought Inheritance: For any two presently available actions, X and Y, where X-ing entails Y-ing, necessarily, if the agent ought to X, then she ought to Y.

Outcome: The outcome of your acting in a certain way is the possible world that would be actual if you were to act in this way. That is, the outcome of an action is the complete state of affairs that would obtain if it were performed.

Overall Value: The intrinsic value-simpliciter of a complete state of affairs.

Patient: The one on whom an action is performed.

Permissible: An action is permissible if and only if it is an action that is not impermissible. An agent's presently available alternative has the property of being permissible if and only if (and because) the set of intrinsic reasons for performing it have a combined strength that is at least as strong as the combined strength of the set of intrinsic reasons for performing any of her other presently available alternatives.

Possible World: A complete state of affairs. The actual world, for example, is a possible world—a complete state of affairs—that obtains.

Pragmatic Encroachment: When the practical encroaches on the epistemic. For example, when practical considerations are relevant in determining whether or not a subject is justified in believing a certain proposition.

Predicate: A term that tells us something about the subject of the sentence. For example, in the sentence "The tire is round," the portion "is round" is the predicate. The predicate tells us that the subject (the tire) possesses a certain intrinsic property (roundness). Predicates can also be used to tell us that there is a certain relation between two things. For instance, in the sentence "The car is north of the city," the portion "is north of" is the predicate. It tells us that the subject (the car) possesses a certain relational property (being north of the city).

Property: A property is a feature, characteristic, or quality a thing might have. The tire has the intrinsic property of being round, and your cup might share this property. The car has the relational property of being north of the city, and your relatives might share this property.

Proposition: The content of an indicative sentence. For example, "Snow is white" and "Schnee ist weiß" express the same proposition.

Qualitative Hedonism: One's welfare depends solely on one's experiences of pleasure and pain. The extent to which a pleasure or pain is intrinsically good-for or bad-for the subject experiencing it is the product of its intensity times its duration times some quality rating, e.g., whether the pleasure is higher or lower.

Qualitative Parsimony: A theory is more qualitatively parsimonious than another when it posits fewer types of entity to explain what needs to be explained.

Rational Control: One has rational control over an act just when she can perform this act by responding to what she takes to be the reasons for or against it.

Reactive Attitudes: Attitudes concerning the involvement with others in interpersonal relationships, e.g., resentment, gratitude, forgiveness, anger. Such attitudes are expressed in holding others morally responsible.

Reason Properties: A property that can be ascribed with a reason predicate, e.g., is a reason for, is a reason against, is a strong reason, is a weak reason, is a decisive reason.

Reflective Equilibrium: The state achieved when, by resolving inconsistencies among one's beliefs, they are mutually supporting. When this state is achieved, one's doxastic structure is coherent and stable.

Repugnant Conclusion: Compared with the existence of many people whose quality of life would be very high, there is some much larger number of people whose existence would be better, even though these people's lives would be barely worth living.

Required: An action is required if and only if it is the uniquely permissible action available; a permissible action that is not optional.

Self-Effacing: An ethical theory is self-effacing if it requires an agent to possess an attitude whose object falls within the ethical domain; but, if the ethical theory were true, this attitude fails to accurately represent its object.

Simpliciter: Without qualification.

Soundness: The property of an argument that is valid and has true premises.

Standard Story of Action: A subject's actions are those of her bodily movements that are done because she wants certain things and because she believes that she can achieve those things by moving her body in the ways she does.

State-Given Reasons: A reason is state-given if and only if it is a consideration that counts in favor or against holding a certain attitude in virtue of the state of affairs in which that attitude is held.

Sufficient Condition: A condition p is a sufficient condition for q when the truth of p guarantees q. That is, p's being true is enough for q's being true. For example, if one is a mother, then one is female. Being a mother is a sufficient condition for being female.

Supervenience: A kind of property X supervenes on another kind Y if and only if any two things that share all their Y properties must also share all their X properties; it's impossible for a thing to change its X properties without changing its Y properties.

Traditional Consequentialism: An agent's presently available alternative has the property of being permissible if and only if (and because) the performance of any of her other presently available alternatives would not have brought about a complete state of affairs that's better overall.

Utilitarianism: An agent's presently available alternative has the property of being permissible if and only if (and because) the performance of any of her other presently available alternatives would not have brought about a complete state of affairs with a higher sum total of pleasure minus pain. In its complete form: An agent's nonentailed action has the property of being permissible if and only if (and because) the performance of any of her other nonentailed actions would not have brought about a complete state of affairs with a higher sum total of pleasure minus pain. An agent's entailed action has the property of being permissible if and only if its performance is entailed by a permissible nonentailed action.

Utility: A measurement of welfare.

Validity: The property of an argument with a form such that if all of the premises were true, then its conclusion must be true. A valid argument is truth preserving by virtue of its form.

Value Non-Inheritance: For any two presently available actions, X and Y, where X-ing entails Y-ing, it is not the case that, necessarily, the goodness of the outcome of X-ing is equal to the goodness of the outcome of Y-ing.

Value-For You: Some fact is good-for or bad-for you if and only if it is personally good or personally bad.

Value-Simpliciter: Some fact is good-simpliciter or bad-simpliciter if and only if it is impersonally good or impersonally bad.

Volitional Control: One has volitional control over an act just when she can perform this act at will.

Welfare Monism: There is only one type of thing that is intrinsically good-for welfare subjects, and only one type of thing that is intrinsically bad-for welfare subjects.

Welfare: Intrinsic personal value, covering both well-being and ill-being.

Well-Being: What makes a life intrinsically better-for the subject living it. Personally good-for makers.